Dynamics of Idealism

White Activists in a Black Movement

N. J. Demerath III
Gerald Marwell
Michael T. Aiken

DYNAMICS
OF
IDEALISM

Jossey-Bass Inc., Publishers
San Francisco · Washington · London · 1971

DYNAMICS OF IDEALISM
White Activists in a Black Movement
    N. J. Demerath III, Gerald Marwell, and Michael T. Aiken

Copyright © 1971 by Jossey-Bass, Inc., Publishers

Jossey-Bass, Inc., Publishers
San Francisco, California USA

Library of Congress Catalog Card Number 75-148656

International Standard Book Number ISBN 0-87589-100-4

Manufactured in the United States of America
    Composed and printed by York Composition Company, Inc.
    Bound by Chas. H. Bohn & Co., Inc.

JACKET DESIGN BY WILLI BAUM, SAN FRANCISCO

FIRST EDITION

Code 7126

The Jossey-Bass
Behavioral Science Series

General Editors

WILLIAM E. HENRY, *University of Chicago*
NEVITT SANFORD, *Wright Institute, Berkeley*

To the children of
Martin Luther King, Jr.,
for this is a study of a new generation

PREFACE

The interregnum, *during which the forces balanced each other fairly well, is now at an end. . . . As American Negroes became educated and culturally assimilated, but still found themselves excluded, they grew bitter. . . . We are now in a deeply unbalanced world situation. Many human relations will be readjusted in the present world revolution, and among them race relations are bound to change considerably. As always in a revolutionary situation when society's moorings are temporarily loosened, there is, on the one hand, an opportunity to direct the changes into organized reforms and, on the other hand, a corresponding risk involved in letting the changes remain uncontrolled and lead into disorganization. To do nothing is to accept defeat.*

Gunnar Myrdal,
An American Dilemma

Perhaps, in the words of Gunnar Myrdal, societies proceed from one "interregnum" to another through a host of intermittent agonies and lost opportunities. But if Myrdal was correct in prophesying an age of turmoil, even he may not have foreseen the lengths and depths this turmoil was to reach. It would have been virtually impossible to predict the events of the 1960s from the vantage point of the early 1940s. Indeed, the decade of the 1960s may become a major watershed in the political history of this nation. Once the societal corpus was examined for its racism, a host of other pathologies was revealed as well. And as the problems took on new dimensions so did the response to them. Despite a myriad of competing labels the 1960s may ultimately be known as the decade of political activism—and of student activism in particular.

In increasing numbers, students have ceased to be passive receptacles of pedagogy and have begun to actively educate others to their visions. And as activism has expanded from a few schools to many the issues have proliferated along with the participatory options. These now range from the Peace Corps to protest against the war in Vietnam, from volunteer work in local tutoring programs to efforts to revolutionize the structure of the university, and from traditional nonviolence to violence itself. For all of this the Civil Rights Movement was a beginning, and those students who went south in the early and middle 1960s were the vanguard.

Dynamics of Idealism is an account of part of that vanguard and deals with the 1965 Summer Community Organization and Political Education (SCOPE) project of the Southern Christian Leadership Conference. One of the largest projects of the southern campaign, SCOPE involved more than three hundred volunteers from all over the country in a two-and-one-half-month voter registration effort in counties scattered through six states (Alabama, Georgia, Florida, North Carolina, South Carolina, and Virginia). Initially buoyed by an idealistic commitment to change a nation, the project had results which are instructive for their commentary on the problems at issue and for the light shed on activism as a social process and activists as social types. In fact, this book resists any quick categorization of either audience or subject matter. It is written not only with an eye to sociological scholars interested in race relations, politics, and social movements but also as a cautionary tale for the many (whether community organizers and protesters or community officials and university administrators) who are directly embroiled in change as it continues to unfold.

Dynamics of Idealism is hardly the first account of student activism or even of student civil rights volunteers. Journalists and social scientists alike have given increasing attention to student protest in its various forms. The celebrated Council of Federated Organizations (COFO) project in Mississippi during the summer of 1964 produced a profuse literature as did the Free Speech Movement at Berkeley during the following fall and the more recent antiwar activities of the Students for a Democratic Society, to name but a few of the benchmarks in the changing face of American politics. Social scientific studies include those of Philip Altbach, Lewis Feuer, Richard Flacks, Kenneth Keniston, Charles Levy, S. M. Lipset, and Alphonso Pinkney. It may help to indicate briefly how our research both shares and departs from some of the characteristics of this literature.

First, most of the previous research on student protest has concentrated on describing the distinctive attributes of the activists themselves, that is, their economic backgrounds, their family relations, their views of the world, and their personal aspirations for the future. These considerations are certainly important, and we follow suit. Yet we consider activism as well as the activists and analyze it as a political movement unfolding over time. Although the individual volunteers can hardly be ignored in this effort the emphasis is not so much on how the volunteers shape the movement as on how the character of the movement and its context shape the volunteers.

This emphasis leads, in turn, to a second respect in which our research differs from others'. For the most part, studies of activism collect data at only one point in time, generally after a particular activist episode is either well underway or played out. Because we wanted to focus on social processes over time, we collected data at three distinct points. We administered questionnaires immediately before and after the summer experience. In them we asked many of the same questions so as to gauge changes that had occurred. The third point of data collection occurred four years later when we conducted telephone interviews with a small subsample of forty volunteers to get at least a rough impression of what had happened in the interim.

The use of questionnaires also distinguishes this study from much of the previous research, which relied upon either journalistic interviews or psychological probings in depth. To some extent our own study relies on all three sources. We used some journalistic materials, particularly transcribed field interviews conducted by the staff of the Stanford radio station during the summer. We also made occasional depth probings during our experiences as participant observers, and we have had access to several diaries and personal documents. For the most part, however, the questionnaires were the primary data source. More than 80 per cent of the volunteers completed the first questionnaire during the SCOPE orientation sessions in June. Although a precise response rate was impossible to calculate because of late-comers, early departures, and the consequent difficulty of calculating an exact base, the rate was certainly higher than that obtained for the physical examination required by the SCOPE project. Later, 71 per cent of our previous respondents completed the follow-up questionnaire administered by mail in the fall, and another seventeen volunteers answered only the follow-up.

We have no illusions that questionnaires are the only path to truth or even a necessarily sure path. Data always require interpretation, and our interpretations often do more to prod speculation than to supply definiteness. And yet, questionnaires do have the particular virtue of calling attention to the rich heterogeneity of a group as large as SCOPE and one exposed to as many variant conditions. Hopefully such data cut through stereotypic absolutes (whether rhapsodic or vilifying) in search of accurate relative proportions. Not all the volunteers fit any single description, and any understanding of the movement depends upon a grasp of this variety.

One last preliminary comment concerns the timing of the study. It has taken five years to complete this report, and who now recalls the years of the middle 1960s, when progress seemed a reality rather than an illusion and when so many were caught up in the drama and enthusiasm of the southern movement? Many consciences momentarily eased have been agonized anew. And as the movement has changed and fragmented, the line between radicals and liberals has become a division of enmity rather than labor.

In part, then, *Dynamics of Idealism* is about yesterday. Perhaps this is inevitable in any social science research as opposed to journalistic accounts. It was certainly inevitable in our case since the project was sufficiently controversial at its inception to preclude a large-scale research grant that would lift our routine professional commitments until the job was done. But there are advantages to the time lag as well, some virtues to be salvaged from the liability. Because of the interval between the events and their analysis, we have had access to hindsight in assessing the movement. For example, had we written quickly on the heels of 1965, we might have spent a good deal of time trying to account for the unusual success that the movement seemed to be generating. Now, however, the premise of success seems more dubious, and we are led to assay the factors that account for the frustrations of the movement as well as its fulfillments. Indeed, we suggest that short-run success but long-run failure is common among movements that depend upon students, intellectuals, and outsiders for their manpower.

Finally, the study seems to us to retain its relevance in dealing with issues that have become chronic and recurrent in American politics. Our prime objective was never just to describe one group of volunteers

but rather to examine phenomena and relationships that are more enduring. For example, the study deals with the beginnings of black power in
an organizational context, and it highlights violence and apathy as two
quite different responses to oppression within Negro communities. We
examine a number of facets of student movements as a generic political
form and note many of the dilemmas and tensions which beset any
precarious venture seeking radical change. Because we are discussing a
scene in which such issues were manifested and articulated so clearly, we
may be able to increase understanding of the future as well as of the past.

The summer of 1965 was only one chapter of an unfinished saga
that envelops us all. The Civil Rights Movement has become much more
than the effort of blacks to win acceptance from whites. It has had far-
reaching impact on the quality of American political life and has produced new styles of political participation that are burningly relevant to
everything from war to education. But none of this developed overnight.

The Civil Rights Movement was born far earlier than the middle
1960s or for that matter the middle 1950s with the fabled Montgomery
bus boycott. A glance at the movement's more distant past suffices to
indicate that its current agonies are not unprecedented. In fact, there is
a sobering periodicity to the history of Negro protest.

Consider, for example, the now familiar phenomenon of demonstrations which seem more futile than productive in any ultimate reckoning. Quite apart from the slave revolts in the ante-bellum South, men
like Frederick Douglass were initiating boycotts, pickets, mass marches,
and so on, in the North before the Civil War. And even at that time de
jure victories were often de facto defeats, such as a penalty of one cent
awarded in a successful suit against a railroad. Nor is there anything new
in the tendency for frustration to produce reactions (in the form of all-
Negro institutions, for example) which inhibit subsequent integrationist
efforts. If this tendency is true for the current black power movement,
it was true in different ways for the Negro churches in the late eighteenth
century, Negro business firms and schools in the late nineteenth century,
and the Black Muslims in the early twentieth century. Each of these
black institutions developed vested interests which could be threatened
by integration.

The participation of whites in the movement is also anything but
novel. Both the NAACP and CORE depended upon whites for their inception and grew to be dominated by whites at later periods. There is
some precedent for the despair of militant blacks who see little hope for
real progress as long as whites are in a position to compromise the goals
of the movement and to impede its autonomous development.

But it is sometimes all too easy to debunk the present by recalling
the past. The phase of the Civil Rights Movement at issue here, beginning

roughly with Mongomery in 1957, did indeed have new aspects that are important to understand. For one thing, it occurred shortly after the United States Supreme Court had put the legal quietus on the separate but equal justification for segregation. This change gave new motivation to blacks acting in their own behalf, and the motivation increased with the realization that court decisions alone would accomplish little since "all deliberate speed" translates to much less than a snail's pace. To use a well-worn phrase, there had been a revolution of rising expectations coupled with a revealing stagnancy of action; the discrepancy between the two provided crucial impetus.

Another distinctive aspect of the movement between 1957 and 1965 was its southern roots. Much of the earlier civil rights effort had been grounded in the North to take advantage of existing legal and political machinery and the local spirit of liberal reasonableness. And yet northern tokenism could be used against a movement rather than in its favor, that is, as a concession to halt further progress. In the South, where the situation was at its worst, there was an opportunity to discredit the prevailing system altogether. By stripping away the legitimacy of state and local authorities for the rest of the nation to see, the way was prepared for national forces to step in with legislative and executive action. Insofar as the southern movement had success at all—and clearly it did with respect to public accommodations, though much less so with regard to education, employment, and the vote—the principle of discrediting local officials was all important. Indeed, if revolution is at all possible in a putative democracy, it may depend upon demonstrating the immorality and duplicity of elected authorities. This strategy is the genius of nonviolence itself, in which leading with a nonviolent heart provokes a violent club in response.

Violence on the part of white officials toward southern blacks was hardly new. But there were new aspects to this particular violence. One concerned the occasion for it as a reply to demands that were constitutionally unexceptionable, highly specific, and clearly communicated. The movement was asking for things—integrated seating on city buses, integrated lunch counters, integrated interstate terminals, equitable voter registration—that were not easy to dismiss as too much too soon. A system reacting brutally to such requests was suspect to its core. And this was particularly the case considering the people who were being brutalized. Not only did they include whites for the first time, but the Negro victims were far more visible as relatively high-status students in the midst of public political activity.

February 1, 1960, is often regarded as the beginning date for this activity. On that day, four Negro students from the Agricultural and Technical College of North Carolina went into downtown Greensboro and sat at a lunch counter awaiting service only to receive vituperative resistance. The sit-in movement spread quickly, and by May the Student Non-Violent Coordinating Committee had been formed. Ultimately, SNCC moved from lunch counter privileges to a host of other grievances. In each area it provided a goad for the established civil rights organizations (SCLC, CORE, NAACP) and elicited national attention by provoking local authorities. Police brutality became a way of life, and the young civil rights workers began to forfeit bail and serve their sentences to lend further meaning to their actions. All this was exacerbated when SNCC moved into Mississippi in 1961 to battle segregation at its apogee. In 1963 SNCC joined with several other groups to form the Mississippi Council of Federated Organizations (COFO) and to work with the Mississippi Freedom Democratic Party on the assumption that the course of state politics could be changed with a massive campaign of voter registration. At this point whites became a conspicuous element of the new militancy. Here were whites working not as prestigeful lawyers, educators, and financiers in the parlors of northern power, but as canvassers, picketers, and marchers in the dust of southern streets.

Although a few whites were working within the southern movement from the beginning the first major influx of northern white students came to Mississippi in the fall of 1963. These were largely from Yale and Stanford and were organized by Allard Lowenstein, who was later elected to Congress in 1968 and defeated in 1970. The experiences of these students in 1963 were a harbinger of things to come. In the summer of 1964 Mississippi played host to an estimated five hundred white students who stepped up the pace of voter registration activities considerably. This was the fabled "long, hot summer" whose drama was made tragically clear at the outset by the deaths of James Chaney, Andrew Goodman, and Michael Schwerner near Philadelphia, Mississippi, in June. This was a summer in which liberals everywhere waited anxiously for the evening news, hoping not to hear of more deaths but expecting them just the same. And although this was also the summer in which Congress and the nation were stirred, however temporarily, to produce a major civil rights act concerning accommodations, it was clear that COFO was only a beginning rather than a culmination of a new stage of the long-standing Civil Rights Movement. The white volunteers of this period helped greatly, particularly in a symbolic capacity. Not only did they provide lines of communication between the southern movement and the rest of the nation but they also pricked the consciences of a new generation of students and prodded many into an activism that may still be short of its peak.

The next chapter recounts our abortive effort to study the 1964 Mississippi movement, an attempt that suddenly foundered only hours before our questionnaires were to be distributed at the June orientation session in Oxford, Ohio. But 1965 presented another opportunity. This time SCLC was to sponsor student volunteers in Alabama, Georgia, Florida, South Carolina, North Carolina, and Virginia. The program was called SCOPE, and since COFO had retrenched its forces, SCOPE was the largest and most variegated of all summer civil rights programs during that year. Here our general historical overview can end, and our detailed research story can begin.

Unlike most researchers, social scientists often incur a special debt to their subjects who provide so much for so little. Such a debt is especially obligatory here. This study depended from the start on its very nonrandom respondents, volunteers who gave their trust and cooperation not only by completing tedious questionnaires under trying circumstances but also by taking us into their confidence for informal conversations before, during, and after the summer at issue.

We are also grateful to the staff of the Southern Christian Leadership Conference and its SCOPE project, without whom we would not have learned so much or experienced so richly. The late Martin Luther King, Jr., Bayard Rustin, Andrew Young, and Hosea Williams would all have been fitting persons to whom to dedicate this book. Others within the movement also offered great help and insight, including James Bevel, Norman Hill, and especially Mark Harrington, who served as our liaison with the SCOPE staff throughout the project, always helping with details and always nurturing our illusions of contributing by responding readily to our analyses. Surely we have taken much more than we have given; the royalties from this book are a scant measure of our debt to SCLC.

We are also indebted to those academic colleagues who supported us during the SCOPE orientation when our research was hanging by a slender thread. Walter Johnson, James Shenton, Samuel Surace, and C. Vann Woodward were especially sustaining and strategic. Margaret Long, a woman born of magnolia who has flowered as an olive branch, provided strength and charm throughout the experience. And August Meier has been a special and continuing source of ideas and reinforcement.

Then too there are those who provided the funds without which this study might never have been completed. Most of these people gave far more than money since they also supplied personal encouragement and valuable suggestions. This is certainly the case with the late Kenneth Underwood, director of the Danforth Study of Campus Ministries and a man whose life was dedicated to the mingling of scholarship and values. It is true of Jack Harrison, who managed to find small sums from his Institute for Christian Faith and Higher Education to finance the study at crucial moments. It is true as well of Vernon Eagle of the New World

Foundation, which provided the largest grant for the study and then waited patiently for a book that came too late to give direct assistance to a phase of the movement that ended so soon. We are also grateful to the National Science Foundation for funds granted the University of Wisconsin Research Committee to allow use of computation facilities. We especially appreciate the University of Wisconsin Research Committee's prompt award of an emergency grant, which funded the first, abortive attempt at this research in 1964. Even though that attempt failed it ultimately led to the study launched in 1965.

The study has depended on a number of research assistants and part-time clerical helpers. K. Ray Stubbs, initially one of the volunteers, was a valuable source of recollection and analytic skill. Chanita Stillerman did yeoman service at the data collection stage. Connie Kolpin was invaluable as typist and girl Friday throughout the writing.

Finally, since this study was done largely on an off-hours basis, we thank our families, from whom we took much of the time required. No other project would have won such ready acquiescence from them or from us.

Washington, D.C.   N. J. DEMERATH III
Madison, Wisconsin   GERALD MARWELL
Louvain, Belgium   MICHAEL T. AIKEN
June 1971

CONTENTS

Dynamics
of Idealism

White Activists
in a Black Movement

Notes from a Research Diary

F_{or} *Negroes who substantially are excluded from society* [*social*] *science is needed even more desperately than for any other group in the population. For social scientists the opportunity to serve in a life-giving purpose is a humanist challenge of rare distinction. Negroes too are eager for a rendezvous with truth and discovery.*
  Martin Luther King, Jr.—*Seventy-fifth Annual Convention*
    of the American Psychological Association

Fellow Social Scientists . . .
It would appear that social scientists, whatever they may feel or do about the Civil Rights Movement as private citizens, have a special interest in, and responsibility for, understanding these great events of our time. It behooves us as professional social scientists to be involved with history as it is made and to do what we can to understand events even as they occur. . . . Doubtless we could do more; but it seems impossible to believe that we should do less. It would be ironic indeed if our disciplines had to study these events retrospectively and at second-hand.
  Irwin Deutscher, *president, Society for the Study of*
    Social Problems
  Alvin W. Gouldner, *editor-in-chief,* Trans-Action
  Herbert C. Kelman, *president, Society for the Psychological*
    Study of Social Issues
  Pitirim A. Sorokin, *president, American Sociological*
    Association
  William F. Whyte, *president, The Society for Applied*
    Anthropology
      Trans-Action, Spring 1965

One of the most frequent demands on the contemporary scholar is to maximize his "relevance." The charge is especially clear for social scientists. And yet relevance is sometimes easier to espouse than to effect. This chapter is an account of the difficulties encountered in this study and describes the complex and often turbulent events surrounding our efforts to gain access to the action. Of course, the history of this research is not as important as the history of the movement, and it is only to us that it seems as long.

It is not always simple to offer a straight-forward chronology of a convoluted research process. For one thing, research seldom proceeds according to the lofty canons of a proper science. For another, it is difficult to be candid about oneself and one's embarrassments. Finally, it is not always clear how much to say about others. With few exceptions we have decided to use the anonymity traditionally expected of the social scientist so that we can be as candid as possible. Certainly the roles and behaviors are more important than the identities behind them.

1964 COFO CAMPAIGN

Although the empirical materials in this book deal exclusively with the southern civil rights volunteers during the summer of 1965, our involvement began in the spring of 1964. It was clear then that in the history of the Civil Rights Movement the forthcoming COFO summer project in Mississippi was to be a landmark, a massive program with massive objectives. Some one thousand volunteers were to be recruited with the primary goal of attacking American racism at its sorest point. Because research designs must be made in advance, we began to develop our plans even as COFO was developing its own.

Our first step was to approach the student head of the University of Wisconsin branch of SNCC, who in turn called COFO headquarters in Jackson, Mississippi, for their reactions to the study. Unfortunately, the director of the COFO project was not in Jackson at that time, so we sent a copy of our detailed proposal to the COFO office and waited for approval. More than a week passed. Since this was already May each passing day was crucial in delaying the drafting and printing of the questionnaires to be distributed at the volunteers' training session in early June. This was the first but hardly the last instance in which we were to wring our hands and keep a wary eye on the calendar while awaiting word from the movement. Finally we called COFO and heard the good news that the director would grant us access to the students during the training sessions.

Meanwhile we were advised to contact a staff member of the

Commission on Religion and Race of the National Council of Churches. The National Council was financing and providing administration for a good part of the summer project, including the training sessions. The staff member was enthusiastic and cooperative and thought filling out the questionnaires so important that it might be scheduled as a training activity in its own right. He asked Michael Aiken (who was to be in charge of questionnaire administration) to attend staff meetings before the training began so that final arrangements could be made then. We were heartened, but we also had a deadline to meet since the questionnaires and all arrangements had to be ready within two weeks.

Contrary to the view of most questionnaire respondents, constructing a useful set of questions is not easy. One must cover an obstacle course mined with such booby traps as the loaded question, confusing response categories, the question that is really two in one so that a single answer is necessarily ambiguous, and the problem of predetermining responses either by creating response sets or by more blatant forms of bias. Good questionnaires also require a notion of what one wants to examine and, indeed, what one expects to find. In this case we had to anticipate what the relevant issues might be in the minds of the volunteers and in the civil rights experience itself. We also had to speculate on the kinds of variables which might be linked to them: Is it worth including a personality battery? How much emphasis should be placed on the ideological and status characteristics of parents? How much do we really need to know about the volunteer's wider concerns and aspirations? These considerations took all the time available.

Aiken arrived in Oxford two days before the training was to begin. The next day the Steering Committee met to discuss the research and to make the final arrangements. Unhappily for us these proved to be no arrangements at all. The composition of the Steering Committee was an important factor in this impotence. The director and the seven district field workers were black but the remaining committee members were white, including the staff representative from the National Council of Churches, several social scientists from the National Training Laboratory, and a psychiatrist who served as an advisor to COFO. Not surprisingly, the Steering Committee was split along lines that were partly racial and partly status, and in some respects based on the degree of one's experience on the civil rights firing line. This factionalism was reflected even in the seating; the representatives of the National Council of Churches and the members of the National Training Lab sat on one side of the circle and the Mississippi COFO staff sat on the other, with Aiken and the psychiatrist linking the two groups at each end. Polarization was perhaps inevitable.

From our standpoint the meeting went from bad to worse. The COFO director, a man of enormous charisma among whites and blacks alike, did not recall his prior approval of the research even after a reminder from his assistant. Once the topic was reopened he was provided reasons for doubting the worth of the study. The psychiatrist indicted questionnaire research generally and stated that our work had no strategic value for the COFO project. He felt it could even be unnerving to the students. Rebuttal from the social scientists of National Training Labs was to little avail, as was a statement of the National Council of Churches representative to the effect that an appropriate commitment had been made and should be honored. The COFO director concurred with the negative advice of the psychiatrist and ventured the further thought that social science had done nothing for the movement before and would not in the future. His thoughts were supported by his staff, and the decision was made without ever taking a vote; consensus emerges spontaneously in participatory democracies.

Some reasons for the decision were voiced later. Although Aiken had promised to let the staff be our guide concerning the use of the materials and their publication, it was feared by some that the information was potentially too explosive. What if the data revealed that even a fraction of the students were self-confessed members of the Communist Party and such information fell into the hands of the FBI, the House Un-American Activities Committee, or some similar federal or Mississippi agency? Indeed, what were the guarantees that we would not hand over such information? After all, we had four strikes against us from the start: we were white; we were scholars rather than volunteers; two of us were native southerners (one from Mississippi); and all three of us were near thirty.

From the standpoint of the COFO staff leaders the decision was justifiable. Regardless of what social science may have done to expose the perniciousness of segregation and poverty, it has done little for the movement itself. To argue that we could provide a service by correcting widespread fallacies concerning the volunteers, by providing criteria for future recruitment, or by supplying insight into the friction and tension that were inevitable in a project of this sort was understandably hollow to men who were leading a venture in which survival itself would often be in doubt. Nor did it help to point out that the questionnaire could aid in the orientation by making the volunteers aware of the contingencies they might face. This was the task of the veteran field workers. From their perspective any indirect tutelage from an outside source would have been a poor substitute for and perhaps even subversive to their crucial expertise and authority. But above all we were white, and black-white tensions were conspicuous within the project even then. The goal of the orientation was precisely to take the white student volunteers out of the pedagogical hands of their white professors and place them in proper relation to the black staff. It was important to sever rather than to strengthen the volunteers' ties to academia, at least temporarily.

This, then, was the abortive end of our first attempt to do the research reported in this volume. There was little bitterness on either side. Everyone concerned with the project, including the COFO director and the psychiatrist consultant, went out of his way to apologize for the confusion. We were disappointed but resigned. While the COFO workers trekked south to Mississippi only a few days after the tragic and foreboding disappearance of Andrew Goodman, James Cheney, and Michael Schwerner, Aiken limped home to the safe confines of Madison, Wisconsin. We returned funds to the University of Wisconsin Alumni Research Foundation, which had generously granted them on one week's notice. We had no plans for any future efforts. Those were only to develop six months later.

FROM COFO TO SCOPE

The summer of 1964 was as dramatic as the nation had been led to expect. The COFO task force went a long way toward accomplishing some of its objectives. Surely it provoked national attention and made southern civil rights a conspicuous and festering sore in American society rather than a hidden virus. The response of local authorities to the COFO volunteers discredited southern authority everywhere and forced the federal government to take at least small steps, such as the 1964 Civil Rights Bill. COFO helped a generation of college students to see the possibilities of activism. Finally, COFO signaled to millions of blacks that passivity was past and redress was in the offing. In short, if one lists the landmark years in the slow development of civil rights in this country, 1964 takes its place alongside 1954, and COFO was very much responsible.

Ironically, however, the summer was not a portent of bigger and better campaigns from COFO itself. COFO was a contrived coalition from the beginning; under the internal and external stress of the summer its cohesion began to loosen. The relations between its constituent parties, SNCC, CORE, the NAACP, and SCLC, had been smouldering for some time, and they became increasingly inflamed as the four carried unequal weights and represented quite different organizational styles and goals. For example, both the NAACP and SCLC tend to be run from the top with a clear structure of authority and a premium on long-term planning. On the other hand, SNCC depended less on authority and more on

ideology and charisma for its cohesion; it emphasized the role of the
grass roots and participatory democracy as matters of principle. Although
CORE tended to follow the NAACP and SCLC organizational modes in
its national affairs, its field officers in the Deep South were relatively
autonomous and used this autonomy to move in SNCC's direction. And
because CORE and SNCC were dominant within COFO, their own
predilections carried the day. Thus, the COFO director reflected SNCC's
antipathy to structured authority by resigning at the end of the summer
and even going so far as to change his name as well as his location to
escape the burdens of his role. Because of his centrality within COFO, the
coalition virtually disbanded with his withdrawal. But there were other
problems. Many of the permanent field workers felt that they had invested
too much time in training volunteers for too little return since most of the
students went back to their homes and colleges in September. Many field
workers also felt that the volunteers were a liability rather than an asset;
they continued to expose the project to danger but remained unable to
relate effectively to local Negroes. Here were the roots of at least one
version of black power. Black field workers were coming to feel increasingly that blacks alone must gain control over their own destiny and build
a movement that could endure without white help.

For all of these reasons, then, COFO rather quickly disintegrated.
By early 1965 it was questionable whether the next summer would witness
a repeat performance by white students. SNCC and CORE were doing
virtually no recruiting. Would another organization fill the gap? In
March SCLC announced that it would take on the task. No organization
seemed better equipped to do so. For all of the charisma generated within
COFO, SCLC had more with the late Martin Luther King, Jr., as its
president. It is true that King provoked some resentment among the
young veterans of CORE and SNCC (who mockingly referred to him
as "de Lawd"), and SCLC was suspect for its traditional religious rhetoric,
its tendency to instruct rather than consult the grassroots and, perhaps,
above all, for what was seen as a tendency to move into situations just in
time to make the final push and receive the ultimate credit. Nevertheless,
King retained sufficient respect within the movement for SCLC to operate
flexibly. Surely his wide respect beyond the movement helped to make
SCLC the most stable and financially well off of all the indigenous southern civil rights groups. In these respects SCLC was ideal as the successor
to COFO, and it was perhaps the only organization equipped to take on
the task alone.

It was characteristic of the SCLC style to create a new sub-
organizational unit within its staff to do the job. Thus was born SCOPE
with voter registration as its principal charge. In March SCOPE began

to recruit volunteers, aiming for five hundred or more. It sent a number of permanent staff members to campuses around the country and sought to enlist faculty members as local sponsors and organizers. At this point our research again seemed appropriate, and we began the process of gaining access for the second time.

INITIAL CONTACTS AND CONVERSATION

After our ill-fated experience with COFO why did we decide to try again? The change in organizational sponsorship was one reason. Because SCLC was more stable and secure than COFO, especially in its relations with the white intellectual community, we felt we had a better chance of gaining cooperation without being seen as a threat. After all, SCOPE had thrown in its lot with academia for the sake of recruitment and had even gathered a group of faculty from such campuses as Columbia, Chicago, and the University of California, Los Angeles, to serve as counselors and workshop leaders during the orientation week. Another encouraging factor was the altered image of the civil rights volunteer. In the spring of 1964 the legitimacy of the whole volunteer enterprise was somewhat precarious in the eyes of the nation. It was moot as to how many would survive, let alone succeed. By the spring of 1965, however, civil rights work had become more routinized and accepted. Even the South was less shocked by the coming invasion, although it remained outraged by the Civil Rights Movement in general. Thus, the atmosphere was somewhat less foreboding, and we anticipated less fear within the movement that our data would have damaging consequences. A third consideration concerned changes in our own situation. In 1964 we had virtually no funding save for a small emergency grant. In 1965 limited funds were available in connection with Demerath's study of student values and campus religion for the Danforth Study of the Campus Ministry. The Danforth study also made it possible to gather some identical data on Wisconsin students with whom to compare the volunteers.

Finally, the rejection by COFO of our 1964 study had resulted partly from a series of misunderstandings, our ineptitude in handling organizational tensions, and our failure to think through the research and its contingencies from the standpoint of the movement. We felt that we could now minimize such problems. For example, we now realized that people involved in a social movement under pressure are not likely to be reliable correspondents; anything less than face-to-face communication is easily forgotten in the press of events. We had also learned to make all arrangements with the full and direct acknowledgement of those in ultimate command of the situation. Perhaps most of all we realized the importance of making these arrangements well before events begin to boil.

When a small staff is running an orientation program for the first time with several hundred students to nurture, instruct, and assign to posts all over the South, three sociologists are hardly welcome without ample introductions in advance.

Our first step was to seek legitimacy through religious auspices. After all, it was the Southern *Christian* Leadership Conference. The late Kenneth Underwood, director of the larger Danforth study of which Demerath's research was a part, wrote a letter introducing us to the director of the SCOPE project, with a copy to King. Because the Danforth Foundation is a major source of funds for programs in American Protestantism we hoped that its name might have some influence. A phone call to the SCOPE director dashed our optimism. It was obvious that the letter had received only a glance. Even over the phone the director conveyed a note of organizational disarray, and it was clear that no letter was likely to get an adequate reading, let alone a reply. The orientation was to begin on June 13, less than a month away. The director had yet to complete his staff, and even the staff members on hand had joined him in leaving the Atlanta office for the Selma to Montgomery march at precisely the time when the most pressing details of SCOPE begged for attention. Thus, even with the organizational sophistication of SCLC, when a major event such as Selma occurred it was difficult to leave someone behind to mind the shop. Social movements, unlike bureaucracies, tend to lurch from crisis to crisis, and the commitment they depend on is such that the committed are unwilling to be left out of the major happenings. In any event, it was readily apparent during the first part of the phone conversation that one or two of us would have to go to Atlanta before the orientation to arrange for the research. Accordingly, it was decided that Aiken and Demerath would arrive on May 30 with a draft of the revised questionnaire in hand.

The SCOPE project had been assigned as its Freedom House King's recently vacated home only three blocks from SCLC headquarters in the Atlanta ghetto. The Selma march had exacted its toll. With the volunteer orientation now only two weeks off there was still no orientation site. The staff members were inexperienced and were under extreme pressure exacerbated by a common fear. Southern Negroes for the most part, everyone was made to feel the importance of battening down the organizational hatches before the northern white middle-class volunteers arrived to effect their own organizational style and to exert their own organizational influence.

Finally the director arrived and we were able to see him briefly for a much-interrupted, disjointed discussion. We had only time to present a brief explanation of our research intentions, leave a draft of the questionnaire, and arrange for a longer session to begin that evening. But although our first confrontation was brief it was also revealing. The director shared some of the same doubts and fears of the COFO leader the summer before. He too was concerned about the potential explosiveness of a questionnaire that sought information on political preferences, attitudes towards communists, and religious predilections. Beyond this, his own position as a newcomer within SCLC may have made him particularly concerned about us. But he may also have been wary of dispatching us quickly since others in the organization might value the research.

The appointment for that night never materialized. We returned on schedule for the meeting, but the director was waylaid by a speaking engagement and a series of meetings so we chatted with members of the staff, sharing orange drinks and a poor TV late-show. The director's arrival after midnight brought this reverie to a screeching halt. Faced with a backlog of administrative problems that his staff had been unable to handle, the director himself set to work. He berated his executive assistant for sweeping floors when he should have been answering crucial correspondence. He inveighed against any alcohol in the house, pointing out that many were waiting for an opportunity to discredit the project. Finally, he concluded with a long lament to the effect that all was chaos and all would be lost unless he was given efficient cooperation. The performance was magnificent. It was the stuff of which social movements are made in motivating an inexperienced staff at the risk of alienating them. Surprisingly there seemed to be relatively little alienation, at least among those who had been through so much before in similar style with the director. Meanwhile, our scheduled appointment was restricted to a fleeting conversation as he and his wife drove us back to our hotel at two in the morning. Having decided to involve others in any decision concerning the research, he asked us to see King's executive assistant the next morning.

Predictably, we discovered in the morning that the executive assistant was out of the office and would not return until late in the afternoon. However, we were told that we should see another SCLC staff member. We did so in search of any support that we could muster. His response was basically an articulate, diplomatic stall. He indicated that other areas needed research more and that ours was only one of many similar studies that SCLC was being asked to consider. Still, he agreed to look over the questionnaire and write us his advice. Although he concurred that we should probably still see King's assistant, he was largely cooling us out in sophisticated fashion.

When King's assistant finally arrived he quickly arranged for the SCOPE director to join the conference but did not include the staff member whom we had seen that morning. We found the assistant bright and level-headed—perhaps because he alone of the people we had seen seemed to understand our project, penetrating quickly to the basic issues raised. The potential explosiveness of the data was broached early. He asked whether the House Un-American Activities Committee could subpoena the data, and, if so, how we would react. We replied that the data could indeed by subpoenaed and at the same time offered to sign a pledge that the three of us would face prosecution before relinquishing the material. We indicated plans for security precautions beyond mere anonymity, although we also suggested that the movement might have fallen prey to southern stereotypes in thinking that anything damaging or discrediting would emerge. Still, we asked the staff to go over the questionnaire and to let us know which items might be considered for possible exclusion.

Through all of this the SCOPE director was quiet, allowing King's executive assistant to take the initiative and the responsibility. We said we were eager to serve wherever possible in nonresearch capacities: for example, as members of the SCOPE orientation faculty. After roughly half an hour of such conversation, the executive assistant said simply that there was no way that SCLC could justifiably oppose the research. Truth was important, and they had nothing to hide. He agreed that the volunteers were likely to be a far more respectable group than others had alleged. He then asked how soon SCLC could have the data we collected so as to begin evaluating individual volunteers already committed for that summer. When we replied that this would be an invasion of the promised confidentiality of the questionnaire and that we were aiming for long-term findings and relationships, he quickly dropped the matter.

At the end of the meeting we were cheered but aware that this was not a final decision. In fact, we had learned of a large staff conference during the next two weeks near Washington, D.C., in which final arrangements for SCOPE were to be made. We were afraid that the executive assistant's own inclinations would not prevail in such circumstances. When we raised the matter with him, hoping to gain access to that meeting so that the research would not be dropped because of questions left unanswered, he replied that he was sure the matter would be settled before-hand, and advised us to call him later that week. Told of our need to go to press with the questionnaires as soon as possible, he indicated that we should go ahead. We did.

GOATS AMONG SHEEP: POLITICS OF
ACTION RESEARCH

Because we still lacked a formal decision on the research, we wanted to be on hand at least a day before the volunteers arrived for the orientation. On June 12, we arrived in Atlanta and made straight for the SCOPE Freedom House to get the final word. Alas, none of our previous contacts was available; all were in a meeting with a press conference to follow. Told that they would return to the Freedom House by ten in the evening, we once again planned for a late-night session. But once again the late night session was aborted, and we began to feel that time was running out. We were told that the staff meeting might still be going on in the hotel room of the man who was to run the orientation, so we set out to find the man and the meeting. If a decision was in the offing, we wanted to be present to answer questions. If the research was not on the agenda, we felt obliged to force the matter.

As it turned out, the meeting was in our hotel and our call from the lobby drew a prompt and gracious invitation to join the group in session. Some fifteen people were gathered, awaiting the arrival of the SCOPE director, who finally arrived after midnight. After an hour of quizzing the director, the orientation impresario (a most distinguished civil rights leader from outside SCLC) decided that it was too late to be efficient, and moved toward the bedroom. We stopped him and asked if we could discuss the research. He replied that he was too tired to deal with the issue, and left after suggesting that it wait until the next day.

At this point, the SCOPE director and the staff men who had earlier tried to discourage us began to repeat their doubts. Not only was the issue of political explosiveness raised again, but in addition we were accused of having betrayed a promise to show them a final draft of the questionnaire before going to press. Finally, we were told that even if the governor of Mississippi had submitted a research proposal, he would be entitled to every courtesy extended to us. The orientation leader then emerged to end the discussion for the night, with sides chosen and hostilities apparent.

By this time the prospects seemed grave. The one man within SCLC who had given us support—King's executive assistant—was out of town; the two that had seemed most dubious were in command. In a defeated mood, we went back to our room and went to bed. But neither of us could sleep, and finally our desperation led to an unorthodox move. We guessed that the man brought in to preside over the orientation had more influence with his old friend, King, than anyone else involved. Accordingly, we decided to appeal to him directly. We composed a long, hand-written letter reviewing our investment, our intentions, and our needs. We stated our disappointment, even indignation, at being shunted aside with so little understanding and for reasons that were not only wrong but contrived. We suggested that a project depending upon student volunteers and faculty sponsors could ill-afford to spurn research interest.

Finally, we summoned up the haughty sense of self-importance necessary to indicate that we were more than academic pretenders. The letter was slipped beneath the leader's door at an early morning hour, and we came away knowing that we had gambled. The letter could have been a blunder to end the research for good, but with so little time remaining and tempers shortening, we had no choice.

Before noon, we received a call from the orientation leader's colleague, who had also come to help with the Atlanta training. He asked us to come to the leader's suite immediately. We arrived to receive a pledge of full support, and joined the two in developing a strategy that would achieve acceptance of the research within SCOPE and SCLC. The orientation leader suggested that it was foolish to raise the question in any meeting until the favorable forces were available. He proposed to wait until Tuesday when both King and his executive assistant would be back in town. Although the strategy had the drawback of delaying the questionnaire distribution until the third day of the orientation at the earliest, it was again our only choice and we agreed. Not all of the volunteers arrived until Tuesday, and so by waiting we gained numbers even though we risked having our respondents affected by the orientation itself. In any event, we now had two important allies, and it was clear we needed every friend we could find.

But Sunday had other surprises in store. In our alter-roles as faculty counselors and workshop leaders for the orientation, we attended the "faculty meeting" called for that afternoon. The faculty were almost entirely white historians assembled from the Selma March. The meeting was uneventful until the orientation leader announced that he was appointing a three-person committee to judge our questionnaire and its design from a scholarly point of view. Because the committee included two historians and a southern journalist, our first thoughts concerned the traditional friction between history and sociology over the usefulness of questionnaires. But when we met with the committee after the faculty meeting had adjourned, the display of cross-disciplinary camaraderie would have warmed the hearts of any academician. And, if there was any doubt about the ultimate support of the faculty, it was to be quickly dispelled.

In the first session of the orientation that evening, the faculty members were asked to introduce themselves to the "student body." The first few dramatically disavowed their academic caste and pledged unrequited allegiance to the movement. Those later in line could only reiterate the same sentiments. The SCOPE director then took the floor and, before some 250 volunteers in the Joe Louis gymnasium, proceeded to castigate the faculty and its presumed knowledge as too highfalutin, too white, too middle-class, and too divorced from reality to deserve the volunteers' attention. The speech was little touched by moderation, and its anti-intellectual overtones prompted squirms and murmurs from faculty, volunteers, and SCLC staff alike.

Our own reaction was ambivalent. On the one hand, we actually agreed with some of the substance of the speech. On the other hand, the tone of the speech and the reaction to it made our research prospects more difficult to gauge. It was possible that anti-intellectualism would so polarize SCOPE that SCLC would be forced to support the director by rejecting our research. And even if we were granted access to the volunteers, it was not at all clear how the volunteers themselves would respond to a scholarly questionnaire when scholarship itself had been denigrated. The evening exposed a tension that was to remain throughout the summer.

The actual work of the orientation began on Monday, June 14. Despite the friction, it was brilliantly conceived and executed. The orientation leader produced a dazzling array of outside speakers, including C. Vann Woodward and John Hope Franklin from academia, Charles Morgan from the American Civil Liberties Union, representatives from labor and the civil rights division of the United States Justice Department, and even an unannounced and unassuming talk by the COFO director of the previous summer. Each formal session included a good many freedom songs, sung with fewer inhibitions as the week went on.

Informal workshops occupied most of each afternoon. These were efforts to enrich the volunteers' perspectives on southern race relations through close discussions with the faculty experts. But as the week went on, most of the faculty turned over more and more of the time to veteran field workers, who occasionally used such techniques as role-playing to provide a facsimile of the confrontations ahead. Because all of this was new to so many there was an aura of unreality about the exercise. Here were bright college students suddenly told of their ignorance; here was a phalanx of committed workers suddenly led to doubt their commitments and to examine their motives.

Meanwhile, our behind-the-scenes problems continued. By Monday night the crisis over anti-intellectualism was threatening to fulminate. The orientation leader called a private meeting to allow the SCOPE director and the faculty to reconcile their differences; unhappily, the solution was not that simple. Despite the orientation leader's calm, the SCOPE director and several faculty members immediately began to compete over credentials and commitments. The meeting ended with the orientation leader's diplomatic statement that, of course, apologies are not required among friends.

Throughout this session the research was never mentioned, but it was on people's minds. Once again our reactions were peculiar and divided. Surely the study was jeopardized by the SCOPE director's sentiments. And yet his position seemed more defensible and no more arrogant than those of some faculty members. The faculty, in general, was too quick to anger and too slow to understand. And by this time we had been reinforced in our view that faculty leadership in the workshops was unnecessary since scholarly seminars were not appropriate. We told the SCOPE director later that evening that, regardless of our research interests, we had a good deal of sympathy for his position. He thanked us, but was clearly suspicious of our motives.

Tuesday was the day of reckoning for the research. The appointed faculty committee had decided to support us, perhaps to rally around the embattled banner of scholarship generally. We were reluctantly prepared to make two concessions, neither of which proved necessary: first, to allow SCLC final authorization on any publication, and second to strike some items from the printed questionnaires by hand before distribution. By now, both King and his executive assistant were back, but the decision would have to follow King's address to the volunteers that evening. Meanwhile, we continued to remind the orientation leader of the importance of reaching a decision with no further delay. We made sure that the faculty committee would be on hand. And we made one important addition to our support. Woodward had delivered a superb lecture in an afternoon session, after which he visited Demerath's workshop. While the two had dinner together later, Woodward was told of the research and asked it he would attend the decision-making meeting in our behalf. He agreed.

King's performance Tuesday night was typically inimitable. After beginning warmly with humor and modesty, he moved to his basic theme:

> I have been asked to discuss the question, "Why are you here?" . . . To my mind, the answer is quite simple. You are here because history is being made. A decade ago it was depressingly true that students were the silent and apathetic generation. McCarthyism muted the voices of students, and paralyzed them with fear. It robbed them of youth's most precious privilege: to question the world they inherit, to challenge it, and to act to change it. For most of the last generation of students, the American Dream was to escape to comfort, conformity, and security upon the ample bosom of a large corporation. Its aspirations were as trivial as its spirit. The educational mountains have labored and have brought forth educated mice. However . . . the tactic of nonviolent, direct action, which was the Negro's unique weapon, fitted perfectly in the hands of the new student generation. . . . Together they wrenched from an unwilling Congress the first federal enactments on

civil rights in nearly a hundred years. If the conceivable could happen, if everything were to come to a halt today, the achievements of the Negro-student alliance would nevertheless be monumental. In the decade of the sixties students found a conscience; Negroes found a courageous and ingenious ally; and the nation, suffocating with material corruption, found something in which it could have authentic pride. The civil rights movement had broken the social and political paralyses of the fifties, and freed the students first of all. They in turn gave to the civil rights movement the ingenious sit-ins and became the first of a series of allies who were destined to change history.

At this point King broadened the implications of the movement to include the need to end the Vietnamese war. Then he closed with a characteristic homiletic flourish:

> Together we will build right here in this southland a new and greater situation for all of God's children, where all men will respect the dignity and the worth of human personality, and when this day comes we will all be able to join hands, as I said at the end of the march on Washington, [applause] not just a few people, and when this day comes, all of us will be able to join hands, black man and white man, Jews and Gentiles, Protestants and Catholics, believers and nonbelievers, Muslims and Hindus, and we'll sing together, "Free at last, Free at last, Thank God Almighty, we're free at last."

Few of the volunteers had ever been so close to charisma, and the speech held the rapt attention of everyone in an audience swollen for the occasion. And yet both the substance and the tone of King's remarks left some uncomfortable. At least a few felt that he should have restricted his comments to the common goals of SCOPE rather than raise issues, such as Vietnam, about which there was division of opinion. A number of the volunteers also reported feeling out of place, as if in the midst of a southern Negro congregation for the first time. Many were not used to King's rhythm or to spontaneous responses from the listeners; insofar as the speech was a musical performance, using extended cadences to create tension and to prompt interjections for release, it was still alien music. Still, the speech was short, and King then presided over a rare question and answer session in which his eloquence and magnetism were sustained despite the spontaneity.

We arranged to meet with King on a small patch of lawn behind the gymnasium immediately after his presentation. Here there was very little light but relative privacy from the audience that surged to the podium after the session. The orientation leader began by briefly telling "Martin" something about us and our research and then introducing the others present. King had often quoted Woodward, so Woodward's support was difficult to spurn. King was also aware that the wife of the chairman of the faculty group had recently been clubbed by police in the Chicago demonstrations against the nonintegrationist policies of the school superintendent so the chairman's endorsement may have carried special weight. Finally, Margaret Long, the journalist, may have tipped the balance.

> The young sociologists proposed to the SCOPE director that they distribute questionnaires to the young missionaries to study their backgrounds and attitudes, and at the summer's end pass out other questions to determine the effect the summer experience would have on them. For some reason, the director felt such a study might betray untoward sentiments or endanger the project. The professors appealed in vain, and the director, adamant, said, "I'll just have to leave it up to Dr. King."
>
> "I don't know what's got into him," I remarked, "but why don't I tell Dr. King you're respectable young fellows and friends of the movement?"
>
> My already amiable rapport with the important visitors escalated to awe, until I felt some dismay at presenting myself as a favored handmaiden of "De Lawd" (as Snicks used to call King, a joke he enjoyed as much as the next one). We were to have a meeting with Dr. King where I could speak well of the sociologists, but it was a couple of days before it came-off—in a dark, grassy yard behind the Morris Brown College gym where SCOPE was meeting. . . . The professors and I repaired to the back yard, and I said, "Hello Martin," and he greeted me with his customary sweet and plain cordiality . . .
>
> Then, as if I were his favorite aunt, I put my arm through his and said, "Martin, these are real good, smart boys and they've got what seems to me an important and interesting study, and I wish they could do it."
>
> "Well," intoned Martin in his richest southern accent, "you know I always take yo word."
>
> Of course, I never in my born days presumed to put in my word to Martin Luther King, Jr. on any matter great or small, but he almost persuaded me that we were in weekly communication so he could take my word on matters of grave national urgency, and I reveled in our little act. Why, yes, Martin said, after our fond exchange before the impressed and delighted professors, he thought it would be an important study, and he hoped the gentlemen would get along with their questionnaire. We dispersed, I amid accolades of the professors who exclaimed that I was "just perfect," struck "exactly the right note," and "handled it beautifully." I glowed with pleasure and didn't belabor the point that King doubtless would have welcomed the study anyway.[1]

Somehow we liked to think of ourselves as older, wiser, and more polished than this account would have it, but Margaret Long's charming intercession was indeed important as another of the cards now stacked

[1] M. Long, "Martin Luther King: 'He Kept So Plain,'" *The Progressive,* May 1968, *32,* 24.

in our favor. Neither the SCOPE director nor the SCLC staff member who had previously tried to discourage us was present at the meeting. We mentioned this to King, trying to present and rebut their arguments as fairly as possible. We wanted all of the cards on the table. Finally, the orientation leader suggested that we be allowed to collect the data but that SCLC hold it in a kind of escrow until all parties had been satisfied. King agreed, and the meeting adjourned. It had been fifteen minutes of what seemed high drama to us but what may have appeared to others as melodrama with comic overtones.

We began to administer the questionnaires the next morning. The volunteers were not required to respond, and the crowded orientation schedule precluded a single session in which they might have filled them out as a group. Thus the response rate was an uncertainty. We were aware that many students become questionnaire-shy during college; activists are especially likely to suspect the value of empiricism and to begrudge the time required. For all these reasons, it was quite possible that we would achieve a very poor response rate to subvert the study despite our efforts.

Fortunately, the delay in administering the questionnaire actually worked in our favor. Some students saw the questionnaire as a way of manifesting their respect for intellectualism in the midst of anti-intellectual rancor. Since the orientation leader had gained the volunteers' enormous respect for his lucid, gentle, and wise articulation of real issues and concerns, his support of the study had more leverage than it might have had earlier. Then too, we had been able to make friends among the volunteers and to enlist the aid of the steering committee in eliciting responses. For whatever reason, we were able to achieve a highly respectable rate of over 80 per cent, although it is difficult to calculate it precisely because SCOPE never achieved a fully accurate count since volunteers continued to dribble in and drop out during and after the orientation.

Now only one problem remained: how to get out of town with the data in hand. The orientation was to end on Saturday with the volunteers dispersing throughout a six-state area. The scene was sure to be hectic. Anticipating this, we decided to raise the issue of the data the day before. That evening we approached King's executive assistant in the middle of the gym floor. He told us to go ahead and take the data. Immediately, however, the SCOPE director joined the conversation, repeating his doubts. We interjected a strong rebuttal that was reinforced by the executive assistant, who took the SCOPE director aside for a private talk. After fifteen minutes, he returned to say that he was going to the home of the other SCLC staff member who had been dubious about the project in order to settle the affair. We were left with the SCOPE director, and offered our unsolicited advice that if he was so concerned about the study and its repercussions, his best tactic now would be to wash his hands of any decision so that no ultimate blame would be placed on him. He seemed to agree, if unhappily.

At that point, we left the gym for a small gathering across town at the home of Margaret Long. The orientation leader was also there. He asked and was told about the last obstacle in our path. He then went quickly to the phone and returned fifteen minutes later with instructions for us to take the data and simply send a copy of the response distributions to the executive assistant for his clearance before going ahead with the analysis. The job was accomplished.

We stayed on until the following evening, bidding goodbyes and good lucks, helping to give assurance, and promising to stay in touch. We joined with the more than three hundred people in a large circle in the middle of the gym floor to sing "We Shall Overcome." Tears were as evident as the attempts to hold them back; crossed hands clasped with special strength and meaning. As car after car left for mostly rural communities, we were moved as participants rather than dispassionate researchers. Death was a possibility for each volunteer; both violence and harassment were certainties for many. They seemed young, but destined to age quickly.

SCOPE IN MIDSUMMER

The questionnaire given out at the Atlanta orientation was the first of two called for by the research design. The second was to include items from the first questionnaire in order to measure change and also questions seeking systematic information about the summer itself. Because we needed a good deal of knowledge about the summer to construct such a questionnaire, at least one of us had to travel south in midsummer to get a first-hand impression of the volunteers' lot. For a variety of reasons, including a southern accent that had a habit of returning quickly, Demerath was nominated. A speaking engagement in Virginia allowed him to ease into the experience by visiting two SCOPE projects there before moving on to Alabama.

The SCLC Ninth Annual Convention, held August 9–13 in Birmingham, Alabama, included volunteer representatives from most SCOPE projects around the South; thus it was an opportunity to canvass experiences on a wide scale. But this was not to be conversation in a vacuum. One of the most aggravated confrontations between the movement and white opposition was occurring in Greensboro, Alabama, some eighty miles south of Birmingham. Throughout July and early August, feelings had run high in the town and surrounding Hale County. There had been frequent arrests, beatings, and other intimidation directed against a voter registration campaign that had a good chance of electing Negroes soon. The convention offered a base from which to send reinforcements and encouragement, including King himself, who was to speak at a mass rally in Greensboro on August 12. To prepare for the speech, the SCLC-SCOPE staff decided to send a group of convention representatives to buttress the local workers in turning out the Hale County Negro community as a whole. With a hint of irony, the SCOPE director asked Demerath if he cared to go along for a few days of grassroots campaigning. The response could hardly have been no.

Civil rights activity and the conduct of research share at least one common tendency in honoring rules more in the breach than in the observance. Thus, six people driving to Greensboro on a fetid August afternoon set off by violating one of the most repeated safety rules of the southern movement. They managed to seat themselves so as to mix not only races but sexes on both front and back seats. This situation was a red flag for any passing redneck, and Demerath had a fleeting sense of holding the reins of a transparent Trojan Horse.

Recollections of the stay in Greensboro remain vivid. A meal of pigs' ears stays with one whether it stays down or not, especially when the cook seems to use it as a combined initiation rite and test of gastronomic courage. The same is true of a night spent in a Negro home, knowing that the price of a bed to oneself is doubling and even tripling up the family. This in a home whose walls are penetrable to the finger, much less the fist. The community mass meetings were also instructive. There is a peculiar fear involved in sitting in the rear of a church with open doors and cars slowly driving by within bomb-tossing range. On the other hand, there is added warmth and confidence in singing "We Shall Overcome" while four girls in the pew ahead do a slow frug to its beat.

Most of the white volunteers and local blacks had learned to react almost casually to danger. Seeing a pickup truck wtih a rifle in the rear window was commonplace. So was being tailed by such trucks or having them drive through the dirt roads of a black neighborhood to shout obscenities and then roar away. But having watched too many war movies in which a soldier's open disregard of caution resulted in certain death, Demerath spent a good deal of time calculating his percentages of safety. This was true, for example, when told that he must walk across town at midnight to get from the Negro church and freedom house to his bed for the evening. And yet there were also bizarre moments such as during a walk back to the church in the morning, when he was called to by two elderly white spinsters working in their garden. They said ever so sweetly that his home for the night was on their property and was occupied by a family that had worked for them for years. After their offer of lemonade had been accepted, they told of their alienation from both the movement and the Ku Klux Klan—but of course, "things were moving just too fast." At no point did they threaten reprisals against the tenants, and later the tenants laughed at the possibility and noted the ladies' complete dependence upon them.

The drive from Greensboro back to Birmingham and the trip back north resembled stages in a decompression process. The research mission had been accomplished, but the larger mission remained formidable. This was the last of our direct contacts with the volunteers while they were in the South. When Aiken and Demerath returned to the South the next January, it was to study the first year of token desegregation in the school systems of the Mississippi Delta, and involved no contact with the volunteers. By then, most of them had returned north, leaving the South to resist its medicine and maintain its wounds.

POSTSCRIPT

To some, this chapter may seem a form of chest-baring and breast-beating designed to establish our credentials as insiders within the movement. Much as we might like to manage our impressions accordingly, this has not been the objective, nor could it be. We never were insiders, and the chapter is in large part an explanation of why. On the other hand, we like to think that we were able to develop some empathy with both the volunteers and the movement, empathy alongside admiration. At least we may have been able to get closer than most to the crucial hopes, concerns, tensions, fulfillments, and frustrations of these people. While we were not volunteers in our own right, the experience of that vanguard in those vanguard years lingers with us all the same. Any insights we developed—sometimes slowly and sometimes against our stubborn "better" judgment—will be sprinkled throughout the chapters to follow. In this chapter we have simply tried to point out that research like this is not easy, and that it produces meaningful experiences quite apart from hard empirical data. The chapters which follow are the product of both.

CHAPTER I

The Sources
of Activism

It's kind of like a commitment to history, when I don't want to be committed to history, and I'm wary about making history at all. . . . It's like holding up your hand in front of a freight train and saying, "Stop." You just get run over. The thing to do is to . . . present your body so that you don't get annihilated. There are different ways to commit yourself, and I don't want to be destroyed in the process. I want to be effective, and I didn't feel that I could be, until I became aware of the movement.

A SCOPE volunteer

21

During the early summer of 1965, politicians, journalists, and southerners at large began to dust off the labels that had applied to the civil rights workers of the previous year. Because adjectives are cheap, there were more than one to a customer, and images frequently clashed. The volunteer was alternately seen as "dedicated," a "drop-out," a "true believer," "atheistic," "idealistic," "kick-seeking," "communist," "carpetbagging," "beat," and so on. Stereotyping is a natural response to any social movement that carries the hopes of some while threatening the interests of others. In this case, we find stereotypes of both positive and negative extremes, stemming not only from the man in the street but in some instances from scholars as well.

Let us begin by meeting a few of the volunteers as individuals, for their individuality should not be forgotten in the aggregate descriptions to follow. Here are four reconstructed (but pseudonymous) cases from the questionnaires, chosen with an eye to diversity:

For Jim Schmitt the decision to join SCOPE took only a few days from the first news of the program. He had been considering joining some part of the movement, and had the strong support of his girl, his friends, and his parents. His father, a northern-bred college professor in a southern school, had himself marched for civil rights. Politically, the entire Schmitt family considered themselves independents, although leaning toward the Democrats. Unitarianism had exercised some influence in Jim's life, as it had in the lives of his parents. Joining SCOPE involved no inordinate sacrifice for him, only another summer vacation. Still, Jim was worried about being ineffective or hurting the movement through lack of knowledge; he was also worried about being killed, and about remaining true to the nonviolence he professed philosophically. His basic motivations for joining involved "a desire to see social justice done—freedom for all men, . . . political ideals, wanting democracy to *work,* [and] strong emotional attachments to the movement through friends who were in it." As this last suggests, Jim had left the South for college and was enrolled instead in a large eastern state university "up north," where he was a B-plus student. He aspired to an eventual Ph.D. in history, although at age twenty-one college teaching was only one of several possible career plans. Like many other liberal southerners, Jim was optimistic about progress in civil rights and disapproved of massive federal intervention. Unlike most liberal southerners, however, he believed in preferential treatment for blacks, and had had fairly extensive social contact with Negroes, including a black girl friend.

Penny Aaron's participation in civil rights work was as unlikely as it was persevering. She received anything but support from her parents.

22

Atypically among Jews, the Aarons were strong segregationists, at least in the eyes of their daughter. While attending a large commuter university in the eastern metropolis of her birth, Penny had continued to live at home. But after informing her parents of her intention to join SCOPE, they asked her never to return. Since she had to pay most of her college expenses and could not work during the SCOPE summer, Penny expected to have to drop out of school the next year. Although her father was a clerical worker and she qualified for funds on the basis of need, her B-minus grades would probably not entitle her to a scholarship, and her hoped-for law degree would be delayed. She reported two worries about the summer: "I might not live up to the standards of the movement," and "I might get sick and get sent home—that would kill me." Actually, her emotional attachment to the movement was long-standing and deep. She had already been south for a march and had been in several sit-ins, marches, picket lines, and so on in the North. She had even been arrested once and jailed for four hours. The previous summer Penny had worked full-time in the office of a civil rights organization. But despite this prior involvement, she felt that she had not done enough. She mentioned as one of her prime reasons for joining SCOPE: "It's time I got to the root of the movement after all my demonstrating." She also commented, "I can't sit back and watch the world pass by; I've got to be a creator of the world. . . . I want to be free, and until all Americans are free, I can't be." And yet Penny did not describe herself as a radical. She was committed to the continuation of nonviolence, though she felt self-defense was justified. Matters should be settled by southerners, although she was pessimistic about this happening. Penny shared the belief of other liberal Democrats in more federal spending on welfare, education, and the like, but she was opposed to withdrawing funds from the South as a federal sanction with which to exact compliance. Withal, she felt herself growing more and more liberal and it was possible that radicalism was a future step. The daughter of religious parents, she had already become a committed atheist.

Alice Looven was a radical although a relatively mild one. She had grave doubts about the superiority of democracy as a political system, and felt that the system had shown itself incapable of coping with the problem of discrimination. She was an independent socialist, preferring no party. Among her main reasons for volunteering was to "help achieve a fair economic and social system . . . [and to] help Negroes find personal dignity." Another was that, "I wasn't born in time to fight in Spain." Alice's radicalism was related to a general suspicion of American institutions. She felt southern courts corrupt, the Justice Department, Federal Bureau of Investigation, and mass media generally uninterested in helping, and northern business actually supportive of segregation. She was far from wedded to nonviolence, thinking it would be better to desert the principle than to leave the condition of the Negro as it was. Nor was she optimistic about the effects of the summer's activity. In fact, her general distrust of white Southerners was coupled with a feeling that the federal government should station troops in the South and cut off funds to the area until it stopped discrimination. A graduate student in political science, Alice expected to teach in the area, while focusing her work and writing on peace and civil rights. Although she considered peace in Vietnam even more important than civil rights, SCOPE was nevertheless so urgent to her that she delayed her marriage as well as her career to participate. And since both her parents were dead there was some financial loss as well. Most of her anxieties about the summer concerned physical fear. She mentioned three specific worries: "getting killed, getting hurt badly, getting raped (by white cops)."

Unlike many of the volunteers, going south was part of a larger pattern of life for Tom Cullen. Irish and from Boston, Tom had just finished his first year in seminary, and expected to become a missionary priest. He participated "because of my vocation in life [and] because of my own personal concern. . . . I am a Christian, and it is out of love that I have joined SCOPE." His major worries were "lack of knowledge of the involved situation, money, and family objections." Although his parents were liberal Democrats and his father a lawyer, they had mixed feelings about integration and expressed mild disapproval of Tom's decision. Still, he was very close to his parents. Tom was a strong advocate of nonviolence. Although he did not trust southern whites, he was more confident concerning federal authorities and was very optimistic about the effects of the summer and the overall progress of civil rights. Opposed to preferential treatment for blacks, he felt they were capable of effecting changes in their current status by themselves. Tom had less previous experience with Negroes than most of the volunteers, and expressed some doubts about his ability to relate to southern blacks. He had never engaged in anything more active than raising funds, and that only once. Still, with the support and urging of his campus priest, he decided to go.

These are only four cases out of the 223 cases of our white SCOPE respondents. While it is possible to describe four on an individual basis, it is obviously impossible to assay the larger group in such biographical terms; hence, the utility of questionnaires and empirical techniques. Questionnaires helped us not only to cover a larger number, but to avoid procrustean labels for the diversity at issue. Although the chapter portrays people rather than statistical sylphs, the portraits will be etched in percentages.

And yet knowing, for example, that 60 per cent of the SCOPE workers felt strongly that the United States should initiate negotiations in Vietnam at that point tells us little about how the student volunteers compare with the mass of other students who stayed behind. Surely we learn a good deal more by comparing the 60 per cent of the volunteers with the less than 25 per cent of students generally who felt similarly about Vietnam at that time.[1] Unfortunately, such broad student poll results are not available for other items we shall be considering. As a second best, we did have access to a comparison sample of 1288 students at the University of Wisconsin who were asked many of the same questions only two months earlier.[2] Since the volunteers represented some forty diverse colleges and universities, it is unfortunate that we must depend upon only one school for our comparisons. But we might have done worse. While Wisconsin has a large minority of out-of-state students and has been in the forefront of radicalized campuses, it also prides itself on being one of the few truly democratic universities in that standards for in-state admissions are not high. Thus, Wisconsin students are probably as heterogeneous and widely representative as those at any single school in the country.

The chapter is organized around a number of issues which have been prominent in the debate over the sources of student activism in general, including their background status and parental relations, their religion, their educational status and views, their wider ideological views, and their specific motivations for volunteering. The concluding section digests all these findings with specific reference to other research on student activists.

There are a few basic statistics that are worth citing in advance as part of the sociological kitbag of descriptive data for any population. Our respondents include 120 males and 103 females. Three per cent were seventeen years of age or younger; 84 per cent were between eighteen and twenty-three; 8 per cent were between twenty-four and twenty-six; 5 per cent twenty-seven or older. As for regional background, about equal proportions came from the Middle Atlantic states, the Midwest, and the Far West (24 per cent each); New England claimed 12 per cent; the South and Border States each contributed less than 10 per cent; and the Deep South, only three workers of the total of 223 white respondents. Almost half the volunteers came from small cities of less than one hundred thou-

---

[1] "Campus '65," *Newsweek* (March 22, 1965), p. 53, poll conducted by L. Harris.

[2] See N. J. Demerath III and K. G. Lutterman, "The Student Parishioner: Radical Rhetoric and Traditional Reality," in K. Underwood, *The Church, The University, and Social Policy*, vol. 2 (Middletown, Conn.: Wesleyan University Press, 1969), pp. 88–144.

sand; slightly less than a third from major metropolitan areas; about 17 per cent from small towns or rural areas; 5 per cent were foreign.

Most of these characteristics provide a first documentation of the diversity within the SCOPE contingent. On the other hand, there is one further variable on which the subjects for this particular analysis are homogeneous; they were all white. This is not to say that all SCOPE volunteers who participated that summer were white; thirty-two blacks answered our questionnaire. But because the backgrounds, experiences, and motivations of the black volunteers were quite different from those of the whites we have excluded the blacks from the analysis. After all, thirty-two respondents are hardly sufficient for generalizing to the great numbers of blacks who were involved in the southern movement. Much of our emphasis will be on the particular drama involved with white activists in a black context.

BACKGROUND STATUS AND PARENTAL RELATIONS

Earlier we listed a number of stereotypic images which were applied to the white civil rights volunteers. One of the labels most commonly invoked by white southerners was that of "rebel," a term used in sneering short-hand for a number of other deprecations as well. The motivations of a rebel are, by definition, more negative than positive and more internal than external in their source. Surely it was comforting for many southerners to bask in the suggestion that the volunteers were reacting more to their own problems than to any genuine failings in the South. But if the label is at all accurate, what might some of these more personal problems have been? Two possibilities concern background status and parental relations. Thus, the volunteers may have been venting hostility to their own low status, to unsympathetic parents, or both.

It would be inaccurate to describe the typical white SCOPE worker as lower-class. The fathers of 70 per cent of the volunteers had upper-middle-class occupations (doctors, lawyers, business executives, and so on); more than half of the fathers had completed at least undergraduate educations or had annual incomes over ten thousand dollars (as of 1965). The proportions are about the same among students generally at the University of Wisconsin, reflecting the middle-class reality of American higher education. The point then is not that the volunteers were exclusively high-status or even that they were peculiarly high-status when compared to students at large. Rather, the volunteers were no lower in status than Wisconsin students as a whole, and social class is no real clue to the selection process which produced the civil rights workers as a distinctive group.

In one sense it should come as no surprise that the volunteers were from generally well-off families. Summer civil rights work is not a paying venture, and it must recruit heavily from those who can afford the luxury. Two-thirds of the volunteers reported that the summer would not pose a financial hardship and would not affect their future plans economically. One explained it pithily, while implying much more: "My father's money has been able to buy my idealism." Of course, there were some who sacrificed inordinately for the venture. Ten per cent indicated that the loss in earnings would cause a drastic change in plans for the year to come, and 30 per cent indicated that they would have to take extra employment to pay for what they had planned to do. For most, however, money would be the least of their hardships.

But rebelliousness occurs even among young adults from privileged homes. Those surfeited by affluence during a war on poverty may react out of guilt; they may strike out against the stifling expectations of success itself. This has certainly been a common theme in the speculative literature on the present inflamed generation. Insofar as it suggests a denial of parental values and ruptured family relations, our data are relevant. At first glance the volunteers seem to fit the mold. Many fewer volunteers than Wisconsin students reported that they felt very close to their parents (28 per cent as opposed to 59 per cent). But further inspection of the workers suggests *independence* rather than rebellious hostility. The volunteers' most common response was that they felt somewhat close to their parents (47 per cent); only 6 per cent reported that they did not get along with or were hostile toward their parents. Nor were most rebelling against parental wishes in becoming civil rights participants. Sixty per cent reported that their parents supported their work in the summer program; about 50 per cent felt that their participation would actually enhance their relationship with their parents; less than 20 per cent anticipated negative affects; and less than 10 per cent reported parents with segregationist sympathies.

These data converge with others of recent vintage to suggest a new meaning for the generation gap cliché. Many of the students of the sixties seem to be following parental models forged in the thirties. Thus, after a generation's gap we have returned to student political action and concern. Remarks like the following were common: "They did the same thing when they were young. They were involved in the labor movement. They are left, socialistic. They were both in agreement." "I'd also had a background from my parents, a liberal background where they would talk about civil rights and about liberal politics and so this was always part of me from the time I was born, I think. And it was just to me rather natural to get interested in anything having to do with, let's say, under-privileged people. I thought about the Peace Corps also, but I became more convinced the Peace Corps should be sent down here."

Despite such comments, it is important not to over-estimate the cohesiveness between the volunteers and their parents. Clearly not all of the SCOPE workers were supported by parents serving as ideological models. Even those whose parents had always espoused the values of liberalism were in some cases reacting against their parents' failure to put their words into action. Indeed, there were many volunteers with whom we talked who saw their parents as culpable for society's current ills. Their generation had seen the problems but had not acted soon enough or forcefully enough to combat them. In this respect, the parents repre-sented the failure of American liberalism; it was a failure many of the volunteers were determined to undo.

In some respects these parents may be as interesting as the SCOPE workers themselves. Thus, many were proud of their progeny's participa-tion, but were frightened of the jailings, beatings, and killings that had been the fate of previous workers. In the face of such reactions, many volunteers were also placed in a quandary. Some withdrew at the last minute either to remain at home or to join a safer project in a safer area. Others may have seen their parents' fear but persisted as a form of pun-ishment for their parents' own inactivity. But most of the volunteers per-severed with a mixture of filial compassion and determination. Letters afford particularly revealing evidence of such sentiments, as is shown in the conclusion to a letter written by a 1964 COFO worker to her brother: "Jon, please be considerate to Mom and Dad. The fear I just expressed I am sure they feel much more intensely without the relief of being here to know how things are. Please don't go defending me or attacking them if they are critical of the project. . . . They said over the phone 'Did you know how much it takes to make a child?' and I thought of how much it took to make a Herbert Lee (or many others whose names I do not know). . . . I thought of how much it took to be a Negro in Mississippi twelve months a year for a lifetime. How can such a thing as a life be weighed?"[3] Such sentiments fit our interpretation of the volunteers as generally independent rather than rebellious, and perhaps some of this independence can be explained in very mundane terms. Although the SCOPE workers had about the same proportion of males and females as the Wisconsin student body, the workers had a mean age some two years older than Wisconsin undergraduates.

[3] E. Sutherland (Ed.), *Letters from Mississippi* (New York: McGraw-Hill, 1965), pp. 150–151.

ATHEIST OR WITNESS?

One facet of the rebel image affixed to the volunteers has to do with religion. Civil rights workers were commonly described as a "bunch of atheists." Like most of the stereotypes, this one has a pinch of truth; like all, it includes a dollop of fantasy. SCOPE was, after all, an organ of the Southern *Christian* Leadership Conference, whose leaders are men of uncommon religiosity. SCLC appealed to many religious types, radical as well as conservative. This was certainly reflected in the volunteers' own religious predilections, perhaps the most striking aspect of their diversity.

Heterogeneity is first apparent in their denominational identifications. About 33 per cent were Protestant, 17 per cent Catholic, and 12 per cent Jewish (thus rebutting another part of the stereotype, since the workers were often alleged to be Jewish atheists in particular).[4] The largest single group, however, had no religious affiliation (36 per cent), although most of these came from homes that were at least nominally religious. Only 16 per cent of the volunteers' mothers did not belong to a religious group: 46 per cent were Protestant, 19 per cent Catholic, and 17 per cent Jewish. When compared with national statistics, both the volunteers and their parents are over-represented with nonaffiliates and Jews. But when compared to our student sample, the proportion Jewish is actually *smaller* among the volunteers (12 per cent as opposed to 20 per cent), although the proportion of nonaffiliates is higher for both volunteers (36 per cent to 14 per cent) and their parents (16 per cent to 5 per cent).

The split among the volunteers becomes more evident when one considers their responses to the following four questions, each a measure of conventional religiosity: (1) "I believe in a divine judgment after death where some shall be rewarded and others punished." (2) "The church is holy and not to be equated with other human institutions." (3) "Men cannot fulfill themselves in the world without believing in God." (4) "Jesus was God's only son, sent into the world to redeem me and all mankind." The response options range from strongly agree to strongly disagree on a six-point scale. That many were not conventionally religious is immediately apparent in that seventy volunteers indicated *strong* disagreement with every one of these statements. On the other

[4] This is one respect, however, in which the summer of 1965 may have differed from previous periods in student civil rights work. Apparently earlier phases had larger Jewish representation. Louis C. Goldberg, "The White Northern Student in Montgomery," (Unpublished paper, Dept. of Social Relations, Johns Hopkins University, 1965) argues that this is an important clue to the general recruitment pattern of social movements in that Jews are likely to identify with the cause early.

hand, the remainder of the volunteers were fairly well distributed in their responses, with a substantial group at the most orthodox end of the continuum. For example, 39 per cent agreed that Jesus was God's only son (despite the Jews included in the group); 27 per cent strongly agreed with this statement. These figures are similar to the 50 per cent of Wisconsin students who agreed and the 30 per cent who strongly agreed. Also similar are the 34 per cent of students and 27 per cent of volunteers who accepted a traditional concept of God as "a person who is concerned about me and all mankind and to whom I am accountable."

Overall, the volunteers reflect a bimodal pattern of religiosity. On the one hand, there is a large group representing the very religious. At the other extreme, there is a large contingent of those who are at least agnostic. Few fall between these positions, indicating that the nominally religious students in the vast majority of today's campus population are strongly represented among those who were *not* activists in 1965.

This same pattern is reflected in the amount of contact the volunteers had with their churches and their campus ministries. The volunteers either rejected forthrightly or participated frequently in church activity. Fifty-five per cent never went to church, but 25 per cent went at least once a week. The largest group of Wisconsin students (40 per cent) fell between these extremes. Similarly, more than 25 per cent of the volunteers indicated moderate or high involvement in a campus religious group, as compared to less than 10 per cent of the students. Indeed, more than 25 per cent of the volunteers cited their campus clergyman as a positive influence in their decisions to participate in the movement. In fact there were several instances in which religion and the campus ministry were instrumental in persuading atheists to join SCOPE: "I talked to one of the campus ministers and told him I was an atheist. He said describe that. I said God is people . . . working together. He said he had the exact same feelings. There is no God in the sky, in the mind. God is in every person. I think that is the only real religious value I have. After this discussion, the minister came to the conclusion that God is the *We* in 'We Shall Overcome.'"

Actually many students today (and perhaps the activists in particular) shy away from a formal religious affiliation and the mainstream churches yet maintain a respect for doctrine, ethics, and religious radicals in campus ministries who are often far more involved than their parent churches in social fermentation. Thus, almost 66 per cent of the volunteers as well as 63 per cent of the students said: "I often find myself in agreement with religious doctrine but opposed to the policies of churches and ministers." One SCOPE worker elaborated his feelings this way: "I'm not against organized religion per se, but I am against the present institutional structure of the church. I really feel that if the church is going to survive, it must find new forms of expression. I think it's very much a dying institution now. This does not mean that the faith which it supposedly proclaims is a dying thing, but I feel that its present forms— the parish—just do not meet the needs of a modern, urban world."

This is the death of God in its intended theological sense. It is not to be confused with the death of religious ethics but rather as an enabling event in putting ethics into action. From this perspective, only a few of the volunteers were actually antireligious. It is possible that just as they were in the vanguard of political change they also harbored many in the vanguard of religious change. Their views point to a far-reaching radicalization of the church, since only a revised institution can provide them with a meaningful religious identity. But then there are also those whose religion brooked no institutional trappings and persisted individually and independently.

VANGUARD ACTIVISTS AND THE UNIVERSITY

It is, of course, no accident that the term *Alma Mater* suggests a link between the university and parenthood. The parallel is more than metaphoric, and in the case of the activists it is particularly clear that the university elicits the same types of ambivalencies associated earlier with their parents. Certainly, the reaction to the university should change as the individual activist changes and matures in his own rights. Just as certainly the reaction to the university should change on the part of the student movement as it develops through new stages and frustrations. Indeed, if there is any single bellwether of changing political activism in the sixties, one could do worse than the changing image of higher education in the eyes of politically concerned students. The university began as a womb for the cause, but for many it has become a principal target.

It is important to examine the significance of the university for political activism as of the early summer of 1965. The object is not only to provide a historical benchmark but also to continue our pursuit of the distinct characteristics of the SCOPE volunteers. How different were they from other students in appraising academia? Were they poor students, intellectual failures, and college drop-outs as the southern stereotypes frequently alleged? Did they harbor the disenchantment and disdain which would make them the leaders of later events? To what extent were they eschewing a meaningless educational quest to seek real issues and the real world elsewhere? The SCOPE summer fell on the heels of the first major contemporary campus blow-up, the Berkeley Free Speech Movement. The issues had already begun to surface.

Make no mistake about it, these were students. Fully 95 per cent had completed at least some college. Many had just graduated with B.A. degrees, 56 per cent were still pursuing their undergraduate laurels, and about one-fourth expected to attend graduate school the next year. Along with their heterogeneity on other matters, however, the volunteers attended a wide range of institutions. Interestingly, the two largest categories were the most prestigious large universities (30 per cent) and the relatively unknown, comparatively poor small schools (22 per cent). More than one-fourth went to religiously affiliated colleges, half of which were Catholic. Less than 5 per cent of the SCOPE workers could be considered drop-outs in any conventional sense. In fact, what is most remarkable about the contingent is its high level of academic aspiration. Fully 80 per cent planned post-graduate study, and more than 33 per cent aspired to a Ph.D. These figures are considerably higher than the comparable percentages for our Wisconsin sample. So were the grades of the volunteers. More than 75 per cent had averages of B-minus or better; more than 33 per cent were B-plus students or higher. In short, the volunteers were committed to education; college commanded a central position in their lives.

But commitment to education means little unless we know their views of what education is and should be. Here the differences between the volunteers and the Wisconsin undergraduates were particularly great. We asked both to select one of eight statements representing the main purpose of college education. The most popular responses fell into two main clusters, the first emphasizing education as a fount of values and social service ("help develop meanings and values for my life" and "preparing myself to serve others and remedy major social problems") and the second emphasizing the development of more practical occupational skills or the acquisition of a degree as an end in itself. Fifty-three per cent of the volunteers chose values or service. All but 19 per cent of the Wisconsin students opted for the practical.

Of course, people committed to a more liberal, less instrumental view of education will be impatient with a program that fails to deal with social problems. This may account for the volunteers' tendency to major in sociology, history, political science, psychology, and social work. But beyond such matters of formal curriculum, one can question the extent to which their college experiences actually measure up to these ideals. The answer is: surprisingly well. Most felt that their courses *did* discuss controversies over basic values (67 per cent), that their professors *were* concerned about social problems (71 per cent) and that what they learned in class *was* valuable outside of college (74 per cent). Perhaps this is why a majority of the volunteers shared a scholarly orientation more typical of professors. They were willing to countenance "knowledge for knowledge's sake" (66 per cent) and, contrary to the current battle cry, they were not insistent on restricting teaching to intimate, socratic dialogue, since 78 per cent agreed that substantial learning can take place even when the professor and the student do not have personal contact with each other. Finally, 58 per cent actually identified themselves as intellectuals.

But the roots of recent events among the activists of yesterday are nevertheless discernible. First, almost half of the student volunteers found their college at least somewhat depersonalized. Second, there was a substantial minority of approximately 20 per cent for whom the answers to *all* of the questions above reflected basically negative attitudes. Even then some were saying what many are saying now. In fact, Stanford University radio station KZSU interviewed two who sounded very contemporary indeed:

You go to a school like Columbia and you see . . . 95 per cent of the people interested in getting through themselves and who just don't give a goddam about what's going on two or three blocks away. If you've ever been to the school, Harlem is here and Columbia is here; they're separated by a park. If you try to get organized on campus, you get these business students and law students all dressed up in their pretty clothes and plaid jackets who come over, and they just despise us. People who would want to do something feel bad about that.

I think the straw that broke the camel's back was the Selma demonstrations when we were at the Federal Building in Los Angeles and there was protesting and marching and everything. . . . I guess I was really kind of infused with this whole spirit of what was happening there and how real that thing was and how great those kids were. Then when I got to UCLA and walked down there and saw all those pretty sorority girls, I didn't know whether to laugh or cry. I just wanted to scream at them, "Do you know what's happening?" I mean word was coming in every minute about the beatings and they didn't know, and even if they knew, they wouldn't have cared. I remember talking to some of my friends, and it was a big joke; it meant nothing to them. . . . I wanted to be doing real work. School never was really important to me and I don't know if it ever will be again.

It is clear from the foregoing statistics that these quotations are atypical of the mood of the volunteers on the eve of the SCOPE experience. And yet the sentiments are harbingers of a chorus that would begin to crescendo the following fall. In retrospect, there seemed to have been many students for whom 1965 was the university's last chance. By the end of the year, as optimism soured with respect to civil rights and poverty and as United States participation in Vietnam accelerated despite academic opposition, higher education had lost both pedigree and credibility among some of the activists.

ATTITUDES ON RACIAL AND POLITICAL ISSUES

Unfortunately we did not ask the Wisconsin students why they had *not* gone south with the civil rights movement. The question had not seemed appropriate in context, and even if we had considered it we would probably not have bothered because of our confidence that we already knew the answer. Surely the prime source of distinctiveness of the civil rights volunteer was his position with respect to the issues of race and racism. Or was it?

It is true that the typical volunteer was far more dedicated to the cause of civil rights than most Americans, but was his position much different from the views of a large pool of northern students who chose not to participate? Although the data measure more the content than the depth of conviction, they suggest that volunteers may not have been as distinctive on this matter as we had expected. It is true that only 8 per cent of the students expressed any agreement with the proposition that, "In view of past discrimination Negroes should now be given jobs ahead of whites." But then the rate of agreement is only 29 per cent among white volunteers themselves, and short of preferential treatment, most Wisconsin students (indeed most northern students) favored racial equality. More than 80 per cent of the student sample believed that the federal government should intervene on behalf of the Negro in the South. Almost 70 per cent indicated their basic sympathy with civil rights volunteers who work in the South, despite the negative stereotypes that had penetrated some of the campus as well as society at large. In fact, fully 20 per cent of the students indicated *very strong* sympathy with civil rights volunteers, and if even 10 per cent of these committed students had volunteered themselves, the University of Wisconsin alone might have provided a phalanx of workers as large as the total number that actually did participate during the summer of 1965. Attitudes on civil rights thus provide no magical key to the puzzle of the volunteers' ideological motivations.

With this in mind, let us consider some other political attitudes that may demarcate the volunteers more clearly. As it happens, the SCOPE workers were distinctive on many other ideological issues of the day. For example, 71 per cent felt strongly that a large proportion of the federal budget should be devoted to poverty, medical care, education, and so on, as compared with less than 30 per cent of the students; over half of the volunteers strongly agreed that we should continue to give economic aid to developing areas, as compared to only 20 per cent of the students; as noted earlier, 60 per cent of the volunteers strongly agreed that the United States should try to initiate negotiations in Vietnam, as opposed to only 20 per cent of the Wisconsin students; finally, almost half of the workers felt that there was at least a fifty-fifty chance of a nuclear war in the next ten years but just over 33 per cent of the Wisconsin student sample shared that feeling. It is in this broad political area that the workers emerge as most distinctive when compared to their campus colleagues. Recall too that we are comparing the volunteers to students at the University of Wisconsin, and although only a tiny minority of these students are radically active on the left, Wisconsin students in general may be slightly more liberal than students on many of the other campuses represented by the volunteers.

In contemporary terms, perhaps one-third of the volunteers might have been described as alienated from American society. These include those who agreed that "the continuing plight of American Negroes has caused me to have grave doubts about the superiority of democracy as a political system" (33 per cent); that "the American system has proven itself incapable of coping with the problem of discrimination against Negroes" (34 per cent); and that "most northern state and local judges are usually willing to go along with a frame of anyone who they consider to have dangerous ideas" (26 per cent). Forty-two per cent expressed agreement with the shibboleth of the left that "American culture is sick and moving along the road to destruction." Although we do not have comparative data for all of these questions, we know that only 20 per cent of the Wisconsin students agreed with the sick diagnosis for American culture generally.

Yet much of the SCOPE workers' alienation was tentative and not central to their lives and beliefs. For the most part, the alienated tended to *agree* rather than *strongly agree* with the statements at issue. The vast majority of the volunteers identified with the Democratic party or considered themselves independents. One in five considered himself a socialist, but like Alice Looven, most took some pain to say things like "democratic socialists" or "nonparty oriented," and several identified themselves as both socialists and liberal Democrats. Perhaps one in twenty considered himself a radical, demanding wholesale political and social upheaval. Most were not. Although there were more of the alienated among the volunteers than among students generally, it is important to remember that the great bulk of the SCOPE contingent continued to believe in the society and its basic political processes. But while most were not apocalyptic militants, they were distinctive in their tendency to be *more* concerned about *more* problems in a *more* left-wing direction than most members of the Wisconsin student sample.

All of this discussion suggests that many volunteers were motivated to join the project as much by a concern over nonracial issues as by a

commitment to civil rights per se. Put another way, although problems
of nuclear war, foreign policy, and domestic poverty may have vexed
the volunteers as much as race relations, in 1965 it was only in the area
of race that one could enter the fray with consequence. The civil rights
movement offered the rewards of mounting success; it recruited without
regard to bureaucratic standards and pedigree; and its operations in the
South were sufficiently removed from home to increase the adventure and
brand it as more distinctive. In a real sense, then, the civil rights movement offered a structured political identity to those with broad-ranging
political concerns.

For supporting evidence, consider the volunteers' responses to the
following question: "Let's assume that this summer's project is only one
among many projects, all devoted to quite different problems but with
the same odds against success and the same personal risks. How would
you evaluate projects for each of the following goals in comparison with
this summer's campaign?" Eight alternative projects were suggested,
ranging from world nuclear disarmament to ending capital punishment.
Even the least popular alternative, "increasing student rights," found
18 per cent thinking it equally or more important than southern civil
rights. Four of the eight were judged equally or more important by large
majorities. This should not be interpreted as a downgrading of the volunteers' commitment to civil rights. Rather it suggests the full range of
issues that had aroused their consciences and provoked their participation.
But before we fall victims to stereotypes of our own concerning the volunteers' motives, let us hear the volunteers' own testimony. It adds a good
deal to the motivational portrait.

SOCIAL CHANGE AND THE TEST OF PERSONAL WORTH

The issue of motivation was a major source of agony for the
white volunteers. This was certainly apparent during the SCOPE orientation week in Atlanta. Many were unclear as to why they were there;
others competed to articulate the "right" reasons in the most convincing
fashion. For example, during one of the afternoon workshops, a young
black veteran of the field staff asked a volunteer why he had decided to
participate. The student talked at some length on the extent to which he
felt the deprivations of segregation in the innermost depths of his soul.
Gradually the affirmation grew embarrassing in its length and seemed to
indicate a sense of guilt. Finally, the student broke off his soliloquy, whereupon the staff member smiled kindly and indicated that no one motivation was necessary and that it was not expected that white volunteers
would share all of the sentiments of the Negroes themselves. Indeed,
many Negroes were suspicious of white civil rights workers who sought

to pass by going black in the sense of counterfeiting not only motivations but also food preferences and vocabulary.

Our questionnaire asked the volunteers to use their own words in describing the three most important reasons behind their decision to participate. The quotations below are representative:

It would be difficult for me to have any self-respect if I did not participate in some way.

I feel this is what God wants me to do.

To get training helpful to me as a future sociologist.

Something is basically wrong with America—I want to do something about it.

I wanted to destroy my myths about Negroes.

I'm using this summer, I'm using the experience for my own ends. I don't see why I should feel guilty about that, because that's the way I live life. I want to get as much out of everything I do as possible. And I'm certainly not hurting anyone.

To present a different side of the white man to the Negro.

I wanted to see whether I would be able to spend a summer working for others; I might want to make this a career.

More clean-cut, Christian, middle-class girls are needed.

Personal fight for equality due to father domination.

Glory.

Of course, it is always risky to quantify such diverse sentiments. Still, we extended at least a loose empirical net over them. After inspecting the open-ended responses, we arrived at a categorization that essentially distinguished between self-oriented and other-oriented motivations, each of which was further subdivided on substantive grounds. The distinctions are by no means clear-cut in all cases, but the basic difference between self- and other-orientations is revealing. The self cluster involves those motivations that essentially involve the summer as a means to a more personal end, however noble those ends may be. The other orientations essentially view the person himself as a means to broader ends from which he does not stand to benefit directly.

The most popular first reason falls into the category of other-oriented humanism, a diffuse motivational theme that involves an effort for change in the name of mankind everywhere. It was a major motif among the white SCOPE workers, but was it really dominant? Self-orientated motives predominate among the second and third reasons. Perhaps the distinction among first, second, and third preferences is not as important as the questionnaire's form would suggest. If one weighs them equally, self-motivations emerge as the most commonly mentioned.

Of course, this does not mean that the white SCOPE volunteers were simply using the movement for personal therapy or aggrandizement. Nor does it mean that the workers had only casual allegiance to civil rights; there were probably many who did not mention the obvious reason for their participation (to aid the Negroes) because it seemed obvious or because they felt patronizing. Even if we accept the findings at face value, one must be careful not to interpret self-motivation as selfish motivation or to convert a percentage difference between self and other motives into the inference that volunteers had either one or the other but not both. Finally, even those who were most concerned with others were sometimes the most confused about their own sense of individual worth and justification as civil rights volunteers. In one of many late-night bull-sessions, a white volunteer expressed his doubts this way: "Look, I'm not really sure how hard I can work to integrate the Negroes into my kind of society. I come from a respectable home with loving parents giving me all those great middle-class advantages, but one of the reasons I am here is because those respectable advantages aren't worth a damn in a society that is as materialistic and hypocritical as this one really is. How can I work to integrate the Negroes into the same sick scene? Shouldn't my real job be to warn them of what lies ahead underneath all that white wrapping paper and tinsel? Shouldn't I really be telling them not to accept integration into the white society unless that society has been changed radically first?" At this point, a listener responded that it was as if the Negroes had been standing in line for generations to see a much ballyhooed technicolor musical; suddenly, just when they are afforded the chance to get in, they are met by several whites coming out who tell them the film is not worth it after all. The listener asked if the real issue was not that blacks deserved the opportunity to decide for themselves, and perhaps even to enjoy the film despite its faults. The conversation produced no resolution, but it represented the kind of soul-searching that was so common during the orientation.

Despite such ambiguities and ambivalences, it seems clear that many of the volunteers saw participation in the movement an opportunity to test their personal mettle under stress, to infuse their life with a broad meaning, or to inject a note of meaningful excitement into lives that seemed relatively meaningless and lackluster. In one sense, of course, this comes close to the southern stereotype of the volunteers as kick-seeking and selfish; and it also resembles Stokely Carmichael's later charge that many of the volunteers "went South as members of the Pepsi generation to be where the action was."[5] While there is some truth to this image shared by radicals and reactionaries alike, it is hardly the whole truth. If the civil rights movement offered "action" and a crucible in which to forge one's identity, it was strikingly different from the beach parties and drag races so often associated with the self-hood of the soft-drink commercials. As we have seen, similar projects with similar opportunities for self-engagement with respect to other social and political issues would have attracted many of the same volunteers for many of the same reasons. The facts are, however, that no similar projects existed and that even the self-oriented motivations of these workers could not have been satisfied without attachment to a major social cause. It is precisely the notion of participating in such a cause that was so important to many; 60 per cent expressed agreement with the sentiment: "Almost nothing that can happen in the South this summer would make me feel my summer's work was not a success."

SCOPE IN THE CONTEXT OF STUDENT ACTIVISM

We have examined our 223 white SCOPE volunteers within the double context of stereotypes held by white southerners and comparison with nonactivist students at the University of Wisconsin. In this summary section we use still another context: namely, a comparison of our findings with those of other studies of activists.

In what follows, a number of references will recur, and it may help to introduce them beforehand. Two books command special attention, largely because of their frequent, if unacknowledged, conflict. The first is Kenneth Keniston's widely cited *The Young Radicals*,[6] an intensive social-psychological study of fourteen members of the Vietnam Summer Project in Boston during the summer of 1967. The second is Lewis S. Feuer's *The Conflict of Generations*,[7] a mammoth comparative and historical examination of student activism in various countries during the nineteenth and twentieth centuries. Not the least of the differences between these works concerns the stance of the authors with reference to activism itself. While Keniston is clearly sympathetic, Feuer is much less so. This, in turn, may contribute to a fundamental difference in interpretation; while Keniston stresses activism as a response to a wider political crisis, Feuer sees it more as a response to the activist's own psychological needs.

[5] S. Carmichael, "What We Want," *New York Review of Books*, 1966, 7, 5–8.

[6] K. Keniston, *Young Radicals* (New York: Harcourt Brace Jovanovich, 1968).

[7] L. S. Feuer, *The Conflict of Generations* (New York: Basic Books, 1969).

Several additional studies have specific reference to white civil rights activists. Alphonso Pinkney's *The Committed*[8] reports on a questionnaire study of active supporters of the Civil Rights Movement during the spring of 1964. While the data are not restricted to student activists and were collected before the COFO summer of 1964, Pinkney does provide a lucid description of the characteristics of white civil rights protagonists in general. A second book on white civil rights workers is Charles Levy's *Voluntary Servitude*,[9] a participant-observation study which focuses especially on the dilemmas of volunteer white teachers in southern Negro colleges. Because Levy focuses on the particular problem of communicating across the racial boundary, we postpone consideration until we confront these issues specifically in Chapter Three. Samuel Surace and Melvin Seeman[10] studied civil rights activists in the Los Angeles area; and Maurice Pinard, Donald Von Eschen, and Jerome Kirk collaborated on several studies[11] of the participants in Freedom Rides and sit-ins of the early 1960s. We also have had access to the unpublished work of Louis Goldberg on white students involved in the Selma-to-Montgomery march.[12]

There are a number of studies of activists in noncivil rights contexts. Several concern Berkeley's Free Speech Movement, notably the questionnaire analyses of Robert H. Somers,[13] of James W. Trent and Judith L. Craise,[14] and of William A. Watts and David N. E. Whitaker.[15] Even before FSM, Frederic Solomon and Jacob R. Fishman had done a before-and-after study of student peace demonstrators in 1962,[16] as well as an earlier study of Negro students who participated in the celebrated

[8] A. Pinkney, *The Committed: White Activists in the Civil Rights Movement* (New Haven: College and University Press, 1968).

[9] C. J. Levy, *Voluntary Servitude: Whites in the Negro Movement* (New York: Appleton-Century-Crofts, 1968).

[10] S. J. Surace and M. Seeman, "Some Correlates of Civil Rights Activism," *Social Forces*, 197–207.

[11] D. Von Eschen, J. Kirk, and M. Pinard, "The Conditions of Direct Action in a Democratic Society," *The Western Political Quarterly*, 1969, *22*, 309–325. Pinard, Kirk, and Von Eschen, "Processes of Recruitment in the Sit-In Movement," *Public Opinion Quarterly*, 1969, *33*, 355–369. Von Eschen, Kirk, and Pinard, "The Disintegration of the Negro Non-Violent Movement," *Journal of Peace Research*, 1967, *4*, 215–234.

[12] Goldberg, *op. cit.*

[13] R. H. Somers, "The Mainsprings of the Rebellion: A Survey of Berkeley Students in November, 1965," in S. M. Lipset and S. S. Wolin (Eds.), *The Berkeley Student Revolt* (Garden City: Doubleday, 1965), pp. 530–557.

[14] J. W. Trent and J. L. Craise, "Commitment and Conformity in the American College," *Journal of Social Issues*, 1967, *23*, 34–51.

[15] W. A. Watts and D. N. E. Whitaker, "Some Sociological Differences Between Highly Committed Members of the Free Speech Movement and the Student Population at Berkeley," *Journal of Applied Behavioral Science*, 1965, 2.

[16] F. Solomon and J. R. Fishman, "YOUTH and PEACE: A Psychosocial Study of Student Peace Demonstrators in Washington, D.C.," *Journal of Social Issues*, 1964, *20*, 54–73.

1960 sit-ins in Greensboro, North Carolina.[17] We have also had pre-publication access to James Elden's work on the California Peace and Freedom Party[18] and to the research by M. Brewster Smith and his colleagues on Peace Corps workers.[19]

Apart from studies of specific movements and groups, several important pieces comment upon and synthesize these monographs. The review by S. M. Lipset and Philip G. Altbach[20] is perhaps the most general and inclusive. Richard Flacks,[21] Edward Sampson,[22] and Keniston[23] himself have similarly important articles of this sort in *The Journal of Social Issues* (July 1967). So much, then, for a very brief introduction to the literature. In what follows we do not always single out every study that is relevant on a given point since several of our findings are universally supported by this literature. Indeed we can begin with precisely such a finding.

There is no more frequently reported characteristic of the student activist than his relatively high social class background. Indeed, no study disputes the general pattern, although both Pinkney and Elden note that older activists tend to combine high status in occupation and education with low income—a pattern of status discrepancy that has been traditional among the intellectual left.[24] With regard to the high over-all status of

[17] F. Solomon and J. R. Fishman, "Youth and Social Action, II: Action and Identity Formation in the First Student Sit-In Demonstration," *Journal of Social Issues*, 1964, *20*, 36–45. See also, R. Searles and J. A. Williams, Jr., "Negro College Students' Participation in Sit-Ins," *Social Forces*, 1962, *40*, 215–220 for data and argument to the effect that the early black participants were students who had begun to identify with white middle-class standards and were struggling more to enter the system than to revolutionize the society as a whole. By and large, this seemed to be the case with the black student volunteers in SCOPE.

[18] J. M. Elden, personal communications on research in progress.

[19] J. Block, N. Haan, and M. B. Smith, "Activism and Apathy in Contemporary Adolescents," in J. F. Adams (Ed.), *Understanding Adolescence* (Boston: Allyn and Bacon, 1968). For other work on Peace Corps volunteers specifically, see L. H. Fuchs, *Those Peculiar Americans* (New York: Meredith Press, 1967); M. I. Stein, *Volunteers for Peace* (New York: Wiley, 1966); Robert B. Textor (Ed.), *Cultural Frontiers of the Peace Corps* (Cambridge: The Massachusetts Institute of Technology Press, 1966).

[20] S. M. Lipset and P. G. Altbach, "Student Politics and Higher Education in the United States," *Comparative Education Review*, 1966, *10*, 320–349. See also Altbach's extremely useful, "Student Politics and Higher Education in the United States: A Select Bibliography" (Cambridge: Center for International Affairs, Harvard University, 1967).

[21] R. Flacks, "The Liberated Generation: An Exploration of the Roots of Student Protest," *Journal of Social Issues*, 1967, *23*, 52–75.

[22] E. E. Sampson, "Student Activism and the Decade of Protest," *Journal of Social Issues*, 1967, *23*, 1–33.

[23] K. Keniston, "The Sources of Student Dissent," *Journal of Social Issues*, 1967, *23*, 108–137. Reprinted in Keniston, *Young Radicals, op. cit.*, Appendix B.

[24] The relationship between status discrepancy and political extremism has been in plausible currency at least since Marx's discussion of the importance of the defecting members of the bourgeoisie to the proletariat. Several scholars have sought to quantify matters and provide an empirical demonstration of the point. Un-

the student activists, however, there are differences of interpretation despite consensus on the facts. The major difference concerns the importance of social class as a causal agent producing activism. Some, like Flacks and Keniston, regard affluence itself as a burden on the student with a conscience who finds himself caught in the discrepancy between his own comfort and the oppression he detects among others. Flacks cites a Students for a Democratic Society meeting in which the leader mimicked the techniques of a revivalist in requesting his followers to come forward and pay penance for their parents' sins of status: "My father is the editor of a Hearst newspaper; I give twenty-five dollars."[25] But while Flacks and Keniston pay particular attention to social class, others tend to assign it less importance. High status is only one of a series of variables related to activism, and less urgent than others. After all, we found that the volunteers were not peculiarly high status but only no lower than the rest of our middle-class students. And in one sense, high status is simply an enabling factor bringing the student into contact with a campus culture and providing him with the leisure and the opportunity to indulge his politics. Of course, not all high-status students are activists, and because high status characterizes right-wing members of the Young Americans for Freedom as well as those on the left, the question is raised of what accounts for the particular thrust and direction of those inclined toward the sort of activism at issue here.

Researchers agree that the student's relations with his parents are crucial, but the dynamics of the relationship form perhaps the central dispute in the literature. Here Feuer is cast as devil's advocate with his thesis that students derive their activism from an animus against their parents and use political means to serve a more personal rebellion. This position has long enjoyed some currency, notably in Harold Lasswell's view that political agitators are generally acting out problems stemming from their childhood.[26] Feuer's thesis, like Lasswell's, substitutes a more psychological emotionalism for the thrust of idealistic political commitment and invokes the kind of psychoanalyzing that has always seemed unduly prying and patronizing to its subjects. The stress on self-destruction in psychoanalytic theory is an important factor in Feuer's analysis of the destructiveness of activism itself.

Those who identify more closely with the positive aspects of activism are disinclined to Feuer's cynical perspective. Flacks argues that

---

happily, a number of methodological problems have plagued the effort. Because a full bibliography would take us too far afield here and anything less would be misleading, we have not provided specific references into this academic morass.

25 Flacks, *op. cit.*, p. 55.

26 H. D. Lasswell, *The Political Writings of Harold D. Lasswell* (New York, The Free Press, 1951).

the activists may actually be *closer* to their parents than most other students and that the spark of activism comes from the discrepancy between the comfortable liberalism of the parental womb and the abrasive shock of society in general and its educational agents in particular. Our own data do not substantiate the claim that the activists are any closer to their parents than other students, and neither does any other study with which we are familiar. Pinkney found that two-thirds of his activists reported no serious family conflict, but those include adult activists as well, and he did find that conflict is somewhat more common among the young. We find that, if anything, the SCOPE volunteers are less close to their parents than University of Wisconsin students generally. And yet there is little evidence of an outright rupture in the typical relationship, hence the term *independence* in preference to *rebellion*.

There is a related point on which our findings are supported by virtually every other inquiry: the activists are most often products of liberal rather than conservative homes. In fact, our proportions are similar to those reported by Solomon and Fishman for 1962 peace demonstrators, less than one-quarter of whom lacked parental support or could be termed in ideological opposition to their parents. Keniston found much the same pattern among the Vietnam activists five years later. And Lipset and Altbach cite numerous other studies in corroboration while pointing out that a small but substantial portion (one-sixth in a study of Samuel Lubell's[27]) come from homes with long histories of radicalism and past associations with the Communist Party of the 1930s. Although the party rarely had more than one hundred thousand members at any given time, its annual turnover rate of roughly 90 per cent insured a much larger base to serve as the parents of current radicals.

But is such evidence wholly sufficient to rebut Feuer's theory? Not quite, in our view, and apparently in Keniston's. In fact, he presents two quite different models of the sources of activism without fully supporting or rejecting either. The first is the radical-rebel syndrome which approximates Feuer's diagnosis, although without the psychoanalytic trimmings; the second is the red-diaper-baby thesis that today's activists are the political progeny of the activists of yesteryear. While the bulk of Keniston's own data and observations tend somewhat closer to the second model than the first, he is unwilling to endorse either as interpretive gospel.

Rather than push the two models to irreconcilable extremes, however, let us consider the possibilities of rapprochement. For example, one can salvage much of the credibility of the radical-rebel, generational con-

---

[27] S. Lubell, "The People Speak," news release, April 28, 1966.

flict model by some very simple amendments in light of the evidence. Thus, it is possible for even a liberal parent to spark a reaction in his offspring. There are no doubt many students who are suffocated with liberal understanding and tolerance. These students must go to extreme lengths to manifest their independence by seeking a distinctive identity that is only signalled by parental concern, puzzlement, and opposition.[28] Another amendment concerns those activists who are reacting precisely against the failures of the rhetorical liberalism of the past and its inability to translate noble sentiment into effective action. Finally, it may be myopic to identify all generational conflict as a function of parental problems. The volunteers with whom we talked described the pathologies of middle-class adult life with the sometimes grudgingly admitted proviso that their own parents were exceptions to the rule. In this respect, generational conflict and rebellion may be a particular instance of a more general phenomenon: the revolt against a discredited authority identified with generations past and rejected in the name of generations to come.

This last formulation provides a basis for reconciling not only the specific interpretive conflict at issue but also the wider debate between the Freudians and Marxians in offering understandings of the dynamics of social protest and change. Just as Ralf Dahrendorf has suggested that Marx's theory of economic conflict can and should be generalized to a theory of conflict against authority of all sorts,[29] so have Bronislaw Malinowski and the neo-Freudians suggested that Freud's theory of family psychosexual conflict be interpreted as conflict against authority of a wider variety.[30] The problem of authority is thus a confluence between Marx and Freud, just as it represents a convergence between the two interpretive models at issue here. Activists are indeed rebels from a kind of authority with quite personal needs, as we have seen. At the same time, these personal needs are tied to perceptions of a wider political authority that has betrayed its liberal promise and now requires drastic change. The link with the older generation is more complex than either model alone suggests. It is ambivalent precisely because the parents' generation has both fostered and frustrated visions that matter.

And yet activism develops out of more than just high status, liberal parents, and a sense of societal malaise. If activism is to be more than a frame of mind, it requires intervening social settings which provide the

[28] G. Marwell, "Adolescent Powerlessness and Delinquent Behavior," *Social Problems*, 1966, *14*, 35–47.
[29] R. Dahrendorf, *Class and Class Conflict in Industrial Society* (Palo Alto, Calif.: Stanford University Press, 1958).
[30] B. Malinowski, *The Sexual Life of Savages* (New York: Harcourt Brace Jovanovich, 1929).

structures for participation and serve to mobilize disenchantment in a politically viable form, a point well-made by Pinard, Von Eschen, and Kirk. Of course, the classic intervening structures of the industrial work place and the union are not the answer for these youth of the middle-class. And although religion and the church have occasionally performed the role, our findings and those of others indicate that the students are not generally in the ranks of the angels. It is true that there is a minority for whom religion is a prime activating agency (our proportion of those who are very religious is quite similar to Pinkney's 32 per cent), but most of the volunteers are not highly religious in the sense of doctrinal ortho-doxy or church membership, and a small group are explicitly non-religious. While most are intensely moralistic and often seem involved in a secular quest, it is apparent that many find political activism an alternate to traditional religious activities, especially as these activities are tied to a status quo that is suspect to all and repugnant to many.

Clearly it is the university which serves as the intervening com-mon denominator and mobilizing agency for most of these student vol-unteers. And again our findings converge with others to indicate that activists are among the most responsive members of the university com-munity in terms of grades, further educational aspirations, and immersion in an ethically vibrant student culture. Of all of these characteristics of *student* activists, good grades are the most commonly cited but not necessarily the most strategic factor. After all, Lipset and Altbach[31] point out that right-wing student radicals are also high academic achievers, suggesting that grades may be simply an indicator of a responsiveness that can be directed in several ways. And while Watts and Whitaker have challenged even this idea in suggesting that there were no differences between the FSM and a cross-section of Berkeley students, it may be that the FSM had reached such large proportions that it was no longer typical of the vanguard in the small activist movement.

In any event, it is plain that something besides sheer intellectual-ism is at issue here. Sheer dedication to civil rights is also not the answer. Our finding that the volunteers are not distinctive in their dedication is corroborated by Surace and Seeman in their study of Los Angeles activists. Perhaps part of the answer lies in Keniston's insight that the activist students seem to be distinguished by a sense of their own "special-ness" as well as a tendency to go beyond.

Here it is worth noting that other observers have also alluded to such vicariousness as a distinct quality of student activism as compared

[31] Lipset and Altbach, *op. cit.*, p. 334.

to more traditional variables. Solomon and Fishman note that even the middle-class black students involved in the initial sit-in movement were sometimes unable to sustain their commitments because their future occupations would take them away from the scene. Keniston comments more broadly, "The protester rarely demonstrates because his *own* interests are jeopardized, but rather because he perceives injustices being done to others less fortunate than himself." This statement is certainly relevant to our own findings with regard to the SCOPE workers' specific motivations and wider political views. It helps to elucidate the amount of self-orientated motivation we found among the volunteers and the agony experienced over the motivational issue in general. Perhaps because idealism was so much a part of their lives, the volunteers were distinguished less by a thorough-going and pessimistic alienation from American life and more by an optimism concerning the ultimate direction of the society and its political institutions. In this regard, they were similar to Pinkney's civil rights protagonists of 1964 who were described as sharing an elemental "faith in nature." Although Pinkney noted that 67 per cent of his respondents "reject the two conventional parties in the U.S.," this was an older group than ours, and the figure includes 26 per cent who were independents possibly straddling the two parties rather than rejecting them. Some of the more recent studies of activists report less optimism and more despair concerning the society and its future.[32] In large part, this may be a product of intervening years which encouraged idealism only to crush it into a sense of disillusioned futility. The SCOPE volunteers were indeed participating at a time that seemed to offer hope. In fact, our conclusion that the volunteers were aroused with respect to a number of issues, although civil rights was the only one which offered a personal sense of efficacy, is also reinforced in other studies. As Solomon and Fishman note, many of their 1962 peace demonstrators later "emphasized the feelings of personal effectiveness obtainable via involvement in the student civil rights movement as compared to that gained in the peace movement." It is worth observing, however, that some of the activists of the later sixties found the tables reversed. Keniston mentions that his fourteen activists were afflicted by an accumulation of "weariness, rage, and resistance," and that they were particularly despairing over the "fear-filled apathy or hostility of large portions of the Negro community" as experienced in the civil rights movement.

Certainly this despair is a possibility for the SCOPE workers them-

[32] A. Venable, "Generational Aspects of Liberal Activism," Senior Honors Thesis, Department of Social Relations, Harvard College, 1966.

selves. But before we leap ahead to consider the mood at the end of the project, let us examine in more detail the mood which the volunteers brought to its beginnings. We have seen that, by and large, our statistical portrait of the SCOPE workers fits well with the collated description of student activists in general. Now we want to go beyond the social psychological roots of activism to delve more deeply into activism as an on-going social drama.

CHAPTER II

Hopes, Fears, and Expectations

I *mean how bad can it be? We're people; they're people. Sure I'm scared but not just about violence. I'm also scared that somehow I will fail them and fail myself.*
A SCOPE volunteer

In many respects, the SCOPE orientation session in Atlanta offered a preview in microcosm of the difficulties, challenges, and emotions that were to become routine over the course of the summer. Imagine more than three hundred diverse volunteers gathered in the Joe Louis Gymnasium during a week teeming with pressure as well as with the Georgia heat. Constantly warned of the rigors that lay ahead; constantly besieged with a sense of the alien culture to which they would have to adapt; constantly reminded of the importance of their tasks—the volunteers digested these messages in various ways. Some sought the company of college friends with whom they had come; others seemed withdrawn as isolated individuals. Some affected a swashbuckling air to parade a confidence that may have been more superficial than self-convincing; others were manifestly afraid. We recall, for example, one girl whose weight was unprepossessingly close to two hundred pounds. Throughout the orientation, she gave loud voice to her fears that she was sure to be raped. It was clear to most, including the psychiatrists who quietly sent her home, that her fear was leavened with pathetically wistful anticipation. This is a bizarre instance of the intermingling of fears and fondest hopes that characterized so many of the volunteers.

If such reactions are natural for anyone embarking upon such a venture, they were all the more understandable for those who were embarking with such meager experience. The term *rookie* is well-established in American sports, but it has increasing application in American politics as well. The SCOPE volunteers came to the movement with relatively little knowledge of the day-to-day life of the southern civil rights worker. In Keniston's terms, this was a "calling" and not a "job,"[1] but it was a calling from afar and one which gave little sense of what lay ahead.

PRIOR EXPERIENCE WITH NEGROES AND ACTIVISM

Consider the degree to which the white workers had had prior contact with Negroes. It is true that they probably had more contact than most white students or white Americans; indeed Surace and Seeman find that inter-racial contact is a better predictor of white civil rights activism than an integrationist ideology.[2] And yet some among the volun-

[1] K. Keniston, *Young Radicals* (New York: Harcourt Brace Jovanovich, 1968). The distinction between a "calling" and a "job" connotes a good deal of Keniston's emphasis on the sense of "specialness" which characterizes the radical youth, even before his radicalism begins as such. Thus, a job is routinized and can be performed by virtually anyone with training; a calling is far more individually compelling.

[2] S. J. Surace and M. Seeman, "Some Correlates of Civil Rights Activism," *Social Forces*, 1967, *46*, 197–207.

teers had had virtually no contact with blacks at all, and most of the contact that had occurred was restricted to the North and probably to middle-class Negroes. We asked five relevant questions on this score to form an implicit scale—How many times (never, once or twice, several times) had they: attended small social gatherings with Negroes (74 per cent said several times or more); worked with Negroes in situations requiring sustained cooperation (61 per cent said several times or more); had Negroes in their home as guests or been guests in Negro homes (54 per cent, several times or more); lived with Negroes in close quarters in dormitories, barracks, and so on (47 per cent, several times or more); or dated a Negro (23 per cent, several times or more). It is difficult to evaluate the ambiguous phrase "several times or more" since it can mean three times or a lifetime of contact, nevertheless it is clear that there was wide variance among the volunteers. Many had enjoyed substantial contact with Negroes, but a significant minority had kept or been kept at a considerable social distance.

Next consider the extent to which the volunteers had participated in prior political activism. The questionnaire asked each respondent to indicate whether he had engaged in seven specific forms of participation and left him space to include any other forms not mentioned. We asked about picketing, fund raising, circulating petitions, organizing boycotts, freedom rides, sit-ins (pray-ins, wade-ins, and so on), and working in a civil rights organizational office. In addition, we separated northern from southern activism so as not to confuse the two. Northern activism predominated, and even though the great majority of the white volunteers had participated in some form of prior activism, this could be quite minimal and still qualify. Thus, while 60 per cent had participated in northern fund-raising only 18 per cent had been involved in such confrontations as sit-ins and the like. Less than 20 per cent had participated in any form of southern activism, and most of this was apparently on the sidelines rather than on the ramparts. While the volunteers no doubt had more experience on this count than most students (unhappily we have no comparison data on this point), few were battle-scarred veterans and roughly one-fifth had no prior activist experience whatsoever, even so much as circulating a petition.

There is an obvious reason why the volunteers scored so low on southern activism; very few had been in the South at all. Fully 45 per cent had never even visited the South; another 28 per cent had spent total time ranging from one day to one month in the region; and only 7 per cent had lived in the South for more than ten years. In fact, even these figures may exaggerate the extent of experience in the South since the questionnaire defined the South as including Maryland, Virginia, and

Texas—three states where a white could visit or live without becoming directly involved in segregation and resistance.

A CATALOGUE OF CONCERNS

In order to get a general assessment of the volunteers' confidence in themselves, we asked their reactions to: "Those of us who are here are the best possible people for this particular job." Some 82 per cent expressed disagreement, and because at that time they had had little opportunity to become acquainted with their colleagues this might be taken as an expression of self-doubt. Later, however, we asked the volunteers a battery of questions to ascertain their self-doubts concerning specific situations. Here the results are more favorable. It is true that 44 per cent expressed doubts about their ability to convince elderly Negroes that they should register to vote, that 43 per cent were concerned about their effectiveness in teaching unmotivated southern Negro youths, and that 33 per cent doubted their ability to work effectively with moderate white southerners. On the other hand, only 11 per cent were apprehensive about their capacity to adapt to poor living conditions or their response to police brutality against a Negro woman whom they had personally persuaded to register to vote. Overall, the volunteers expressed more confidence than not, but then the extent of their confidence increased only as the hypothetical challenges moved from the interpersonal to the impersonal or to the purely personal ability to control one's own emotions, as in the response to police brutality.

As one more way of tapping their concerns, we asked them to list in their own words the three most important worries about the summer ahead. As always, there is variety, but there are some common worries too:

(1) I might not be able to cope with pressures; (2) my errors could hurt, even kill citizens; (3) wonder if I can remain nonviolent and see a woman beaten.

(1) that I will not be able to "turn the other cheek" when a crisis occurs; (2) that I will not be as accepted in middle-class clothing than if I wore SNCC outfits; (3) that my family in New York and army relatives in Atlanta and Little Rock will not understand the project.

(1) being ineffective or damaging through lack of knowledge; (2) being killed; (3) staying nonviolent.

(1) being raped; (2) measuring up to the attitude of the community; (3) doing too much directing rather than following.

(1) not being adequate to learn and live and give all that I might;

(2) having too much sympathy and too little initiative; (3) finding myself using cant and cliches and manipulating people.

(1) lack of ability to communicate effectively; (2) being persistent in the face of apathy; (3) losing sight of my ideals and my identity.

(1) living as part of the community, "communicating," and being persuasive; (2) being resourceful, energetic; (3) getting drafted.

This is only a small and unsystematic sample of the range of comments elicited from the volunteers. We converted the full assortment of worries into quantitative categories. Expressions of self-concern far overshadowed other-concern by more than three-to-one. But then the relatively personal nature of the question no doubt had a good deal to do with this patterning. Certainly it is not fair to infer that the volunteers had no concerns for the project itself, or even that these concerns paled into insignificance beside their self-anxieties. While the count does indicate that personal anxiety was at least a major counterpoint to anxieties over the ultimate success of the movement, it does not allow us to judge the relative weight of the two. Indeed, it is more reliable to assess different types of worries *within* the self and other categories. Within the "other" cluster, concern over success of the project was articulated most often (by 26 per cent), and concern over family problems (for example, "My parents may never really understand and the summer may put a gap between us") and the safety of persons affiliated with the project came next (14 and 13 per cent, respectively). Turning to the more extensive list of worries related to "self," the two most prominent involve personal safety (78 per cent) and personal success as a worker (69 per cent), although the problem of acceptance and communication also loomed large (36 per cent).

THE THREAT OF VIOLENCE

Because nearly four-fifths of the volunteers evidenced concern over their own safety, a word specifically about fear is in order. Certainly it was understandable. The specter of violence and harassment was a constant factor in the orientation. The volunteers were constantly aware of the murder of Chaney, Goodman, and Schwerner the summer before in Mississippi. In fact, many had a tendency to look around the room and wonder who would play those tragic roles in 1965. More than one-third expected that there would be at least a few purposeful killings during the summer, and an additional 25 per cent anticipated that some volunteers would suffer very serious bodily injuries. At a more personal level, 38 per cent thought there was at least a fifty-fifty chance that they themselves would be involved in violence during the summer, and although another 40 per cent thought it somewhat unlikely, only 22 per cent felt it very unlikely. There were some who felt that violence was almost a precondition of their success; 23 per cent tended to agree that the program "would not be a success unless several dramatic incidents focused the attention of the world on the intolerable conditions of the southern Negro"—and surely few things are more dramatic than violence itself. And yet the volunteers expected other forms of harassment as well, especially from the southern police. More than two out of three thought there was at least an even chance that they would be arrested and spend some time in jail.

The fear of violence was not only understandable, it was also constructive. The SCOPE staff and veteran field workers went to great lengths to point out the virtues of caution and to urge effective rather than heroic actions. Fools not only rush in where angels fear to tread, but fools are beaten and even killed for the best of intentions. The staff knew very well that they would expend a good deal of effort simply herding the novice volunteers within the margins of safety. In fact, some of the most dangerous personnel—to the project as well as to themselves— were often the most dedicated. Clergymen were particularly vexing because many were convinced that even the roughest redneck was reachable through sweet reason—and a disproportionate number of clergymen were brutalized while reasoning to deaf ears.

From the standpoint of the volunteers, much of the meaningfulness of the venture depended on a certain personal risk. In the previous chapter we noted that many sought a test of character under stress, and physical fear was an undeniable part of that stress. As the volunteers were soon to learn first-hand, however, there are many different types of fear. The following letter is from a COFO volunteer in Mississippi during 1964. We quote it as particularly eloquent wisdom of hindsight and as a good delineation of the various forms of anxieties that would beset many of the workers during 1965:

To my brother,
        Last night I was a long time before sleeping, although I was extremely tired. Every shadow, every noise—the bark of a dog, the sound of a car—in my fear and exhaustion was turned into a terrorist's approach. And I believed that I heard the back door and a Klansman walk in, until he was close by the bed. Almost paralysed by the fear, silent, I finally shone my flashlight on the spot where I thought he was standing. . . . I breathe deep, think the words of a song, pull the sheet up close to my neck—still the tension. Then I rethought why I was here, rethought what could be gained in view of what could be lost. All this was in rather personal terms, and then in larger scope of the whole project. I remembered Bob Moses saying he had felt justified in asking hundreds of stu-

dents to go to Mississippi because he was not asking anyone to do something that he would not do. . . . I became aware of the uselessness of fear that immobilizes an individual. Then I began to relax. "We are not afraid. Oh Lord, deep in my heart, I do believe, We Shall Overcome Someday" and then I think I began to truly understand what the words meant. Anyone who comes down here and is not afraid I think must be crazy as well as dangerous to this project where security is quite important. But the type of fear that they mean when they, when we, sing "we are not afraid" is the type that immobilizes. . . . The songs help to dissipate the fear. Some of the words in the songs do not hold real meaning on their own, others become rather monotonous—but when they are sung in unison, or sung silently by oneself, they take on new meaning beyond words or rhythm. . . . There is almost a religious quality about some of these songs, having little to do with the usual concept of a god. It has to do with the miracle that youth has organized to fight hatred and ignorance. It has to do with the holiness of the dignity of man. The god that makes such miracles is the god I do believe in when we sing "God is on our side." I know I am on that God's side. And I do hope he is on ours.[3]

Civil rights workers are hardly the first troops to experience the efficacy of virtue in combating fear. But few soldiers have felt their virtue more strongly. As Keniston has put it, "The issue of violence is to this generation what the issue of sex was to the Victorian world." This is evident in the volunteer's resolve to meet violence with nonviolence. Led by Martin Luther King, Jr., the most celebrated nonviolent general in the country's history, the SCOPE workers were united almost to a man. In order to measure their belief in nonviolence, we included on the questionnaire four statements concerning the concept of nonviolence (see Appendix) and asked the volunteers to agree or disagree with each. Few departed from the nonviolent pattern on any item. In fact, the most common response to all four was strong agreement with the nonviolent position, and almost half the volunteers were strongly opposed to using even the *threat* of violence.

So firm was most volunteers' commitment that they expected to hold themselves in check even under the most provocative circumstances. Earlier we mentioned a battery of hypothetical situations designed to gauge their self-confidence. One of the challenges included their ability to "remain nonviolent in the face of police brutality against a Negro woman whom you have personally persuaded to register for voting." Almost 60 per cent expressed confidence here, and although 17 per cent expressed a lack of confidence, the rest were unsure. Of course, even those who manifested a commitment to nonviolence did so for what may have been quite different reasons. While some were wedded to it as a matter of

[3] E. Sutherland (Ed.), *Letters From Mississippi* (New York: McGraw-Hill, 1965), p. 151.

deep moral conviction, others were persuaded more by its tactical expedi-
ency. No doubt there were many who had not thought through all of its
philosophical implications; some may have viewed nonviolence as a
bridge to secure solidarity with King and hence a check on their anxieties;
there were probably a few who felt that a violent response to the hypothetical policeman would itself require more courage than they could
muster. For whatever reason, the overwhelming majority of the SCOPE
workers was far more confident of controlling violence within themselves
than of controlling the potential violence among white southerners. Only
one in four was confident that he could stop "a small group of drunken,
hostile white youths" from committing physical harm if he had to face
them alone. Since these anxieties were related to the volunteers' views of
the South, let us turn to a more detailed consideration of those views.

IMAGES OF THE WHITE SOUTH

In the previous chapter we assessed some of the white southerners'
stereotypes of white civil rights workers. But of course, the workers re-
ciprocated with stereotypes of their own. In general, the volunteers'
images of southern authority were far more severe than their views of
southern whites as individuals. To invoke an ironic term from Ralph K.
White's social-psychological analysis of wartime attitudes towards the
enemy,[4] the volunteers tended toward a "black-top" conception of the
South in attributing the most heinous aspects of the scene to a set of
malevolent leaders as opposed to their relatively innocent followers.

Not surprisingly, the most bitterly resented part of the southern
establishment was the police. Of seven southern institutions or organizations which we asked the volunteers to rate for their effectiveness in behalf
of segregation, the police were cited most often as strongly effective (by
66 per cent). Seventy per cent of the volunteers felt that southern police
were "generally recruited from among the least qualified segments of the
population," and higher levels of law enforcement were not held in much
higher esteem. Eighty-six per cent agreed that "most state and local
courts in the deep South tolerate illegal police methods"; 96 per cent
disagreed that "when the case does not concern Negro civil rights the
Negro usually receives a fair trial in a state or local court in the Deep
South." Half of our white SCOPE volunteers thought that southern courts
were strongly effective forces for segregation; only 5 per cent thought
they were working for integration. And almost two-thirds of the volunteers rejected some of the laws of the South. That is, they disagreed with

[4] R. K. White, "Misperception and the Vietnam War," *Journal of Social
Issues*, 1966, 22, 1–164.

the proposition that "the civil rights campaign should continue to work within the existing southern laws, although the movement should seek changes in them."

In light of these findings, it is predictable that most of the volunteers were opposed to having the South develop its own solution to its race problem through its own institutions. Outside interference was deemed crucial, particularly interference from Washington. Nine out of ten disagreed that "the racial crisis in the United States should be resolved on a local level without the intervention of the federal government." Most even favored the use of economic sanctions, since more than three-fourths felt that "federal funds for public projects should be withdrawn from segregationist areas." Indeed, some volunteers were willing to go much further. Forty-six per cent expressed some degree of assent with the notion that "federal troops should be stationed in hard-core segregationist areas on a semipermanent basis to guarantee civil rights."

On the other hand, most volunteers felt that such external coercion would produce only a temporary solution and that "any lasting changes in civil rights in the South will have to come from the southerners themselves rather than from outside pressures." Fifty-six per cent agreed with this statement. Many of them could agree because they were more optimistic concerning change in the white southerner than in his institutions. Eight out of ten expected more than token progress in the ten years to come. Almost the same proportion felt that "most whites in the Deep South know that society is changing and that they will have to go along with integration in the end." Indeed, almost half of the volunteers expressed agreement with the following propositions: "Most whites in the Deep South feel a good deal of shame about segregation and would like an easy way to end it without a loss of pride" (43 per cent), and "Most whites in the Deep South are willing to integrate in many areas but they are prevented from doing so by the white power structure" (45 per cent).

This more charitable view of the southern white may reflect a tendency for some of the students to see their destiny as so manifest as to be apparent to the southern whites themselves. Although a substantial minority of the volunteers harbored stern antipathies (for example, one-fourth expressed agreement that "most southern whites are actually anxious to use violence"), the central pattern remained in viewing the southern white as largely a creature of the institutions which manipulate him. It is the power structure and not its pawns which stands between segregation and progress. "The southern segregationist," said three out of four, "is to be pitied rather than scorned, because he is a victim of his circumstances."

None of this implies that the volunteers expected to have much positive contact with southern whites. After all, to say that individuals are the victims of a system is not to deny the system's constraints. It is true that about half of the volunteers thought there was at least an even chance of having a few honest discussions with local whites concerning the issues between them; about one in four disagreed that the differences between them would "preclude any pleasant or constructive contact." Beyond conversation, however, the volunteers were more united in expecting disaffiliation—even segregation—from the local white community. Only one in five thought there was any reasonable chance that they might develop a lasting friendship; only one-third saw any prospects of attending a white church. Less than one in ten thought the odds were in favor of their dating a white southerner.

In fact, most felt that their relations with local whites would be so tense that considerable effort would be required to protect the SCOPE public image. This expectation, together with the religious conservatism of a number of volunteers, meant that they were unusually severe in setting self-standards. More than two-thirds felt that "since civil rights workers are in the public eye, they must abstain from *all* nonmarital sexual activities in order to maintain high standards of personal decorum"; half felt that "alcohol must be avoided in any form." If the volunteers were going south for fun and games, many had a monastic view of merriment. This is one sense in which the summer was seen as a sacrifice, and as excitement only in a very special and demanding sense. However, there was one regard in which the volunteers were considerably less concerned about their image. While the question departed from the previous two in mentioning nothing about being in the public eye, two-thirds said that they would not be greatly disturbed if some of their colleagues were "self-declared Communists," although none of the volunteers met the description. But let us go on to examine another set of images and stereotypes concerned with the southern Negroes and their leadership.

EXPECTATIONS OF THE BLACK COMMUNITY

It was into the black, not the white, communities of the South that the volunteers had been invited. Accordingly there was very little disagreement as to the contact expected here. Virtually all anticipated visiting or living in a black home, attending a black church, discussing civil rights and other matters with blacks, and developing lasting black friendships. These activities were to be a part of the job with its pleasures and its triumphs. Only on the question of dating local blacks was disagreement evident; 53 per cent thought it unlikely, and the rest were divided between those who were unsure and those who thought it probable.

The black community was to be their community. Of course, some white students found this intimidating as well as inviting; recall that a major worry about the summer concerned lack of acceptance and an inability to communicate with members of the black community. Still, approximately six out of ten were confident they could teach an unmotivated southern Negro youth or communicate with an older southern Negro woman who was afraid to register to vote. About the same proportion disagreed that "most Negroes in the Deep South will be afraid to be associated with the summer project," and "that a lack of cooperation from local Negroes will be a major obstacle to the summer project."

These attitudes were not a patronizing function of noblesse oblige. Many of the veteran black workers were concerned that the white students might take over the movement, but the volunteers had no such intentions. Although black power was yet only a glint in the eyes of the more aggressive militants, the students felt that the blacks were the real leaders, and heroic at that. More than 80 per cent of the volunteers expected most of the permanent field workers in the South to have "developed extraordinary sensitivity to the needs and wants of other people." And although the volunteers were hardly the sort to give blind obedience, 56 per cent were willing to say that "under no circumstances whatsoever should a participant place his judgment above the judgment of the project leaders in determining how to act." Clearly, their attitude was respect for the leaders rather than anticipated submission to a well-oiled bureaucratic organization. On the latter point, the volunteers had few illusions. Eighty-three per cent disagreed that the project would be a "highly efficient and well-coordinated organization." In fact, many of them would not have had it any other way. Only 25 per cent wished the movement would model itself along the efficient lines of American business organizations. To members of an antibureaucratic generation, organizational efficiency could hardly be foreseen as a crucial indicator of political success.[5]

Despite the volunteers' somewhat equivocal confidence in themselves, they did expect success for the SCOPE project as a whole, largely on the strength of its black leadership. Certainly this was the case with the primary goal of voter registration: almost three out of four expected the summer campaigning to produce a "politically momentous increase in registered voters." Apart from registration itself, almost half went further to predict a "dramatic increase in militancy among southern Negroes," and more than a third even expected "a very large number of whites

---

[5] Once again the theme of individualistic independence is important here. Not only is it discernible among our SCOPE volunteers and Keniston's young radicals, *op. cit.* in the Vietnam Summer Project, but it also applies to the idealism of the Peace Corps worker. Indeed, the pursuit of individualism and the escape from the bureaucratized society is a major theme of L. H. Fuchs, *Those Peculiar Americans* (New York: Meredith Press, 1967).

in the Deep South to move to more moderate positions as a result of the summer's activities." Finally, as a minimum accomplishment, six out of ten agreed that "even if things are not changed much in the South this summer, what happens there will speed up integration in the North."

Clearly, many of these white students felt that they were riding a crest of change from which they drew both comfort and exhilaration. Just as clearly, the blacks were to be the leaders and the source of those rare virtues on which successful political movements depend. Indeed, the contact with southern blacks and the movement was so important to these white volunteers that for some it was an end in itself. As we saw in Chapter One, more than half felt that "almost nothing that could happen in the South this summer would make me feel my summer's work was not a success."

INTERRELATIONSHIP OF BACKGROUNDS
AND EXPECTATIONS

So far our introduction to the volunteers has been more descriptive than analytic, more poll-like than sociological, in presenting merely the breakdown of volunteer responses to single questions. Here we consider some of the more important variables in seeking the relation between the volunteers' backgrounds and their specific views and expectations of the summer.

Of course, one could go to great lengths and inspect whole chains of relationships, linking ten or more of these variables in elaborate formulations. We have opted for parsimony in two respects. First, we restrict ourselves to two-variable relationships because the sample size and number of uncontrolled conditions make more complex analyses inadvisable. Second, although up to this point we have used distinct items to capture distinct nuances, we now are more concerned with larger dimensions of the volunteers' backgrounds and expectations. Thus, we often use aggregate measures of these dimensions, combining several different questions into a single scale. To take a very common example, we use an equally-weighted combination of the father's education, income, and occupational status to produce an over-all measure of the respondent's social class background. In the same fashion, we use an equally-weighted combination of all four items pertaining to nonviolence in Table 1 to form an aggregate scale of nonviolence as a single entry in the matrix here. The Appendix provides the details of all the scales presented in the matrix and describes the statistical technique of inter-battery factor analysis used to assure that a single dimension is involved and to determine its components. Meanwhile, each cell in Table 1 represents a Pearson product-moment correlation coefficient. A superior "a" (ᵃ) denotes relationships

Table 1. INTERRELATIONSHIPS AMONG BACKGROUND CHARACTERISTICS AND ATTITUDES

Attitudes and Expectations	Religious Conservatism	Political Liberalism	Scholarly Orientation	Prior Contact with Negroes	Female Sex	High Socio-economic Status	Poor Relations with Parents	Prior Activism in North	Prior Activism in South
Expectation of a high degree of involvement with whites	.16[a]	−.02	.02	−.03	.03	−.12	−.02	−.07	.13[a]
Expectation of a high degree of involvement with Negroes	−.17[a]	.13	.07	.13	−.03	.06	.16[a]	.12	.05
Has high self-confidence	.08	−.02	.01	.19[b]	.01	−.10	−.02	.12	.08
Expectation of harassment	−.05	−.07	−.01	.17[a]	−.17[a]	−.01	.07	.05	.02
Belief in nonviolence	.27[c]	−.08	−.17[a]	−.04	.08	−.05	−.04	−.06	−.08
Attachment to American political institutions	.08	−.26[c]	.04	−.13	−.02	−.02	−.16[a]	−.12	−.09
Concern with worker's public image	.40[c]	−.28[c]	−.26[c]	−.10	−.01	−.08	−.15[a]	−.16[a]	−.07
In favor of outside intervention in the South	−.21[b]	.22[b]	.22[b]	.15[a]	−.03	.11	−.04	.16[a]	.06
Unfavorable image of southern courts and police	−.23[c]	.18[b]	−.04	.11	.09	.05	.03	.09	−.06

Antipathy toward white southerners	$-.02$	$.07$	$-.03$	$-.15^a$	$-.06$	$-.03$	$.00$	$-.02$	$-.16^a$
Cynicism about project personnel and organization	$-.20^b$	$.10$	$.25^c$	$.05$	$.02$	$.04$	$-.04$	$-.01$	$.08$
High expectation of project success	$.25^c$	$-.06$	$-.13$	$.15^a$	$.08$	$.00$	$.04$	$.08$	$.14^a$
Salience of safety as a worry	$-.13$	$-.04$	$.22^b$	$-.07$	$-.10$	$.07$	$-.16^a$	$-.01$	$-.12$
Saliency of personal success as a worry	$.02$	$-.07$	$-.02$	$.01$	$.01$	$.02$	$-.01$	$.05$	$.04$
Expectation of cooperation from local Negroes	$.20^a$	$-.09$	$-.20^b$	$.03$	$.13$	$.02$	$-.06$	$-.02$	$-.04$
Belief that Negroes should be given preferential treatment	$-.06$	$.10$	$-.04$	$.21^b$	$-.04$	$.15^a$	$-.06$	$.16^a$	$.15^a$
Do not favor negotiations in a situation like Vietnam	$.39^c$	$-.21^b$	$.08$	$.02$	$.01$	$-.13^a$	$.02$	$-.09$	$.09$
Index of political pessimism	$-.17^a$	$.29^c$	$-.07$	$.08$	$.05$	$.01$	$.07$	$.12$	$-.01$

[a] $p < .05$

[b] $p < .01$

[c] $p < .001$

Note: These correlations are normally based on 223 cases except where data are missing.

that would occur less than five times in a hundred by chance alone; a superior "b" (^{b}) marks those that would occur less than one time in a hundred; and a superior "c" (^{c}) indicates those that would occur less than once in a thousand. Of course, we also present relationships that are not statistically significant because even the lack of relationship can be theoretically important, and we want to present as much information as possible for the use of future research in the area.

So much for the methodological prologue. Turning to the substance of the table, let us begin by asking which background variables produce the most significant correlations with views and expectations pertaining to the project. The answer is perhaps predictable from our finding in Chapter One that the volunteers were more widely split on religion than on any other characteristic. Thus, the most potent variable here is the index of religious traditionalism. The measure is positively related to high expected involvement with whites but low expected involvement with Negroes; high assent to nonviolent principles; concern with the decorum and public image of the project; a tendency to feel that the South can ultimately handle its own problems with regard to segregation; a more charitable and trusting conception of southern authorities, courts, and police; lack of cynicism concerning the project; high expectations for project success; high expectations for local Negro cooperation; a hawkish position concerning Vietnam; and low political pessimism in general. In sum, religious involvement seems to be related to an optimistic, if not Panglossian, view of the southern scene and the movement within it. Perhaps this is because religiosity represents a wider traditionalism which runs counter to a radical mood of confrontational crisis overlaid with pessimism. Surely such a mood is the other side of the coin just described, and it is a side that has turned up with increasing frequency since 1965.

But the religious measures do have some contenders for statistical prominence in Table 1—for example, self-estimated political liberalism, scholarly orientation, and prior contact with Negroes. The more liberal volunteers were less charitable in their views of southern courts and police; more reluctant to permit the South to solve its own problems; less concerned with the public image of the volunteers and their projects; had a distrust of American political institutions; were pessimistic about the future political life of their country; and were dovish on the Vietnam issue. But beyond such broad political correlates of liberalness, it is important to note that the volunteers' self-affixed political labels were largely unrelated to specific expectations or beliefs about the summer ahead. Where particular anxieties and anticipations were at issue, there was a great deal of diversity even among the volunteers of a single political stripe.

The next most potent variable in Table 1 is something of a surprise. The measure of scholarly orientation includes the value placed on knowledge for knowledge's sake, agreement that significant learning can take place without personal relationships between faculty and student, and the volunteer's tendency simply to think of himself as an intellectual. In characterizing the scholar in the den of activism, six significant correlates are revealed in reading down the column. First, the scholars tended to be less drawn to the tactical philosophy of nonviolence. Perhaps this is because they were intellectually wary of clasping any philosophy to their bosom without more critical examination. Perhaps it is also because their orientation made them more skeptical of the movement generally and SCOPE in particular. For example, the more scholarly also tended to be more dubious about the South providing its own solution to segregation without outside interference; they tended to have less faith in the project personnel and organization; and they were less concerned about the need to project a favorable public image by maintaining scrupulous decorum. Certainly the scholars were less sanguine in their expectations for Negro cooperation. They were also more worried about their personal safety, and scholarly orientation bore a suggestive, if not significant, negative relation to expectations of project success generally.

Of course, it is tempting for authors who think of themselves as scholars to see scholarly respondents as brighter, more realistic, more candid, and more perceptive than other respondents. This may be true, but the present data offer no assurance, and we must await later chapters which ask of the volunteers' actual experiences. Meanwhile, it is worth noting that the scholars were not necessarily the political radicals among the volunteers. These two background characteristics are virtually unrelated $(r = .05)$, and even their correlates differ. Thus, although scholarliness and political liberalism are similarly related to little concern about the project's public image and to favoring outside intervention in the South, the two bear different relationships to such matters as imagery of southern institutions, Vietnam, and the degree of over-all political pessimism.

The amount of prior contact with Negroes also has several significant correlates, but the profile is clearly different from political liberalism and scholarly orientation. Those with more contact tended to favor preferential treatment of Negroes in light of past discrimination. They also expected to encounter more harassment in the summer ahead, yet they were more confident about coping with a variety of possible contingencies and hence to expect the project to be a success. Although those with more prior contact with blacks were more in favor of outside intervention in the South, surprisingly, they harbored less antipathy against white southerners.

But lest we give the impression that there are a number of well-

crystallized syndromes of attitudes and expectations in relation to background factors and predispositions, it is important to remember that most
of the possible relationships between the four background factors just
discussed and the various dependent variables in Table 2 are not statistically significant. Indeed, for the last three variables discussed (political
liberalism, scholarly orientation, and prior contact with Negroes) only
one-third of all of their possible relationships depart reliably from zero.

This raises one of the most striking findings represented in the
table; namely, the lack of findings which qualify as significant. For example, two of the veteran workhorses in the sociological stable—sex and
socioeconomic status—are remarkably unproductive. It is true that females
are less likely to expect harassment, but this virtually exhausts the impact
of sex. Only two attitudes—belief in preferential treatment for Negroes
and dovishness with respect to Vietnam—are related to higher social class.
In part, this failure of the stock-in-trade may reflect the recruitment
funnel into the movement, one which insures more homogeneity than the
volunteers' surface characteristics would indicate. Without impugning anyone's femininity, the movement is not a place where women are women
in the frilliest sense of the phrase, and status differences also tend to have
attenuated import in such special circumstances. Much the same might
be said for relations with parents, for which the table indicates only four
significant correlates. Those having poor relations with their parents were
less attached to American political institutions, less concerned about the
worker's public image, less inclined to worry about personal safety, and
expectant of greater involvement with Negroes. These latter three items
make intuitive sense in suggesting that political involvement may be a sur-
rogate for family involvement and that a concern for safety is more common among volunteers close to parents who are themselves concerned.
Still, these correlates are only a fraction of the many that were possible,
and the larger implication is that parental relations tend to be over-
whelmed by more immediately salient items around which the volunteers
cluster more meaningfully.

Two last examples of surprising statistical impotence concern prior
activism in the North and South respectively. Prior activism in the North
is positively related to a belief in preferential treatment for Negroes and
favoring outside intervention in the South; it is negatively related to a
concern with the volunteer's public image, perhaps because prior experience with activism indicates that activists can only be people rather than
saints. As for southern activism, it too is positively related to a belief in
preferential treatment for Negroes. But in addition it is associated with
an expectation that the project will be a success and with generally
favorable attitudes toward white southerners and toward the expectation

of a high degree of involvement with white southerners. It may be that prior contact with the southern movement teaches one that the opposition of whites is more a reflection of social structure than of personal malevolence. But again the more important conclusion is the lack of statistical impact for these two predictor variables. Apparently those who had known prior activism had not been distinctly marked, perhaps because they had not experienced it deeply enough.

Our discussion of Table 1 has concentrated on the relative effects of various background variables. But there is another way to summarize the mass of correlation coefficients; namely, to ask what is the relative *vulnerability* of the assorted views and expectations to the influence of background variables? Instead of examining the table column-by-column, this requires a row-by-row inspection. Actually, the most vulnerable items or dependent variables turn out to be the index of concern with worker's public image and favoring outside intervention in the South. Each of these has five significant relationships out of nine possible. Only one additional variable—belief in preferential treatment for Negroes has as many as four significant correlates with these nine background factors.

The only clear interpretation of the table as a whole, then, is that it lacks any syndrome of attitudes and expectations that is predictable by knowledge of a volunteer's background or experience. These were people seeking to assuage their fears and to fill in their ignorance concerning the months ahead. At the orientation session in Atlanta they hungrily sought information from veteran field workers about expected harassment, about likely cooperation of local Negroes, and about the daily routines of voter registration—precisely those matters about which they had the least knowledge and experience. To repeat the point with which the chapter begins, most of the volunteers were new to the movement and frankly displayed both the befuddlement and the anxiety of the novice. Although there are a few important relationships with background characteristics, the experience departed too much from that background for it to bear consistently high relations to their anticipations. This, of course, is an implicit hypothesis in itself, since we would expect the domains of attitudes and evaluations to tighten up considerably as the rookies become more seasoned during the summer that awaited them.

SUMMARY

This chapter represents more a stepping stone than an end point in the analysis. In depicting the white SCOPE volunteers on the eve of their experiences, it has sought to describe their mood while delineating a few of its internal patterns and some of its relationships to background factors discussed in Chapter One. While the correlation technique with which the chapter ends discharges the twin obligation of seeking relationships and presenting maximum data for those interested, it does so at the expense of an uncomfortable and digressive abstraction from the reality of the volunteers as individuals. Of course, any single description of so many individuals can hardly avoid abstraction. But let us close the chapter with a risk in the opposite direction. Instead of probing for the heterogeneity that exists, let us portray the typical volunteer going into the field. What were the feelings and misgivings that were to inform his activity and his perceptions? What were the views and the attitudes which might be subject to change as a result of the impact of the summer upon him?

We saw in the previous chapter that the typical volunteer was relatively high status, seeking independence rather than rebelling from parents who were by and large supportive. He was a high academic achiever with high academic and career aspirations. While he had a good deal of appreciation for the world of scholarship on its own terms, he also sensed that his college experience was relevant to the issues of the world as it was and might be. Turning to these issues more specifically, the typical volunteer was more likely to be irreligious than devout, and yet regardless of his beliefs he felt that the churches had not acted on the dictates of religious ethics. Politically, he was obviously a liberal on civil rights; however, he was not in favor of preferential treatment for Negroes because of their past oppression. Perhaps more important than his views of civil rights, however, was his attitude on a host of other issues. Whether on nuclear disarmament, capital punishment, or the war in Vietnam, he was more liberal than his student peers. Indeed the evidence suggests that the sum of his concerns and disillusionments on these issues had pushed the typical volunteer to a point where he had to do something constructive to honor his commitments. The civil rights movement was the one structured opportunity available, and within it, SCOPE was the most active in seeking recruits in 1965. But one last motivational strand remains in seeking to understand our hypothetical subject. His own testimony indicates that, in addition to the obvious political and humanitarian reasons for his participation, he viewed the project as a crucible in which to find and to forge his own identity under stress. In this sense, the movement offered both an opportunity and a challenge; as such, the experience elicited an ambivalent combination of fear and adventure, each of which was essential to the meaningfulness of the summer itself.

As for the typical volunteer's attitudes and expectations concerning the movement and its context, he was scornful of southern courts and police and pessimistic that the South can contrive its own solution to segregation without massive external influence. Although he expected to have little contact with southern whites, he tended to view them not as personally malevolent but rather as tragic subservients in a system due to collapse. On the other hand, he obviously expected a great deal of personal contact with southern Negroes and expected them to be both cooperative and courageous. Certainly he had the highest regard for veteran field workers within the movement, seeing them as especially sensitive to the needs of others. He held this view despite his skepticism concerning the organizational efficiency of SCOPE.

Even though our volunteer anticipates a great deal of harassment and has more worries about his personal safety than anything else, he nevertheless assented to nonviolent philosophy and tactics, and he had a great deal of confidence in his ability to handle a number of specific although hypothetical situations. He was greatly concerned about protecting the public image of the project, one that might be threatened by the presence of Communists, alcohol, or illicit sex among the members. Withal, he was optimistic about the ultimate success of the project. He expected a momentous increase in voter registration, although he was less sanguine about increasing the militancy of southern blacks or converting southern whites to more moderate positions.

This concludes both the simplified portrait of the typical volunteer and this two-chapter treatment of the personal and intellectual baggage which the volunteers as a group brought to the South. By now the reader may be as anxious to get to this actual experience as were the volunteers themselves at the end of their orientation. Now we follow them into the field, relying on their own recollections as well as on the quantitative items in the second questionnaire administered the following fall.

CHAPTER III

Confrontation Camp

More and more, I'm just horrified at the extent to which environment and culture can deplete a man of all sorts of reserves and let him fall into a condition, not of despair, but such absolute resignation. I'm just frustrated by it every day, and irritated by it. I just want to shake the people and say, "It doesn't have to be this way." And yet who am I to say that because maybe it does have to be that way. I'm trying to tell them it doesn't, but I can't blame them, given their past experience, what they've grown up with. The other day I met a girl who was twenty-one and had never been to school. When we told her she should register to vote, she didn't know what we were talking about. We were trying to explain, and finally we said would she have a car to get up to Orangeburg, and she said, "Orangeburg?" as if she'd never heard of it. Slowly she realized where it was. She said, "But how would I get out of here?"

A SCOPE volunteer

It is a sad commentary on social science that there is a burgeoning literature on who the activists are but only scant materials on what activism entails. What does it mean to be an alien agent for change in a society clinging to a status quo? What are the fears and anxieties of marked men among marksmen? What are the joys and satisfactions of the day-to-day life? What are its frustrations, and to what extent are they psychological, interpersonal, organizational, or ideological? To answer such questions requires more than a study of one summer within a single episode of political protest. But we can examine the case before us with these queries in mind. This chapter makes a beginning as it follows the volunteers into the field to recount their experiences, often in their own words. Our object is to describe how they lived, sometimes in contrast to how they had expected to live. In the process we shall emphasize their social context and their relations to local blacks and local whites.

FROM THE BOWL TO THE GRIDDLE

The morning after the orientation ended foreshadowed what was in store for the volunteers. Nearly three hundred of them had to be started toward points throughout the South. Adequate transportation, sufficient funds, and clear project leadership had to be checked. There were trivial but exasperating problems on every count. Confusion held sway, and departures were delayed. The routine of activism had begun. And if this presaged the events to follow, such events were to be enacted in six different states.

Of the 182 white workers answering our questionnaire, forty-eight were distributed among fifteen Alabama counties; another fifty went to fourteen counties in Georgia; South Carolina was granted forty-seven, scattered among ten counties; North Carolina had eleven workers in two counties; Virginia claimed seventeen in six counties; and north Florida received four volunteers in two counties. The destinations of five volunteers were not ascertained.

Traveling from Atlanta in overburdened cars and innocent southern buses, some of the volunteers arrived that same day and others the next. Anxiety, excitement, and wishful anticipation no doubt filtered their early perceptions. But to get a sense of the scene, let us cite one setting in Mississippi as it was described by a COFO worker the previous summer:

Dear Anne,
It's a hot lazy Sunday afternoon. I want to try to give you a description of Itta Benna, and the place where we're staying.
The Negro neighborhood is literally "on the other side of the railroad tracks." To get over to the white and downtown areas you have to

either walk past several warehouses, small factories, etc., or cross the railroad tracks. The Negro neighborhood hasn't got a single paved street in it. It's all dirt and gravel roads. The houses vary from really beat-up shacks to fairly good looking cottages. The beat-up places predominate. There are lots of smelly outhouses and many of the houses have no inside water.

During the day it seems as if there is nothing but small children, hordes of them, and old people sitting on porches. There are quite a few churches. These have the most uncomfortable benches imaginable. I really can't do a good job of describing it; but then I don't have to—you've seen places like this town in movies and magazines a hundred times. But to see the place in the real is so different from seeing pictures of it. It's really there—you feel the heat, breathe the dust, smell the outhouses, hear the kids and the chickens.

John and I are staying with a sixty-seven year old woman named Rosa Lee Williams. She owns her place, so she doesn't have to worry about being thrown out.

Her house is on East Freedom Street. The street runs along the railroad tracks. Across the street is a row of corn and then the railroad tracks and a cotton field beyond. The house has a living room, with double bed that John and I sleep in, a bedroom where Mrs. Williams sleeps and where we eat, then a small kitchen. The only running water in the place is in the toilet. No sinks are hooked up, so we wash out of buckets, etc., but at least we have a flush toilet. Those outhouses are too much!

Mrs. Williams gets $4 a week from each of us for a room. Originally she said she wasn't going to cook for us, but she's always doing it anyhow, so we're giving her another $4 a week. She said she didn't want the extra money, but she's on a pension and welfare, so she probably needs the money. She's really gotten crazy about us. She calls us "Lil' Bro' " and "Big Bro' " (Bro' is brother). She had a broken leg which wasn't set quite right, so she sort of limps. She also has an improperly set collarbone; it was broken when she was fighting with someone over a shotgun. She's still mad at the Deputy Sheriff for not giving her back the shotgun.

There's an old preacher, Mr. Bevel, two doors down. Another preacher in Itta Benna decided that it would be better for John and me to move in with him because he has a phone. When we mentioned it to Mrs. Williams, she was furious with Bevel for trying to take us away and we had to stop talking about it for fear she'd start a fight with him.

She's really a fiery and fast-moving old woman. The first night we were here, Willie, John, and I moved the bed into the living room. She was in the bedroom about three seconds before us and had the bed half apart before we were in the room. While we were setting it up in the living-room she was running around mopping under where we were putting the bed. Before we went to sleep she brought in a can and put it under the bed. She said it was for "spittin' " (she chews tobacco).

She keeps as clean a house as is possible with all the dust from the road blowing in. She's meticulous about flies and mosquitoes and usually sprays the place at night.

She's sort of a lonely old woman and I guess she enjoys having people around the house. She said that the last of her children died after the influenza epidemic of 1918. Her husband was a preacher and she's a retired midwife.

John and I both started having diarrhea last night. Must be due to new bugs in the water, food, etc. It should be over in a few days.[1]

How does the description compare with our data from the SCOPE workers in 1965?

Virtually all (89 per cent) of our respondents lived in local Negro homes. Almost 40 per cent of these report that a woman was head of the household. This proportion is more than one might expect, although it squares with the current notions of black matriarchy and a feeling of many that women were more supportive of the movement than men.[2] Living conditions were clearly below the standards to which most of the volunteers were accustomed; 34 per cent described them as "much worse" and another 45 per cent said "somewhat worse." The situation was not purely physical since psychological unease and ambivalence were common. For example, one volunteer told a roving field reporter from the Stanford University radio station, KZSU, that, "The only problem I've had is, like, living here; the dirt drives me out of my mind. In most houses, if you see dirt in the sink you just clean it up, it's no big thing. But here, the whole house is so filthy all the time, I'm scared to clean up after things for fear it'll look insulting." The anthropologists might call this culture shock. So did one of the volunteers in Alabama, although he was reacting less to housekeeping than to kinship: "When I came here and saw the things that happen here, it was a shock. The people here, oh it annoys me still and I'd like to do something about it more than anything. The families here are just unbelievable. One of the girls was pointing out in the street one day . . . to one of the local girls and said, 'there's my half-sister.' I said, what do you mean your half-sister? She said, 'Well, you know my dad likes to step out every once in a while. I've got half-sisters all over the town.' It's such a regular thing around here, and it bothers me, because I think one of the big problems around here is family life and family planning." Such reactions were common. And yet most of the volunteers were able to adjust and perhaps even thrive on the drama of the occasion. There is a certain gratification in simply meeting such

[1] E. Sutherland, *Letters From Mississippi* (New York: McGraw-Hill, 1965), pp. 39–40.

[2] D. P. Moynihan, "The Negro Family: The Case for National Planning" (Office of Policy Planning and Research, United States Department of Labor, March, 1965). Of course, the "Moynihan Report" is both famous and infamous, depending on the circles in which one is traveling. For a probing account of the politics involved in its interpretation, see L. Rainwater and W. L. Yancey, *The Moynihan Report and the Politics of Controversy* (Cambridge, Mass.: The Massachusetts Institute of Technology Press, 1967).

people and living on their own terms. One volunteer who lived with both a lower-class and a middle-class black family during the summer compared them this way: "I lived with a Negro family in one of the most difficult areas in this county, and it was difficult to take. No water, no plumbing (not even an outhouse), and over-crowded—three family members plus the four of us. But in comparison to now with this middle-class family, that was much finer, much more fascinating. This is like living anywhere in the country, but they were unsophisticated, even toward the civil rights movement: 'Why are you down here?' 'What makes you white people different?' These people were so poor, so destitute, but the ties between them . . . well, there was so much love and how anybody can have so much love when they have suffered so much is beyond me. Here there is more comfort, but the feelings are repressed." This remark hints at a complaint that was frequent among volunteers assigned to middle-class homes. Many hungered for the "real" experience of poverty. They were removed from the locus of the problem and its possible cure.

Meanwhile, it is important not to bloat the matter of living conditions out of proportion. Not only did a good many workers live in middle-class homes, but even the majority in more stricken circumstances were able to cope. Sixty-eight per cent reported no trouble adapting at all, and another 31 per cent indicated that they had a few problems which were quickly overcome. And if it is true that the spirit of any army derives from its belly, the volunteers were apparently well-off in this respect. Soul food had not yet become faddish fare for fund-raising dinners, but the volunteers were more than satisfied. Fifty-three per cent described the eating as "good," and another 23 per cent called it "excellent." As one respondent put it, "The food was great when I ate with a Negro family, although it was damn poor when we cooked for ourselves around the project office." Of course, some of this enthusiasm for eating in Negro homes may reflect the romance of activism generally, and there is no doubt that many volunteers ate especially well because they were treated as guests, sometimes at the family's own dietary expense. Still, there is something to be said for southern cooking and many of the SCOPE workers returned home saying it.

In any event, it is apparent that living conditions were among the least of the volunteers' problems. Although a few became increasingly annoyed with the lack of privacy and accouterments previously taken for granted, most were quick to indicate that this annoyance was largely because of the frustration in other more important respects. Two key sources of the frustration were the volunteers' relations with local blacks and whites respectively.

RELATIONS WITH THE HOST COMMUNITY

SCOPE did not simply thrust its workers onto local communities. The volunteers went only where they had been requested by an indigeneous black leadership willing to assume control and responsibility. Thus, in moving from Atlanta into the field, the workers moved from under the wing of the central SCLC staff to the more immediate charge of local leaders who had neither national prestige nor professional commitment. Any treatment of the relations between the volunteers and the Negro communities must begin with the local leadership. Perhaps inevitably, this situation was a source of both strength and weakness, wisdom and folly. But if negative judgments seem to predominate in the comments which follow, it is worth noting that not a little courage was required for these leaders to host the volunteers in the first place—somewhat like offering one's home as a dynamite depot. It is understandable that many shied from the cooperation that these men ventured.

Unfortunately our questionnaire failed to include questions directly concerned with the local black leadership. However, we can make inferences from other items and rely on the volunteers' written comments and personal experiences. For example, consider the statement: "The southern Negro is the real current leader in the civil rights struggle." Before the volunteers went into the field, 44 per cent voiced strong agreement with the proposition. One would expect this to increase over the course of the summer if the local leaders had been widely effective in their roles. Alas, the percentage dipped to 32 per cent in the second questionnaire administered in the fall. Perhaps more revealing, and surely more dramatic, is the percentage shift regarding the item: "Under no circumstances whatsoever should a participant place his judgment above the policy of the project leaders in determining how to act." Before their field experience, fully 56 per cent of the volunteers indicated agreement; at the end of the summer the proportion had dropped to 22 per cent. This tentative evidence is supported in interviews and remarks appended to the post-summer questionnaires. One volunteer described an atmosphere of particular tension and suspicion between the local black leaders and their white charges: "Southern Negroes are the leaders of the civil rights movement, as they should be, and are wary of white northerners who believe they (northerners) know how to solve the problem of segregation. Yet I believe too many of the southern Negro leaders are, in a sense, paranoid in this regard. . . . They were so overcome by those apprehensions that their fearful attitudes (both verbalized and subconscious) created a barrier between us and them. It was sometimes difficult for us to resist acting defensively in reaction to their accusations, and a tension was created that might not have evolved had we not felt that we had been unjustly convicted of doing something which most of us had all along been consciously trying *not* to do."

In addition to mutual suspicion and its consequences, some volunteers also described the political results of relying too much on a single established leader. Such leaders were often seen as divorced from the potential followers of the movement by social class differences exacerbated by authoritarianism. One volunteer was suspicious that his particular leader was profiting economically through pay-offs from local whites. Other workers remarked that although their leaders were able to extract concessions from the whites, these were generally symbolic gestures in lieu of more meaningful gains. In some cases the outside volunteers were not alone in their disenchantment with the local black leadership. There were several instances of challenges from within the black community itself.

Clearly, many volunteers saw their local leaders more as a brake than as an accelerator. Yet the matter is both too important and too complex to summarize so quickly. Other volunteers were highly positive in their reactions. And even some of those who were negative may have been partaking of a spirit that some blacks in the movement found inappropriate. As one of the SCOPE staff commented to a volunteer, "Man, you're sure quick to use that term, Uncle Tom. He's a Tom, she's a Tom, everybody's a Tom, but you folks gonna jive your way to heaven. Listen, I don't think you all have earned the right to call someone that 'til you know what it's really like. I got that right, but even I don't call people that as much as you folks been doing it." In his diary, one volunteer leader explicitly recognized that structural factors could often produce tension quite apart from the personalities involved. "Friday morning, July 11: Our local leader really gave us and especially me hell for causing so many problems. . . . But we lack social outlets, and what is worse, some of the Negro community doesn't approve of integrated couples or our being out after 10:00 p.m. There is a lack of communication (e.g., Friday night we had a rally at the park without getting final approval from the local leaders—my fault). I think the main problem is lack of communication. A lot of this is due to the factor that none of them has enough time to be in constant contact with us and I can't get in contact with them." Finally, and perhaps most importantly, the volunteers were sometimes pawns in a power struggle between the local black community

on the one hand and the SCLC authorities on the other. One worker
wrote this about the conflict:

> I strongly disagree with SCLC's apparent policy of strengthening and
> supporting authoritarian Negro leaders and organizations (presumably
> because it's easier to deal with one man, and easier to control huge
> projects like SCOPE if authoritarian techniques of leadership are
> used). But I believe this hurts the Negro communities and is contrary
> to all the ideals of democracy which fill SCLC rhetoric. The policy
> seems to work all right for mobilizing demonstrations as long as SCLC
> has staff in a town to shore up the local leader they're using, but SCLC
> often leaves ruined towns behind when it leaves and the Negroes left
> are no more able or used to active democratic decision-making than
> they were before the movement arrived. This is not just generalization
> from one case. It was true, . . . according to other SCOPE people,
> . . . all over Georgia.

OUTSIDE ELITISM AND GRASS ROOTS DEMOCRACY

The last quotation points to a dilemma that was not only visible
throughout the SCOPE project but is likely to vex any movement seeking
radical change under the banner of democratization. Keniston refers to
the problem as a tension between "power and participation."[3] The radical's clarion cry, "Let the people decide!" is often followed by a realization
that the people's decision is slow in coming, moderate in aim, and conservative in tactic. At this point, the movement has several alternatives: it
may stand pat, begin a program of political education, seek to take charge
of the situation, or try to dismiss one set of local spokesmen in favor of
another set promising more radical decisions. Each of these alternatives
was illustrated at various points in the southern movement, but perhaps
the dominant response was cyclical. That is, the leadership of the movement began by letting the people decide, yet after discovering that the
people's decision did not measure up the leadership began to play a more
authoritarian role. However, this role involved such a departure from the
espoused democratic ideology that it led to guilt and a reversion to the
first stage, at which point the process began all over again.

If we view the movement as a political organization, this cycle
is understandable. The business of politics requires nothing so much as
control over one's political forces. Where that control is lacking, the

---

[3] For a discussion of this problem in the context of the antiwar movement,
K. Keniston, *The Young Radicals* (New York: Harcourt Brace Jovanovich, 1968),
especially Chapter Five. The same difficulty in the Peace Corps context is discussed
in L. H. Fuchs, *Those Peculiar Americans* (New York: Meredith Press, 1967),
especially Chapter Five. As an anthropologist might put it, "going native" was a
temptation for many but an unhappy experience for most.

movement may lose both thrust and efficiency. And yet the term *move-ment* is apt precisely because it suggests a faction moving ahead of the mass and seeking to turn potential support into actual power. The difficulty was not always obvious to, say, an SCLC staff member in Atlanta who spent most of his time communicating with Washington and points north. The problem was greatest at the local level, and it was there that the 1965 volunteers entered the scene. Not only were they often caught up in the dilemma and its dynamics but their soul-searching was complicated when factions emerged among the local leaders themselves.

A surprising proportion of volunteers reported actual hostility from local Negroes. Only 35 per cent indicated that there had been no hostility at all, whereas 45 per cent indicated "slight hostility," 18 per cent "moderate hostility," and 2 per cent "extreme hostility." Thus, at least one in five of the SCOPE workers experienced at least moderate opposition from local Negroes. Although this is not to say that one-fifth of the local Negroes were opposed, it is certainly important to examine the sources of the opposition that did exist. In one South Carolina town, the source was the local mortician, a strong figure in the power configuration of any southern black community because of the church-related burial societies. He was tied in with the white authorities, according to our respondent. Other volunteers reported hostility from local Negro professionals (teachers, doctors, school administrators) who felt that their relations with local whites were important but precarious, and who sometimes refused to supply the workers with cars and supplies, even threatening to use their influence against the project. Many indicated that local clergymen were uncooperative. For example, some did not allow their churches to be used for mass meetings. One volunteer reported that the Negro minister in his Alabama town actually relayed tactical information to whites.

Still another possible source of hostility was the local Negro Voters' League. According to a volunteer who was in Alabama, "Most of the hostility came from leaders of the local Negro Voter Association who thought we were undermining their positions and going too fast. They were very antidemonstration; they were in good with the white power structure and we were antagonizing it. As a result, they wouldn't give us assistance. They told the people not to talk with us, and they even told some people we brought to the polls to register to go home."

Actual opposition, however, was less of a problem than seeming apathy among local Negroes. Of course, much of this apathy was born of fear and fatalism, both derived from a grinding oppression that makes one grateful for small favors and unable to conceive of large demands. To those who would underestimate the effects of poverty, such reality may be harsh and sobering: "I'm a little bit disappointed in some of the reactions we've been getting. . . . It's such a terrific letdown, and the thing I'm referring to is the fact that so many of the Negroes here seem to be not the least interested in what we're doing, or at least they're not going the least bit out of their way to cooperate with us or to help us. . . . I feel like screaming at them, 'don't you realize that we're down here to help you!' " Other volunteers were more analytic in reacting to the syndrome, and many saw Negro religion as both a cause and a symbol.

I realize now that it's not going to be just a matter of holding up our golden ideals and our wonderful equality signs and making them change —it's gonna be tough to do that. I've also realized that the Negroes here have been as ignorant about things as the whites have. And I don't know if it's because they've been kept ignorant—I know that's part of the problem. Fear, I imagine, is another part if they even attempt to change things. It's the ministers who for many years were saying the only way to keep going was to say it's the life in heaven. The ministers in some places are becoming a hindrance. They completely ignore pragmatic values or things they can do on earth now. It's terrible to go to church and see people yelling and screaming about going to heaven when they won't even come to register to vote. This is one of the messages we've got to get across, and this, too, is going to be tough.

Instead of relying solely on quotations, let us consider some of the relevant questionnaire data. At some points, the data challenge the thrust of the qualitative judgments we have considered so far.

CHARACTERISTICS OF BLACK SUPPORTERS

If all of the local Negroes had been willing to support the workers, there would have been no reason for the volunteers to come; an indigenous movement and perhaps the millennium would be at hand. But if many workers were disappointed with black support, they may well have expected too much. Cynics and bigots alike were surprised that there was any support at all. A common refrain from the southern white was, "Our nigras are good nigras and won't have anything to do with that white trash."

Most projects did receive support, however, and we asked the volunteers from which portions of the black community it came. Their impressions are reflected in Table 2. The collective judgment tallies only partially with historical, journalistic and other sociological statements and predictions.

One set of figures in the table clearly stands out as different from the rest. For most of the volunteers, the surest source of support and the numerical backbone of the movement was the high school age youth. Fully 63 per cent of the volunteers judged this group to have given "great support," a figure more than double that for any other segment of the black

Table 2. DEGREES OF SUPPORT FROM FACTIONS OF
LOCAL NEGRO COMMUNITY

	Great Support	Moderate Support	Some Support	Little Support	No Support
			Per Cent		
SEX:					
Male	24	39	31	5	0
Female	27	47	21	4	1
AGE:					
Pre-high school	21	20	29	18	12
High school	63	26	9	1	1
College	16	24	20	27	12
Young adults	12	31	30	23	5
Middle age	10	26	38	24	2
Older	5	16	32	35	12
OCCUPATION:					
Clergymen	25	30	23	20	2
Professional	12	24	20	23	21
Store owners and businessmen	14	22	28	28	8
School teachers	5	13	21	33	28
Domestics in white houses	3	18	37	31	12
Laborers	12	31	35	16	7
Sharecroppers	4	16	27	34	18

community. Ninety per cent of the volunteers thought the youth of either great or moderate support. Such unanimity is remarkable. Here is one speaking for most: "The intensity in the southern movement . . . it's been with kids . . . I mean little kids from twelve to sixteen, to see kids who understand that when they go out they're going to get beaten up or thrown in jail . . . just *know* they're going to do it and go out and do it again and go out singing a song like 'This Little Light of Mine' and get beat over the head and come back with their mouths bleeding and singing 'We Love Everybody.' It's hard to turn away from something like that. . . . This is how I visualize the movement as children." All of this discussion raises the important issue of whether the support of high schoolers presages greater militancy among the adults of the future or whether it reflects a characteristic limited to adolescence. Unfortunately we have no way of answering the query with the present data. But a segment of a recorded volunteer bull-session concerning a slightly older age group serves as a check on any optimism.

First volunteer: The discouraging thing is the young men, the twenty-year-olds and the eighteen-year-olds. But I think whites would be the same. The culture's antipathetic to anything that smacks of being square. "Good citizen," oh boy, that's a real calling card [sarcasm]. I'm talking about twenty-year-old men. What twenty-year-old man in his right mind—

Local Negro: That's why you guys are down here, I think—probably because you're the same age and hopefully you can find a way to talk to them.

First volunteer: No—there's a gulf, a cultural gulf, . . . and there's a cultural gulf even between John [local Negro volunteer] and them too. . . . John's a square too, because he's a good citizen.

Second volunteer: No he isn't. He's a square because of what happened in the last two years. Wasn't square at all to be in the freedom movement two years ago. Man—you stand out there in this park when they integrated the park two years ago, three hundred people around one hundred Negroes with pitchforks and broken bottles. . . . That isn't square.

Third volunteer: The thing is, that was the glory of the movement. This is the hard work.

There is indeed a profound difference between a social movement in its beginning phases and at the stage of "hard work." Moreover, movements by their very nature depend upon aberrant adherents. This means not only that movements tend to develop among the dispossessed and those who identify with them, but also that, among the dispossessed, movements attract those who are least ensconced within the conventional occupational and normative structures. Hence, that the Civil Rights Movement should depend upon the joint allegiance of white intellectuals and black high school students is a commentary on most movements, future as well as past. And to say that the high school student of today is likely to mellow as he becomes an adult is not to deny that the high school students in succeeding years will be more militant than their predecessors. This is especially the case as the revolutionary spark reaches the youth of the northern ghettos.

But if age-related dislocation is a factor in producing militancy, it apparently cannot be generalized to those who are dislocated by old age instead of youth. The image of the wizened, elderly Negro standing at the head of a movement and finally demanding his rights has been a favorite theme of the mass media, perhaps because a photograph of an eighty-year-old Negro couple who are willing to endure hot sun and withering glances to finally register has enormous appeal. Table 2 suggests, however, that such incidents are rare and that the elderly are hardly in the vanguard, without implying that the aged are actively opposed to change. Some may have grown accustomed to the status quo, and many have been terrorized by the prior fates of those who sought to change it. Still others are just so old as to be infirm or ineffective, despite their predilections. After all, sheer physical energy is an important variable in any political activity.

Turning from age to sex, Table 2 is somewhat more ambiguous. It is true that the volunteers gave an edge in support to women, as we mentioned earlier. This partakes of the feminine mystique portrayed by the Lorraine Hansberry play *Raisin in the Sun* and by the fabled *Moynihan Report*. But as the *Moynihan Report* demonstrated (at least to a few), the roots of black matriarchy are largely economic.[4] With specific reference to the Civil Rights Movement, men are more often exposed to the vicissitudes of the occupational market place, and can ill afford conspicuous support of a gauntlet in the face of a white employer. Indeed, looking ahead in the table to the occupational differences, note that although domestics in white homes are almost always Negro women, they have one of the very lowest profiles of estimated support, presumably because of *their* dependency upon white employers. This at least is one among several possible explanations. For another, S. M. Lipset has argued that domestics and others in intimate, if subservient, contact with status superiors actually become socialized to some of the values and political norms of these superiors, even when they run against the grain of self-interest.[5] As Louis Lomax has commented, "God save us from the cook's eye view of the world."[6]

In looking at the full occupational break-down in Table 2, how-

[4] For some impressive documentation to the effect that the roots of black matriarchy and family disorganization are indeed economic, see Moynihan, *op. cit.*, p. 22.

[5] S. M. Lipset, *Political Man* (Garden City: Doubleday and Co., 1960), especially Chapter Seven. The position of the American domestic has long intrigued scholars, particularly European observers such as Alexis de Tocqueville, *Democracy in America*, trans. by George Lawrence; ed. by J. P. Mayer and M. Lerner (New York: Harper and Row, 1966), pp. 550–557. The larger problem of the contingencies of developing "class consciousness" has plagued scholars and activists alike at least since Karl Marx. Indeed, there is a parallel between Marx's own career and the experiences of the student activists. The younger Marx was so convinced that alienation existed on a massive scale that he tended to assume that class consciousness would develop quickly among the proletariat; the older Marx had learned differently and concentrated increasing attention on the variables which govern the problematic rise of such consciousness. Such a contrast might also be drawn between the novice and experienced volunteer.

[6] Lomax made this remark in the context of a television panel show. For a broader account of his perspective, see L. Lomax, *The Negro Revolt* (New York: Harper and Row, 1962).

ever, we note that the results are surprisingly meager. That is, the overall differences in support between occupational or status groups in the
black community are not as great as one might predict, especially after
exposure to the legend of Uncle Tom and the black bourgeoisie and
after listening to the volunteer's own impressionistic contrasts between
low-status enthusiasm and high-status recalcitrance. "There was going
door-to-door, and you could see in the poor neighborhoods people would
drag you in their house and say, 'See this icebox, everything in it is
yours, just come and get it,' and in the rich neighborhoods people would
say, 'We'll give you a dollar if you go away.' Rich, comparatively—
no Negro is really rich."

Of course, part of the discrepancy between this remark and the
empirical findings of the table arises from the idiosyncrasy of the former
and the insensitivity of the latter. But there is a possible resolution as well.
It may be that the volunteers were reacting not so much to the absolute
absence of high-status support, but rather to the gap between what the
high-status blacks might have provided and what they actually delivered.
Because the Negro middle-class has so much more to offer a movement in
skills, monies, contacts, and the like, one would expect more support from
them simply by virtue of their potential. From this perspective, the high-
status groups do indeed fall short.

No single group illustrated this better than the Negro school
teachers and administrators. In fact, no single group in the entire table
was judged to be less supportive. Of course, this is largely because they
were the prisoners of a white status system with exclusive control over
their jobs and over the mobility for which so many longed. The finding
actually replicates those of several previous studies concerning the black
educator. As only one example, Aiken and Demerath found in a separate
study of patterns of Mississippi school desegregation that the Negro school
professionals were the only ones among both whites and blacks interviewed to equivocate on the inferiority of the black schools.[7] This may
have been distorted perception at work, but it was also a vested interest
rearing its head. The way of the educated subservient is not easy.

On the other hand, consider the clergymen in Table 2. Earlier
we mention that clergymen were sometimes regarded as poor leaders
in the local setting and that some volunteers reported instances in which
Negro ministers had frustrated the SCOPE project considerably. Here,
however, the statistics indicate that, compared to other occupations, the

[7] M. T. Aiken and N. J. Demerath III, "Tokenism in the Delta: Two
Mississippi Cases," report to the United States Office of Education, in R. W.
Mack (Ed.), *Our Children's Burden* (New York: Random House, 1968), pp. 41–
107.

black clergymen at large were *more* supportive. The important point then is that not all clergymen were either militant or conservative. Relative to other occupations, ministers were less dependent upon white employers and were therefore freer to participate.[8] Also relative to other occupations, the clergymen were more dependent on the good will of the black community, and because that community was so hobbled in its activism, many saw the minister's participation as a symbol of what they would like to have done but could not.

SOCIAL RELATIONSHIPS

Apart from the formal achievements of voter registration, organization, education, and so on, many volunteers found their greatest fulfillment and excitement in personal relationships with members of the black community. Just the simple act of communicating across enormous class and racial barriers was often the most thrilling aspect of the entire experience. One worker in South Carolina said, "Living with the people and having us learn to understand them was the biggest success of the summer because it helped them to understand us—they had never lived with whites before. Even if no one had registered to vote, the project would have been successful because it built understanding and love." And to draw once again on the letters from the 1964 COFO workers in Mississippi, one described the kind of isolated incident that can give meaning to an entire summer.

> One day when I was canvassing I met Mr. Brown. I told him my name is Ann. He said yes, Miss Ann, pleased to meet you. He is a young Negro teacher in the all-Negro Temple High School and of course he had no contact with white people before, except as Mr., Mrs., "Massa,"—well, I said please call me Ann—and Ran, there was nothing so beautiful as the rest of the conversation. At every opportunity he had, he said Ann—he didn't just say Ann—he rolled the name around his tongue, savored the taste and sang it, listening to the echo in the back of his mind. He played with the word as a child would play with a new and fascinating toy, as a person would delight in the ecstasy of a new-found love. And that conversation has left a

8 A closely cropped analysis of the Negro minister would want to make distinctions within the category. For example, Martin Luther King, Jr., was a Baptist, and this denomination emphasizes the principle of local autonomy, making the minister beholden to his flock for his job and his rewards. Where the parish approves of a given political action, the minister is likely to have sufficient support for undertaking it. On the other hand, consider the ministers associated with other Negro denominations, such as the African Methodist Episcopal. Here power tends to flow more from the centralized office of the bishop; the local minister must often gain the support of a middle-class Negro leader if he is to participate in the movement with impunity. Negro bishops, like Negro school superintendents, have not been known for their militancy.

mark on me. I hear the name—a loved word—the start of something so big, so beautiful, so new.[9]

For such experiences to loom so large, two explanations are plausible among many. First, it may be that more formal triumphs were hard to come by. Second, it is possible that even this sort of informal communication was particularly salient because it was rare for many of the volunteers.

Table 3 considers seven different forms of possible contact which the volunteers might have had with local blacks. The first three forms

Table 3. CONTACTS WITH LOCAL NEGROES

	Daily or Almost	Many	Several	One	None or Two
			Per Cent		
Visit homes	86	12	2	0	0
Spend night	86	7	6	1	1
Attend church	24	61	12	2	0
Friendly and casual conversation	63	24	11	2	1
Honest discussion about civil rights	49	34	15	2	0
Rational discussion about non-civil rights issue	34	40	23	3	1
Date a local Negro	1	14	17	17	50

are hardly surprising in the high frequency of contact reported, including church attendance where 24 per cent attended daily with Negroes despite the paucity of daily services in many congregations. But the next five types of contact deserve more attention. Whereas 63 per cent of the SCOPE workers reported daily, or almost daily, "friendly, casual conversation with local Negroes along the street," this figure drops to 49 per cent for honest discussions about civil rights, and to 34 per cent for rational discussions about non-civil rights issues. Finally note the figures

[9] Sutherland, *op. cit.*, p. 49. Here the objective was to induce the black to drop his accustomed deferential formality toward a white. For an intriguing case of a slightly different type, see H. Powdermaker, *Stranger and Friend: The Way of an Anthropologist* (New York: Norton, 1966), pp. 152–154. In the course of research on Indianola, Mississippi, in 1932–1933, Powdermaker accorded formal titles (Mr., Mrs., and so on) to Negroes, to whom whites generally referred on a paternalistic, first-name basis (and largely still do).

concerning interracial dating. For the vast majority of the volunteers, the summer precluded accustomed dating behavior. While 50 per cent reported no dates with local Negroes, another 34 per cent indicated having dated Negroes several times at the most, and only 15 per cent reported frequent interracial dates. These figures suggest that there were problems as well as prospects with this sort of contact. A volunteer in Alabama described both: "One problem we've had is that a guy became interested in a local girl; white guy, Negro girl. He was very, very careful not to expose the relationship before the watchful and waitful eyes of the old women of the community. Things were going along quite well until we realized that this girl's minister, who happens to be married, is also interested in this girl and the minister started spreading rumors that were totally unfounded and totally untrue. This relationship was completely on the up-and-up; that's the only trouble that we've gotten into so far. . . . The local girls are very aggressive and they're also very pretty and as the summer gets longer and hotter and we get lonelier, our guard slips a little bit."

The over-all pattern of Table 3 is difficult to assess in absolute terms. From one perspective the figures may seem high, from another low. But recalling that virtually all of the respondents were living within the Negro community, the amount of contact was at least somewhat lower than we anticipated. In such a communal setting, where the volunteers lived with blacks and spent most of their time knocking on the doors of black homes, discussion both of incidental matters and of civil rights should have been daily occurrences. That they were not for at least one of three was surprising. On the other hand, the question remains: does "many times" mean three days in five, or one day in ten? If the former, then the number of volunteers who suffered great difficulties in communicating with local blacks was probably less than one in five. If the latter figure is closer to the reality, there were many more volunteers who were substantially isolated from the black communities. And, as the following statements make clear, even face-to-face interaction is no guarantee of communication in its more meaningful sense:

I had this feeling that I would know half the people in the county before I was finished with the summer, and I'm sure that that won't be true. Although I've seen them, you know, you just don't know very many people by name. You know more people by face, but you don't know very many real well. Which perhaps isn't the way it should be, but I don't know how else it could be as the situation is here.

I feel much more at ease, much more rapport, with what I call the northern Negro. The southern Negro—at least the Negroes that I've met—I have only the fact that we're both human beings and we're both living in the same world. Other than that, there's no rapport at all, really.

As I am white, most local Negroes were afraid of me and only too ready to just agree with me and probably forget the whole thing.

The really uneducated people I can't reach. I'm white, and I just don't speak the language, and when I try and speak their language, it's so false, it's so pseudo, it's not me.

Communication between the white volunteer and the southern Negro had to span enormous subcultural gulfs in the patterning and etiquette of self-expression. Perhaps more important was the Negro's deeply inculcated fear of opening himself up to any white man. If the culture of the white college student thrives on verbalization, the culture of the southern Negro regards words as less important than prior emotional understandings. If the culture of the white college student is adept at making new friends out of total strangers, this is hardly the case in a black community where virtually all strangers must be suspect. Friendships are too important in communities under stress to be manufactured lightly.

For all of these reasons, it is not surprising that relatively few close mutual ties were established between the white SCOPE workers and members of the local black community. When asked specifically, 14 per cent of the volunteers reported no ties of this sort. Thirty-three per cent reported one or two, and another 25 per cent claimed three or four, but less than 30 per cent claimed to have established as many as five reciprocal interracial relationships that would be termed close. And only a small proportion of the volunteers were still in touch with their southern Negro friends four years later.

The difficulty was not exclusively racial. Although race was obtrusive, so was social class. Any circumstance in which college students are left to interact with members of the lower class is likely to be more halting than scintillating. Ironically, the middle-class blacks who were so wary of the volunteers were those with whom the white volunteers might have been most at ease. And in addition to both race and social class, religion was a frequent barrier to close contact: "Being an atheist, the God-bit was a problem in a way. I talked a lot to several Negro kids my age who helped us. They always asked my religion. NONE. It really *hurt* and confused them—they couldn't really understand—but they knew that I was honest and tremendously full of joy at life—they couldn't feel I was bad, so they made a very agonized attempt to expand their horizon to include me."

Of course, the volunteers adapted to these interpersonal problems in a number of ways. Two of particular interest were quite different but also quite common. First, some SCOPE workers tried to hurl themselves into the roles and identities of the blacks themselves. As one volunteer suggests, this posed potential problems:

> Every time someone here calls [one white staff member] a "white nigger" he says "white *Negro*." And he has an identity problem, he keeps thinking of himself as a Negro, in a lot of ways, trying to be. He cultivates friendships with people who tear him down because he's white. And bends over backwards; he uses more Negro slang than any Negro I've ever known. He's always "in a trick," and using bad grammar, in what are supposed to be Negro idioms. Just every way possible, trying to be more Negro than the Negroes. And I've known a lot of people like that. It really bothers me. You know, I'm going to be myself whether I like it or not, and not bend over backwards to be something I don't like specially either.

Charles Levy commented on this syndrome in his analysis of white teachers in southern Negro colleges by saying, "When the white discovers that he cannot withdraw from his whiteness by converting to blackness, he withdraws from Negroes."[10] Actually, one might paraphrase Levy and reverse the roles of white and black as a possible explanation of the withdrawal of Negroes into black power.

A second adaptation to the interpersonal problem worth noting among white SCOPE volunteers was that instead of seeking to overcome the gulf, some sought to transcend the matter altogether by rejecting SCOPE's proximate goals in favor of an ultimate vision:

> How can we expect a man who knows nothing but his cotton and local people to care about wider issues when the white who has, for instance, college education, exposure to wider ideas—in other words, who *should* be a responsible, informed, intelligent, aware citizen—when this white man *does not* care? The problem is what we can realistically expect and what we can hold as a goal in an ideal sense, what we should try to strive for. If we want to "make" the Negro into another Mr. Average citizen, it shouldn't be difficult. The basic question is a much larger one of what all people should contribute to and take from their society—and how man can more fully experience life and enrich himself—and this should include all people; race, in this respect, is irrelevant. I suppose what we are doing now is making equal opportunity, within a particular framework, for justice; equal opportunity for injustice, for ignorance, for education, and making it so the social system and all will not be geared in favor of [or] to the detriment of a group based on pigmentation of skin. I would like to think much more

---

[10] C. J. Levy, *Voluntary Servitude* (New York: Appleton-Century-Crofts, 1968), p. 123. Levy's book is organized in terms of four stages of psychological adjustment on the part of whites in a black context: contentment, indignation, awkwardness, and dismay. While most of the SCOPE workers arrived indignant and experienced little contentment, both awkwardness and dismay were clearly manifest.

about *whether* there is any *real hope* for man in general in the future, what it is, if any, and how it may be attained.

These various efforts to cope with the problems of relating to the local blacks left some volunteers exhausted, others with a sense of guilt for claiming closer relationships than had actually developed, and still others with a renewed sense of prejudice. Perhaps no white is more aware of his own prejudice than one seeking to eradicate it in others. A good number of the volunteers seemed to struggle to choke back Negro stereotypes which threatened to surge to the fore. Few were able to admit to the sorts of dislikes, moods of anger, even personal hatred that might have had their moment and then disappeared to clear the air in other circumstances. It was a triumph indeed for many to report sentiments such as, "I met the greatest, kindest, and most inspiring people I've ever met. My life was so greatly enriched that it's hard to write about it." And yet, sometimes in the same breath, this same volunteer gave less articulated expression to other feelings: "At one time . . . a cruel but true thought came to my mind: 'It's great to be white.' " Clearly, there was a great deal of ambivalence associated with this interracial contact. Some were inclined to view the problem as transitory or epiphenomenal,[11] but it seems to us that subsequent events have underlined its agonizing urgency in the changing context of the civil rights scene.

INTRARACIAL CONTACT

Let us move now from dirt roads to paved streets, from the unlighted alley of the powerless to the neon benighted thoroughfares of the powerful—from the local blacks to the local whites as they interacted with the volunteers. In Chapter Two we noted that the volunteers' expectations for southern whites had three principal components. First, they were extremely negative concerning southern authorities and the white "power structure"; accordingly they expected not only arrests and jailings, but also various degrees of violence. Second, the volunteers were somewhat more sanguine in their view of southern whites at large, tending to see them as guilt-ridden over segregation and aware that it must come to an end. But third, the volunteers anticipated very little contact with local whites, save the contact involved in harassment.

Let us begin by considering their interactions with local whites. The volunteers were almost uniformly without previous experience in the South. If their images of it were to change for the better, some degree of favorable contact with southern whites would be necessary. But sus-

[11] See A. Pinkney, *The Committed* (New Haven, Conn.: College and University Press, 1968), p. 205. Compare C. Levy, *op. cit.*, p. 125.

tained contact of any sort was rare. In the absence of more than superficial interaction, one tends to read into faces what one expects to find
behind them:

> You can be out in the country for days at a time and never see the
> white people of the town. And I sort of forget that they exist; I forget
> that we are in hostile territory. Then all it takes is a day in town. You
> know, you just see those white faces and you know where you are
> again. But if you stay in the Negro community you almost start to
> forget. What do white faces look like? To me, I don't know, they all
> look sort of familiar. They look like all of the bad stories I've read
> since I was a little girl. I just see them as like pale ghosts that creep
> down the street and scream boo! and expect you to run. The people in
> this town look so pale and lifeless. It's as though they were all cut out
> of the same book and they just creep around.

Table 4 does for the local whites what Table 3 did for the local
blacks. Again there are seven types of possible contact, and percentages
range along a five-point scale for each. The figures tell a story of general
isolation. Two-thirds of the volunteers never even visited a local white

Table 4. CONTACT WITH LOCAL WHITES

	Daily or almost	Many times	Several times	Once or twice	Never
			Per Cent		
Visit homes	1	3	6	23	66
Spend night	1	2	2	2	94
Attend church	0	3	2	15	80
Friendly and casual conversation	1	2	13	26	58
Honest discussion about civil rights	2	5	18	34	41
Rational discussion about noncivil rights issue	2	8	23	36	31
Date a local white	0	1	1	2	96

home, let alone spent the night in one. Although most of the volunteers
did little or no dating of local blacks, only 4 per cent dated any local
whites. And while almost half of the volunteers were church attenders at
home, only 20 per cent went to southern white churches during the sum-

mer, and then only once or twice for most. A Catholic volunteer in Alabama later recalled her local church-going practices this way:

> When we first arrived in town, we asked the family we were staying with where the nearest Catholic church was. They told us it was twenty miles away, in a somewhat larger town. So the three of us, on Sunday, got up early, borrowed a car, and drove off to Mass. This lasted about three weeks. Then one day we were over in the white part of town and we noticed, plain as day, a Catholic church. We asked our family about it and were told, "Yes, but that's a *white* church." Our going to that church would have meant trouble, especially since one of us was black. Well after that we soon began to realize that it was going to be hard to be a "good" Catholic anyway. For instance, we could hardly insist that our family feed us fish on Friday. So after a while we just gave up—Mass included—for the summer.

Perhaps more important than the lack of such formal contact, however, was the lack of even conversational interchange. Fully 58 per cent of the volunteers never had a "friendly, casual conversation" with a local white, and another 26 per cent reported having only one or two. Honest discussions about civil rights were more common, but still were quite rare. Only 25 per cent had them more than once or twice. And turning to the separate matter of close mutual ties, not reported in Table 4, it is predictable that 86 per cent of the volunteers claimed no friendships whatsoever of this sort with local whites.

Clearly, it is hard to change the minds of others with so little access. However, although contact was infrequent, it did occur, and it could be very meaningful.

> We were in Athens where University of Georgia is, so we had the oddity of meeting a southern white liberal group. Great people—minds so questioning and so hungry for the life of intellectual freedom we've always known. They were thrilled about the Free Speech Movement. I was invited to speak in about twelve classes on campus—mostly political science, sociology, and history. Very interesting response—many kids came to me afterwards, "I'm so glad you said what you believed even if I can't believe or accept everything or even many things." Occasionally, a brave soul, "We should be proud to have her here, and I agree with her," and sad things, "I haven't the courage to do what you do—I wish I did, but I don't." [I was] asked questions about civil rights—*always* my views on intermarriage—my candid "fine, okay with me" answers were hard for them to take—but they did. I felt they were very ambiguous and sort of felt trapped by their position as southern youth. Several of them worked with us in the Negro community after speaking to them in class.

WHITE OPPOSITION

For some volunteers the absence of reasonable positive interaction with local whites might have seemed a lost opportunity. For others it was simply a function of their intended immersion in the black community. Regardless of intention, however, the opposition of whites was hard to avoid. That there was opposition in almost every town is quite clear. Ninety-three per cent of the volunteers report personal exposure to at least one incident of harassment. These ranged from the most common verbal taunts to being followed on country roads or hearing shotgun blasts from a fleeting car during the night. Twenty per cent reported physical violence.

What were the sources of this opposition? Table 5 contains the opinions of the volunteers. Note that the table does not report on differences in segregationist *feelings* but only on the degree to which the actual behavior of different groups was more or less obstructive to the movement. Not unexpectedly, for example, women were judged less actively opposed than men, although women were no more resigned or favorable at the other end of the continuum. Turning from sex to age, Table 5 reveals little of the spectacular differentiation that we saw earlier for black support. If one sums the percentages in the two columns on the right (vocal and violent opposition), the teenage whites seem to be the most overt opponents and the young adults the least. This is hardly a pattern to inspire statistical confidence.

The occupational data offer somewhat more revealing results. Whites in higher status occupations were less often judged to be in blatant opposition to the movement. Of course, this may mean only that professionals, businessmen, and clergymen are more tutored and hence more subtle in their segregationist ways. On the other hand, or in other settings, it may reflect a basic rift within the white community itself. One can at least imagine a community in which the white middle-class is quietly moderate in its racial views but unable to change the tide and tradition set in motion and sustained by lower-class whites and the political officials who pander to their votes. Indeed, this political pressure on elected officials is so strong in the South that the following episode recounted by a volunteer in Georgia is truly exceptional.

> There was an excellent judge in town. For example, the leader of the local KKK threatened to kill us and then filed charges against the Negro preacher we stayed with for pointing a pistol at him. We then charged the KKK leader with obscenity—"black-ass niggers," "nigger-lover," etc.—and disorderly conduct. The courtroom was packed. The judge dropped the charges against the preacher and fined the KKK man, and this was an elected judge no less!

This case is far from representative of the typical whites with whom the volunteers came in contact. Interestingly enough, if one combines vocal and violent opposition, the police were substantially less often

Table 5. Degrees of Opposition from Factions of Local White Community

	Favorable	Resigned	Apathetic	Quietly Opposed	Vocally Opposed	Violently Opposed
			Per Cent			
SEX:						
Male	0	0	2	22	49	27
Female	0	0	10	37	41	12
AGE:						
Teen-age	1	3	8	12	54	22
Young adults	2	1	8	27	35	28
Middle age	1	1	5	22	46	25
Older	0	1	5	19	47	27
OCCUPATION:						
Professionals	0	10	15	34	33	8
Businessmen	1	8	9	34	36	13
Clergymen	3	13	18	31	26	10
Laborers	0	0	2	15	51	33
Poor rural	0	2	8	13	36	41
Farmers	0	0	3	16	45	36
Police	0	7	1	23	35	35

considered obstructive than the poor rural folk, the farmers, or the laborers. All of these groups were widely implicated in the volunteers' accounts of harassment sampled here:

Our office had about forty phone calls making death threats and once was shotgunned very seriously. In fact, I was nearly shot during an election.

I was run off the road while driving; shot at twice; and received numerous phone threats.

Our house was bombed and shot at; I was threatened twice with a gun and threatened numerous times with physical violence.

Shot at twice, almost run over once, car chases by local whites, sworn at by locals, followed around, had phone tapped, mail withheld.

A white youth walked up to a group of four of us on the street in the Negro section and proceeded to beat each of us in turn. I was knocked to the ground and kicked—no major injuries. He made the round of us three times, beating me and another guy, chasing a third. But he didn't touch the only Negro member with us at the time.

There was a Klan rally . . . and we were protesting in order to get the [voter] registration books opened. The Klansmen met us on the street and beat us.

This last instance is the second that raises the spectre of the KKK. But when we asked the volunteers specifically concerning its activity in their county or community, only one in three said it was even "fairly active."

THE POLICE

At a time when the police are under close and controversial national scrutiny, they deserve special attention here. Although they were not seen as the most violent segment of the white community, their behavior was more pivotal to the cause. The police were supposed to represent law enforcement, and when they stood aside to permit violence it was worthy of comment in its own right especially when the cases involved state as well as local police: "I was once knocked down unconscious during a picket-line at a supermarket. Georgia State Patrolmen were present, but offered no protection whatever." "I was picketing an auto parts store with a Negro my own age. A white boy my age approached and knocked me to the ground with his fist while four state police watched."

And yet the police did more than watch. They often stopped the volunteers to ask for their drivers' licenses, occasionally impounding their cars for parking violations, and frequently arresting them for other traffic offenses. There were several instances in which police harassment involved violence itself. For example, one volunteer told of going with a group to swear out a warrant, whereupon the "deputy sheriff whacked me three times with a cane (causing head bleeding)." And another recalls, "A city policeman stopped us and hit me when I told him that his search was unconstitutional."

Again, however, one's judgment concerning the frequency of formal police actions depends largely upon one's expectations. For example, 41 per cent of the volunteers were arrested at least once, a figure that is (or used to be) very high for a three-month period in the lives of such middle-class college youths. On the other hand, a majority of the volunteers escaped further legal embroilment. Twenty-seven per cent were actually taken to court, although almost all of these were convicted of at least one offense and 35 per cent spent at least one night in jail.

Those who were jailed were hardly happy with their keepers. Fifty-six per cent reported verbal abuse from the jailors, not to mention the other prisoners. Seventeen per cent of the volunteers reported actual physical abuse. Such statistics may seem dry and all too matter-of-fact, so below is a lengthy letter home from a SCOPE volunteer immediately after her release from jail in Alabama. We quote it virtually in full as a particularly graphic description of a particularly damnable hell, although we have changed the local names to avoid further recriminations against any of the blacks involved.

Wednesday July 27: On Wednesday, we nonviolent demonstrators were given ten minutes to get out of the streets or be tear-gassed and beaten with billy clubs by local and state police. All we wanted to do was to march five miles to the AME Church, one of Rev. Jones' churches that was burned, probably by the KKK's. We also would travel to another Methodist church which has also been burned. The police had just removed the wooden barricade that was placed across the street Monday. Therefore, the police now were charging us with blocking the public street. No one moved, many joined the group in these tense moments including myself.

After fifteen minutes of determined singing of freedom songs, we stopped to hear the police say time was up and we had better move back to the other AME Church. Rev. Jones said that on Monday they had asked us to go to the church and then in addition to being tear-gassed at the barricade they tear-gassed the very church to which we were to return. A tear gas bomb was also thrown right beside Rev. Jones' eighteen-month-old baby. . . . The Rev. Jones said that we were not moving and if we did move due to tear gas we were not to run but to walk orderly back to the church.

At this point the police must have known that we meant business so they changed their tactics and declared we were all under arrest. Many felt that if it had not been for the TV cameras the police would have really violently attacked us. White SCOPE workers were picked out of the crowd to be among the first fifty out of about three hundred people arrested that day. (About five hundred have been arrested in this week.) After loading us onto five public school buses, we were first taken to the jail for an hour and then on to the state prison. . . . The men were frisked—Rev. Jones and another leader were handcuffed. The girls were told to put all belongings—purses, towels, scarves, jewelry—in a box. I quickly stuck my $2 and my Hong Kong hanky under my blouse, having only to give up my wad of Kleenex.

When I walked into the prison compound one policeman said let me have this one. A prison card was filled out on me. I talked about ten minutes with Sheriff Jim Clark. We all were fingerprinted, a copy to be sent to Montgomery and one to Washington, D.C. The white people could not understand why we six girls were here with 152 other women and 154 men.

We 158 women and girls were placed in a cell twenty feet by forty feet. One side of the cell had windows which were boarded up so that we could not see the men. Fresh air and light on this side of the cell was lacking. We had one toilet (usually stuffed up), no sink or washing facilities, one bucket of water with one common drinking ladle, plus cozy cement floors on which to sleep. We had to pound on the door whenever we needed more water or toilet paper. None of us were fed that day.

Thursday July 28: The next morning, after sleeping with feet and arms in our faces, for the floor space was not adequate for all to lie down comfortably, we were beckoned to pray by Mary Lou. We praised God for coming through the night safely with no tear gas in our cells and for a new day.

Because we had a lady who needed a diabetic shot and a woman who was seven months pregnant, we started asking politely if we could have a doctor and one of the mattresses that was stacked in a corner outside our cell. No mattress. The doctor finally did come and the two ladies were taken out of prison.

We tried time and time again to make a telephone call, a legal right every one has who is arrested. No phone calls were permitted. Our lunch, the first food I'd had for over twenty-four hours, was served at 1:00 p.m.—cold beans and dry corn bread. While the girls ate, the guys sang freedom songs which boosted our morale. We sang then as the guys passed by our cell to the "dining room." Earlier that afternoon we had ripped off the wooden boards along the one side of our cell so we could talk and see the guys and our men leaders.

Before settling down on the hard cement floor we had prayers and songs, "Give Me That Old Time Religion," "Come By Here My Lord," "Amazing Grace." About 2:30 a.m. I woke feeling the need of our one luxury, the stuffed toilet. Naturally, the toilet paper was all gone. After pounding on the locked screen door the jailer finally came and I tried politely to ask for toilet paper. He told me in so many words that it was my own fault for being there. Now I know I was to love this poor environmentally deprived man, that the philosophy of SCLC is to convert those that hate you but at that moment I felt the most hate, frustration, and pure violence against him and other white people. I marveled that if I could feel this way, how must Negroes feel who have had to live under the white man all their lives. It is a miracle that not more violence occurs and it is certainly a godsend that Dr. Martin Luther King, Jr., has been able to be an instrument of love and nonviolent philosophy.

Friday July 29: More people became sick. In an early morning count, I estimated about thirty who had stomach troubles, fifteen with piles, ten with female problems and five with diabetes. Several others were pregnant. People began to faint. Those of us who were blessed with relatively good health helped others who were sick. Again we asked for a doctor. Eventually he came. Fifty persons were allowed to leave. We thought they were going home but instead they were taken to another jail.

Strange aspects of personalities came forth when young girls who were not even sick jammed the cell's doorway to get in with the fifty who were leaving. SNCC, SCOPE, and SCLC workers plus a few others had to sort out the sick older ladies and girls so that they could leave rather than the disillusioned freedom fighters.

Lunch was served around noon—cold beans and dry corn bread plus one pitcher of water and that good old common cup per table.

The morale went up and down that afternoon. Some boys and girls were on a hunger strike. I did not eat lunch mainly because my stomach hurt and beans looked hard. The cozy cold cement floor felt good during times that I felt feverish. Dinner was served around 7:30— cold beans and dry corn bread. As I walked by a guard I said to him, "You know it is getting harder and harder to be loving and nonviolent." He mumbled something. I sat at the table staring at these beans and swearing to myself I'd never eat another bean the rest of my life. I returned to the cold cold cement floor. Some medical supplies arrived like aspirin, etc., and the long overdue sanitary napkins.

I fell asleep. When I awoke I realized Vespers was being held. Everyone said a Bible verse. It ended with the triumphant and powerful song, "We Shall Overcome." Then back to bed on the hard cement floor.

Around 9:30 p.m. the jailor called two names as he stood at the cell door: . . . an Atlanta SCOPE worker, and to my surprise, my name. I sleepily picked up my shoes which I used for a pillow and walked barefooted out of the cell. Having been almost asleep it was an unreal situation when someone said to sign a piece of paper so that I could be bonded out of jail. Nine leaders and we two girls were to be the first bonded out of jail on $100 property bonds each. One white nonuniformed man approached Mary and me and said, "I would not treat my dog the way you all have been treated. Why don't you go home where you belong," etc. We . . . tried to explain about God, equality, brotherhood, but it all seemed to fall on deaf ears. As we were assembling to leave, Charlie Smith drank out of the cold water fountain. One huge white man hit his wooden axe handle on the fountain as Mary and I moved forward to take a drink and he said, "You cannot drink from this, it is state property." We left.

One moment we were in jail, the next moment we were riding on soft car cushions. . . . We were free. It all seemed like a bad dream. But we were not free. The discomfort of others still in jail weighed heavily on our hearts.

It was like homecoming as we pulled into Rev. Jones' home around 11:00 p.m. The psychological let down of all the tensions, fears, and strains released itself in tears as Mrs. Jones gave me a big hug. Someone said I looked like I had been dragged through a wringer—no wonder with practically no food, no clean clothes, no bath, no lipstick, and messy hair. My stomach hurt and I felt hot and cold. A friend gave me a glass of milk, which I sipped slowly. After taking some medicine I went to sleep on a soft couch in the parsonage.

Saturday July 30: Most of the day I spent sleeping, drinking liquids, and gaining strength. The other leaders immediately began the task of getting property bonds for each of the four hundred people still in jail. Bonds could not be made until a list of people's names in jail was known. The sheriff and jail warden would not give us a list. Slowly but surely people were bonded out of the three different jails. Mary Lou, when she returned from jail, talked with me about freedom, and about people who thought they were free. She commented that only selfish people were free. How true!! People who are free do not think of those who are not free. The perfect example of unselfish people was the leaders who got out of jail and immediately realized they were not free until the rest of the other inmates were free. Late Friday, Saturday, and Sunday nights, people who had been in jail worked hard obtaining bonds, getting them signed, driving empty cars to pick up the tired, but soon to be free, Freedom Fighters. Some of the drivers had been on a hunger strike.

OTHER PLACES, OTHER EXPERIENCES

Such a letter compels attention. But it does not represent the experience of all of the volunteers, and cannot stand as our last descriptive word. For most, the daily routine included tension, but not violence. While harassment was an affront to the volunteers and their morality, it was the exception rather than the rule in their experience with the white community. The following quotations provide a better measure of those experiences:

A number of people have nodded to us on the streets. A number of people have recognized us and *not* nodded on the street, and a few people have said nasties to us. But the only real contact we've had has been with the police chief, who invited us in for a chat and to have our pictures taken the first day we got here. And what he said essentially was that he wanted to take our pictures just in case. And that he would watch over us. He said he wanted pictures of all the civil rights workers who came here, but he hasn't followed up on that. So I assume he was just trying to scare us. In any event, it was very reassuring. To me, here's this nice fatherly old man who says, "I'm going to watch over you," and did. I mean, they follow us everywhere we go. You saw the car tonight. That's off-duty policemen, they're not as friendly.

I expected a lot more open hostility. When we first came, we were afraid to sit outside here, and now we sit outside all the time, think nothing of it.

I had a feeling that people were at least going to throw rocks at the house. The only thing that's happened here is that Mr. Cheek had the unfortunate bad luck, or whatever it was, to bounce a check. He was $7 short for some check right after we got here. They hauled him into jail for a day and fined him $50. And it never would have happened if we hadn't been here. He's well-off and has good standing in the neighborhood.

There was little, if any, harassment to anyone [in the project]. The state policemen were indifferent and the local sheriff was too busy fishing and running bootleg.

Throughout these quotations, one senses a mixture of relief and disappointment over the failure of harassment to measure up to expectations. But one volunteer, at least, had another reaction to the southern whites, one of fleeting identification:

A summer in the Negro community can induce *some* sympathy for the southerner's irrational stand. You know the old saying, fifty million southerners can't be all wrong all of the time. . . . And we have come across many of the stereotypes. . . . We have run into many disappointing things and personality traits in the Negro community, which of course can be laid to the system, and are probably easily traced to the system, but they exist, still. And we have seen apathy, terrific, tremendous, unbelievable apathy. We have seen people running out of the office as they're being registered—on the threshold. Intelligent high school graduates, boys, running out of the office like twelve-year-old children. People lie to us repeatedly that they're registered when they aren't—we who have tried to register them very hard. . . . We have seen rather odd behavior from the girls that live here—odd, that is, from middle-class Los Angeles standards. We have seen eighteen-year-old boys who work with us who have six children and aren't married, and thirteen-year-old girls who are married. Most of the homes don't have fathers in them; some have two fathers. Many shocking things have come to our attention. Mothers who don't feed their children. . . . We can have some sympathy for the southerner who doesn't want his children to go to school with children who have this disease or that disease or somebody whose morals are like this or like that.

Although this one volunteer's view was hardly typical, it does provide one more illustration of the variety of reactions of white workers adapting to a black community under local white resistance.

SUMMARY

This chapter has sought to portray the community context of the civil rights worker. The volunteers had many characteristics of the seditious stranger; they were greeted with suspicion by some blacks as well as most whites. By and large, the SCOPE student was not given figurative

olive branches for his heroism in behalf of humanity. Although the scene
was less dangerous than many had expected, it was also more difficult to
adjust to than many had anticipated. This finding suggests the gap between a movement's hopes and its realities, between an ideological view
of the world and actual events as they are played out in the local dust.

However, there is one respect in which the chapter may seem to
contrive homogeneity out of variability. In suggesting that the experience
was essentially the same from one type of southern community to another,
we may seem unresponsive to some crucial differences between community
types. We pursued the matter empirically and, without making a display
of the data, they show that by and large the local scenes were not as
systematically different as one might suppose. It is true that projects in
urban areas as opposed to rural areas were likely to experience more involvement with local whites, less involvement with local blacks, and
somewhat more harassment largely because of the more efficient urban
police force. It is also true that volunteers in communities with high proportions of Negro residents tended to show much more involvement with
local blacks and much less with local whites, suggesting the extent to
which places such as Lowndes County, Alabama, are polarized by racism
and the movement. But these are only a few scant significant correlations
out of many that were possible. Moreover, there is one further distinction
that produced even less impact despite its currency in the popular treatments of the South. The gap between the Deep South and the Upper
South produced little difference in the experiences of the volunteers. This
was something of a surprise to us, although it will not surprise many of
the volunteers who were in South Carolina, North Carolina, and Virginia.
Indeed, one of them expressed a good deal of resentment over our use of
the regional distinction in the questionnaire:

You constantly used the term "Deep South" in the questionnaire. This
really bothers me, because I spent my summer in North Carolina,
which is not considered part of the Deep South, but North Carolina,
particularly the eastern counties, [is] buried in segregation. The Klan
there is not brutal like one might find in Alabama or Mississippi, but
it is the best organized one in the country. Also, the governor of the state
is on record publicly as a segregationist and the state and local government is run so the Negroes are systematically excluded from jobs,
voting, education, opportunity and everything else. So as long as you
all exclude North Carolina, and for that matter any of the other
southern states that SCOPE was in, you are allowing yourselves to be
fooled. North Carolina has hidden behind the "North Carolina Image"
for too long, and until the nation as a whole realizes that it is a bad
state and treats it as being no better than Alabama or Mississippi, it
will continue to hide behind the image. I bring this to your attention
because you of all people should be aware of this and view the total

situation accordingly. The time has come when the South must be dealt with as a whole (hole), and certain states must stop being viewed as "progressive," but rather as just part of the whole stinking mess that is considered wrong. In doing this, hopefully, segregation northern-style will come into perspective, and we will be able to deal with that too.

Of course, this suggests not only that the distinction between Deep and Upper South is more myth than reality, but also that the distinction between the North and the South at large has been overdrawn. Surely this is one lesson that the movement has learned since 1965, as it has taken its demands to Chicago, New York, Philadelphia, Detroit, Los Angeles, and other cities. Indeed, if anything the North may hold even less promise of quick success than did the South. This is partly because the demands have changed, and unlike voting rights and public accommodation integration there are no constitutional guarantees against slum housing and grossly inadequate income. It is also because, with some conspicuous exceptions, northern officialdom has been more restrained and hence more politically effective in fending off the tactics of nonviolence. Finally, the ideological climate has shifted from Negro tokenism to black power, from integration to identity, and from political demonstrations to explosive incidents. In any event and for whatever reason, the North is no longer the promised land at the end of an underground railway. The scene we have portrayed for the southern communities may be increasingly apt for northern communities as well.

CHAPTER IV

Routine of Radicalism and Problematics of Success

Ferguson City will be ours!
A SCOPE diary

The gap between the goals and the accomplishments of radical movements is well-known to cynics and scholars alike. Less recognized is the gap between the radical's rhetoric and his daily routine. Having looked at who the volunteers were, why they went, and the community context of their efforts, we now want to focus on what they did and with what results. There are a number of possible criteria for measuring the relative success of SCOPE as a whole, its separate projects, and the volunteers as individuals. While one evaluation may invoke publicly stated goals and accomplishments, another may reach different conclusions by examining other objectives and assessments. We are just as interested in the criteria the volunteers use to define their triumphs and frustrations as in the degree to which these criteria were met. By assessing both, we hope to learn something about the dynamics of this movement in particular and perhaps other movements in general.

This is not to say that formal goals are irrelevant; in fact, in the first section of this chapter we offer the official SCOPE self-assessment in terms of its prior objectives. But such goals often provide more of a backdrop than a scenario; they are frequently lost sight of, frustrated, or displaced in the heat of confrontation and in the tedium of day-to-day life. Accordingly, we next examine the volunteers' own record of what they did and what they might have preferred to do according to personal bent and strategic importance. All of this is, in turn, a prologue to an analysis aimed at uncovering the most meaningful facets of *overall* project success as subjectively estimated by the volunteers. Finally, we treat one of these facets in special detail; namely, the degree of project militancy.

FORMAL OBJECTIVES AND ACCOMPLISHMENTS

The term SCOPE is itself an acronym for two of its three principal objectives: Summer Community Organization and Political Education. However, it was a third goal which was actually first in priority: voter registration. The Southern Christian Leadership Conference wanted to anticipate and then implement the 1965 Civil Rights Act (finally signed into law on August 6, 1965), which provided for a suspension of literacy and other qualification tests, the appointment of federal voting examiners, and federal initiation of court suits to bar continuation of the poll tax in certain southern states. During the June orientation session the SCOPE director remarked,

> Nothing is more important now than implementation of this voting bill! Not only are we going to gain the little fruits that's going to be created by this voting bill, we're going to show the inadequacy of the voting bill. They still don't have integrated schools, because we did not

get them in the Supreme Court decision in 1954, waitin' around for
the white men to do it. There are still many places in the Southland
that you try and walk in as an integrated team or as a Negro they'll
beat your brains out, because we did not . . . implement the 1964
Civil Rights bill. What we want to do when President Johnson puts
his pen on that voting rights bill is to register Negroes from Virginia
to Texas. You have to understand in Alabama where there's some
places now the courthouse door's open and they will not intimidate
you. And they tell the Negro, "Come on in and register, come on in
and register. But you have to be educated." Now this is the same system, the same society that has denied the Negro an education, and
now it tells this Negro, "Come on in and register, but you *have* to be
educated!" . . . It's kind like if I take one of you, and chain your
hands together, and then nail you up against a wall with a large nail
that you *could* not break loose. Then I set the whole building on fire
and make an announcement, "All you who are interested in savin'
yourselves run out the door." Now that poor fella I've nailed up
against the wall, his problem is not to get out the door. Hell, it's to
get loose from the wall. And this is what Wallace has done to the
Negroes in Alabama.

With respect to this relatively clear goal of voter registration,
SCLC provided specific data for evaluation at the end of the summer. In
all, 68,796 attempted to register, with a net increment of 49,302 success-
fully qualified voters on the rolls. Of course, such figures may seem large
or small depending on one's vantage point. It was undoubtedly significant
to register some 49,000 voters in comparison to the past, but how significant was it compared to the job that remained? As the newsletter that
announced the statistics pointed out, even after the efforts during the summer, less than 300,000 of the more than one million eligible black voters
were actually registered. Should SCOPE have been able to do more?

The late passage of the Voting Rights Act had not helped. For
many projects, it was only after the law had been enacted that registration began to move beyond tokenism. But had the law been passed months
or years previously, other obstacles remained. Not only were disappoint-
ingly few federal voting inspectors assigned to the South, but many local
registration centers skirted the law by confining their open hours to the
few and the inconvenient. In a few project areas, there was no open
registration at all during the summer, and others forced the volunteers to
concentrate their efforts on only two or three days out of each month.

But even if voter registration had gone more smoothly and more
rapidly, the SCOPE leadership did not regard it as a panacea to the
political woes of the southern black. This is precisely where the two remaining goals of political education and community organization enter.
Concerning the need for education, the SCOPE director was very clear.

Now, SCOPE has three objectives: mass voter registration, political education, and community organization. These are the three objectives. Mass registration, I can tell you now, . . . there's no science in registerin' people. I say 80 per cent of the successful . . . voter registration drives are con men's games. You con the person down; you tell him you're gonna give him some pie in the sky; you tell 'em they're not as decent as their neighbor; you tell 'em that they're going to get a better job. You *con* 'em down there. They don't really know what it's all about. You persuade 'em to go down there, you tell 'em they're not a first class American citizen. You tell 'em they're not bearing their rightful share in this democracy. But you can be sure as your life that just as much as you con 'em down to register, they're not going to vote on election day. And this is why we have such a low percent[age] of our people voting. Because we have not taught them *why* they're registered. Now the political education we're speaking about is not the type you're taught in college. . . . I'm not interested in this type. You can't tell a Negro in Democritus, Alabama, about no Appalachian bill when his stomach is achin' for the need of food. You can't go to Albany, Georgia and tell a Negro something about the policy in Vietnam when his children down there have no shoes to wear to school. So I'm talking about political education that the grass root people can understand. I'm talkin' about the kind where you teaches every Saturday, the type your wife puts in the skillet and it's a long white slice. And as your wife begin to cook it, it draws up smaller and smaller and smaller. And by the time she turn it over, it draws up so small by the time she get it done you just got a little thin streak of skin that she puts across your plate. This is something he can understand. "You know why you can't buy the same slice of bacon, the kind that your boss buys? The kind that his wife puts in the skillet and it's this wide, this long, and she cooks and she turns it over, and it's still long and wide?" You just can't realize how many mornings he has sat down that table and thought, "Oh, if I could just get another piece of bacon," *This* is the type of political education. "But this situation prevails, mister, because you don't participate in the government! You're not registered and you're not voting! You know if we had you and all your people registered to vote, we could even have the Food and Drug Administration pass laws that meat like this couldn't even be on the market."

Such political education received repeated emphasis during the orientation, with repeated instruction concerning the difference between success and failure. The lecturing was hardly in the pedagogical style of the academy. To some volunteers, it was another aspect of the director's hostility and antiintellectualism, and it contributed to the friction described earlier in the Prologue. However, many of these same volunteers later came to appreciate remarks that had antagonized them earlier. Thus, the following may have seemed gratuitously degrading in June but prophetic by September:

Say you have a group of individuals in Ludowici, Georgia; you can alienate them the first five minutes, no, the first three minutes. And they'll look on you as one that they have not the ability or the right to challenge. Then you've lost your audience; you've driven a wedge; you've built a wall between yourself and the person you're trying to help attain the necessary tools that will cause them to articulate and govern themselves. One thing is going to be very hard for you to do. . . . And you may feel like it's easy—you say you'd have no trouble at all conversing with my fourth-grade daughter—you'd have no trouble at all. But when we start thinking of political education, when we start thinking of educating the people, that we'll be dealing with largely political issues, and you start thinking of their chronological age, and you start thinking of their education, and when you yourself can take the knowledge that you have acquired, and the knowledge that you will acquire here this week, and break it all the way down that a fourth-grade mind can comprehend it, and yet your teaching allow this fourth-grade mind enough freedom to agree or to disagree or to question—this is not going to be easy for you to do. . . . But you're going to have to find out somehow in order to be able to teach the kind of political education we're talking about.

The SCOPE director was equally emphatic about the need for organization: "See, I guess I'm an organizational fanatic. Because I don't believe you can do anything unless you organize. I don't think you can do anything, accomplish anything, haphazardly. Just loping down the lane of despair, looking—I don't think you're going to accomplish anything. So we gonna have to teach people to organize and structure themselves around a power structure."

If one reads uncritically the figures supplied by SCLC concerning education and organization, the summer program seems spectacularly successful. SCOPE reported 1,026,457 citizens involved in their political education classes, and 666,316 Negroes engaged in the community organization effort. And yet the meaning of these figures is ambiguous. "Involvement" in classes may mean nothing in terms of lasting education— or it may mean a profoundly changed outlook. Community organization may mean voters' leagues and mutual aid or it may mean attending one meeting on a Sunday afternoon to decide that it is all someone else's business. All of these meanings were no doubt represented during the summer. Let us turn to the volunteers for more detail.

SITTING IN SELF-JUDGMENT

Because the subjective success of a political movement is often difficult to define, our second questionnaire used several questions in hopes of surrounding if not capturing it. Table 6 presents the results of two of

Table 6. VOLUNTEERS' JUDGMENTS OF SUCCESS

	Project Success	Personal Success
	Per Cent	
Highly Successful	15	10
Reasonably Successful	43	55
Somewhat Successful	28	28
Fairly Unsuccessful	11	6
Very Unsuccessful	3	1
Total	100	100

these, one concerned with the volunteers' estimates of overall *project* success and the other with their *personal* success as individuals.

In one sense the table reverses a pattern seen in Chapter Two concerning the volunteers' expectations for the summer. At that point, the volunteers were if anything more confident in the project than in themselves; at the end of the summer, they claimed slightly more personal success than project success. Thus, only 15 per cent found the project "highly successful," and although a plurality of 43 per cent deemed it "reasonably successful," more than 40 per cent fall into the bottom three categories of the scale, indicating considerable disappointment. On the other hand, 65 per cent thought themselves highly or reasonably successful.

The tendency to evaluate personal contributions higher than collective SCOPE achievements may relate to our earlier conclusion that many of the volunteers went south in search of a personal identity. Even though the project did not always measure up to expectations, the summer could still be meaningful to them as individuals. Even though the project did not revolutionize the South, it did provide progress on a small scale that became more personally gratifying once the volunteers had learned the odds against revolution itself.

But it is important to note that both columns of figures in Table 6 are somewhat ambiguous. For example, considering the project evaluations, what does it mean to say that the modal response was one of "reasonable success"? It could of course imply very great success indeed, short of a revolution. On the other hand, as suggested above, it could represent more of a rueful realization than a political boast. Clearly, we need to know much more about the contingencies and nuances of the volunteers' activities to grasp their evaluations. Let us begin with an examination of the dominant activity of the summer, voter registration.

VOTER REGISTRATION

We have already mentioned that registration was only one of three SCOPE objectives but that it was first in priority. Table 7 confirms the

Table 7. VOLUNTEER TIME EXPENDITURES

	Per Cent Spending "All" or "Most" of Time
Voter registration	79
Community organization	26
Political education	19
Tutoring and remedial education	8
Protest activities	5
Seeking employment and economic benefits for Negroes	4
General medical care	2
Integrating public accommodations	1
Birth control education and assistance	1

point in terms of time expended. In the second questionnaire, we asked the volunteers to estimate how often they had engaged in each of nine activities, with response categories including "all the time," "most of the time," "several times," "rarely," and "never." Seventy-nine per cent of the white SCOPE workers claimed to have spent all or most of their time on voter registration alone. The next most common activities were community organization and political education with 26 per cent and 19 per cent respectively.[1]

The disproportionate registration effort is understandable on several counts. Not only did the much discussed Voting Rights Act provide both challenge and momentum, but voter registration was well-suited to the more latent organizational needs of SCOPE. For a program just getting under way and trying to prove itself, registration offered a crystallized

---

[1] Results like these may shake the faith of the survey researcher in revealing that respondents often answer without reading questions carefully. A literal interpretation of the results suggests an arithmetic impossibility in the high proportions who say that they participated in one activity "all of the time" but another activity "some of the time" or even "most of the time." Clearly many respondents interpreted the response options in relative rather than absolute terms in keeping with the response formats of previous items in the questionnaire.

goal to serve as both a gauge of success and a motivating mechanism. This was not the case with either community organization or political education, both of which are long-range, amorphous, and difficult to program.

But if voter registration commandeered the routine, what was the routine itself? Several volunteers described their typical day on an hour-by-hour basis. Here, for example, is the schedule of a project leader in Georgia:

> I have to get up about half past seven or eight o'clock. Get a group of people down to the courthouse with cards to write down the names, addresses, and phone numbers of all the people we've brought down to register. I send a group out during the day to the courthouse and around the city and downtown to bring the people down to register. Other groups go out to separate communities in Macon and work there on their educational centers and their family planning, whatever they're doing now. Then we schedule a lunch down here in one of the churches, and we usually go eat about three o'clock. From four to eight we canvass neighborhoods; make appointments to pick them up the next day and bring them down to register. Get records of who in the house is registered, how many people in the house, and so on. At night usually there's a meeting of some kind. And then, about twelve, I write stories and send them home before I go to bed, and then get up in the morning and do the same thing.

Like any repeated activity, registration fell into a common pattern for most of the volunteers. Even the actual interpersonal contacts became standardized and began to follow predictable protocols. Here, for example, are several conversations between SCOPE workers and potential registrants concerning a forthcoming mass meeting in the community:

> We wanted to tell you about the mass meeting tonight, at the Little Rock Baptist Church.
> Yes.
> We were hoping you'd be able to attend.
> Mmm-hmm.
> We're going to have movies on the march tonight, and there'll be talking, and there'll be a little freedom, a little Jesus Christ, and a little of all of them.

> How do you do? Can we talk to you a minute? . . . We came over to remind you of the mass meeting tonight, right up here. Planning on coming?
> No, I'm sick. I been down about fourteen months, can't walk.
> Oh. Could you go, do you think? To the mass meeting.
> No, I have to stay here with my wife.
> Oh. Well, do you suppose you could tell anybody about it? It's very important to everybody that they be there.
> I'd like to go, I wish I could. . . .
> I tell you what, why don't you remember us in your prayers tonight, okay?

I guess I could tell you while I'm holding him [a baby] about why I'm here. Right down here at the church tonight there's a mass meeting. We were trying to go out and tell everybody about it who hasn't heard, or remind them if they have, so that everybody'll—

We know about it, we do. . . .

Well, bring your kids, too, 'cause this is something that they've got to learn about it now, in hopes that they can take over this whole movement when the rest of us are getting married and settling down and can't run around.

That's right.

Okay, good-bye.

Do you know about it? It's eight o'clock and we were hoping you planned to attend?

Yes.

Okay, very good, it's all about what's going on right now, and what we're trying to do, and what maybe you can do, and we can all work together to make this a better world. Okay? Bring your kids, too.

These are hardly the sorts of sophisticated and ideologically charged appeals that one might expect of bright college students selling political wares. But then the volunteers had quickly learned that the SCOPE director had been right in inveighing against sophistication. The problem was not what to communicate, but to communicate at all. The smoothest interchange was likely to be more stylized than substantive and more of an exercise in doorstep etiquette than an instance of political instruction. As we saw in the last chapter, the black-white barrier was always salient and compounded by educational and status differences.

Yet the canvassing did produce small personal triumphs that were meaningful even when they did not produce a registered voter. And there were many times when the personal and the political progress coincided, as in this example from Alabama:

If they're not so scared at seeing you—they go "Yes ma'am, no ma'am, anything you say, ma'am," you know—if they're not that terrified, then they're really intrigued by having a white person come to their door. And if you're alone, or with a colored person, instead of being in a large group, you can usually get very good conversations. I met a lot of really fascinating people that way. People like a music teacher who is eighty-nine years old and has had one leg since she was seven years old —because of an accident. She walks with a stick, and we *carried* her in to register. And when Miss Annie Lewis registered, she was so proud of herself! She had to sit there a minute, shaking, because she is so old and kind of palsied, and she finally could calm down to write and fill out the form, I leaned over her shoulder, and she did a great job; I'm sure she passed. The registrars kept giving us dirty looks for bringing this poor old thing in there.

In addition to such vignettes, other volunteers described triumphs on a larger scale. Here, for example, are two reports—the first from South Carolina and the second from Alabama.

Success Story: We registered about 1,200 Negroes during the summer and the people have continued to register during the past several months. On September 15th there was a municipal election and 25 per cent of the eligible whites turned out. As a result they ousted the mayor and three council men. The factory we integrated the day before we left now employs twenty-six Negroes out of a total work force of 136.

Anyway—we registered about 450 people and did the leg work and pleading to transfer two hundred Negro children to the white schools where— our friends write—they still are, with a tutoring program by college students being set up via the Board of Education! There is *no* comparison between the schools. The white high school is quite good—Negro high school is terrible! Unbelievable. Also, our preacher ran for City Council and lost, but got six hundred votes vs. nine hundred votes and got more anyway than the liberal faculty candidate put up last time against the same bastard. Also, people think the Republican candidate will now seek the Negro vote to defeat him. So, at least the recognition of Negro political power and the old game of concession-support hopefully begins.

Such reports are especially remarkable when one considers the vast amount of effort, money, and even love required for each individual registration. But the reports are also sobering when one recalls again that some 700,000 potential registrees remained among the southern blacks. Moreover, there is the ever-looming distinction between a voter registered and a vote cast, particularly in a society where only 60–70 per cent of all eligible voters participate even in presidential elections.

But lest we confuse the roles of author and cynic, let us cite some of the volunteers' own words concerning their problems and doubts. Describing the backstage complications and frustrations that surrounded the canvassing, one volunteer wrote,

On a typical day, Maggie and I get up at seven, and we get picked up at 8:30, which means that the lady who's going to pick us up arrives usually about nine, and picks us up and takes us to the office. We go get our mail, and go back to the office. We spend from nine until approximately 10:30 deciding where we are going to go, what cars we are going to go in, and who is going to go in which cars, with people squabbling back and forth about "I don't want to go to Uniontown!" "Well, you're going to *go* to Uniontown!" you know, and eventually Henry will assert himself or I will assert myself, or somebody will assert himself and say, "Everybody—you! that car; you! that car" and people will go off. Very often, there are many more people than cars, and the leftover people get to sit in the cafe all day. So then we'll leave the office about 10:30 or so . . . for our destination. Which is, on a typical day, out in the county someplace. Or to Uniontown. . . . If you're in the county you'll stay in the car and go from place to place. Now, having had too many people to start with, you'll have six people in this car. You'll need two. So, when you go to a house, and if it's only one house by itself, two people will get out of the car and the other four will sit there while the two go in and talk; because if six people gang up on somebody it scares them. If there's more houses, you all get out of the car and split up. If you're in Uniontown, you get dropped off. That's a town of reasonable size. We split up and canvass for the twenty-eighth time in the same areas with *nothing* new to say. And we've been trying to set up mass meetings, and there's been area disorganization about when mass meetings are going to be and where. It's been driving us crazy trying to set up these things. Then having plans fall through just when you've got it all organized, something major will go wrong, which is frustrating. . . . At about four, if you're in Uniontown, you'll be picked up again; or if you're out in the county, you'll decide to quit. We never eat lunch for some reason; we stop and drink soda pop and eat ice cream but nobody ever seems to eat lunch. Then we come back to the office, dither around the office, read or whatever, and then go home. Between 4:30 and six, sometime. Whenever there's a car around.

Once again, this is a far cry from the total dedication and compelling urgency generally associated with political radicalism. Nor are reports of disorganization, frustration, and tedium uncommon. There is ample testimony that the registration campaign was not as successful as it might have been, as in these observations from projects in South Carolina and Alabama:

Some of our SCOPE people have been disappointed in the routineness of the summer, the limited and technical goals, and the number of people registered. They came down with grandiose ideas and they wanted to do something broader, rather vague but something more beautiful. And talking to drunks on Broadway and dragging in housewives is not that beautiful. They are rather disappointed, and as a result, they haven't functioned as well as they might have. They don't fill up the time with activities that well; they're rather discouraged. Some have withdrawn almost by themselves; they never help us with the voter registration. They're never seen, just report to us once in a while what they're up to.

There has been a lack of initiative with the leaders and the kids. . . . We tell people that we'll be by tomorrow at this time and you be there and we'll take you down [to be registered]. And you go around and about 70 per cent of the people wouldn't be there. So you'd spend that much gas going ten miles out there and ten miles back and get nobody or get two out of ten people. So one day I drove around for three hours and got nobody and finally I got two people in the street as I was going home. And so I said "Well this is just ridiculous." And what we were doing was going to each neighborhood by each neighborhood, so by August 15th we might be at the last Negro neighborhood, but maybe there there's kids who wanted to help us the whole time. Like one day a kid came in and said, "I'm from South Macon and I'd like to help you." And we weren't going to be in South Macon for four more weeks, so what were these people going to do until we got there. . . . Kids are saying that they want to go where the people really need us (not where a group tells them to go). They all had different ideas about what they want to do. So I said, well, fine, let them do what they want to do. Like if the girls want to tutor little kids, they should do that.

There are a number of common themes running through these reflections, but one deserves particular emphasis. At the beginning of the summer, most of the volunteers felt that the most troublesome obstacles to success would come from the white power structure, and then perhaps from the recalcitrance of blacks in responding to white outsiders. The quotations above suggest a third impediment that often proved at least as salient and perhaps more so; namely, difficulties within the project itself and among its personnel.

This should not be surprising. After all, a political movement is hardly on a par with bureaucratic organizations in coping with niggling exigencies, and it is precisely such exigencies that can cause so much confusion. Because the individual projects frequently found themselves inefficient and indecisive, there was a strain on interpersonal relationships and a stain on the self-images of the individual volunteers themselves. The result was sometimes friction, sometimes withdrawal, and sometimes a tendency to look beyond such technical goals to the kind of action that the summer had seemed to promise at its outset. All of this offers a corollary to our earlier suggestion that the specific goal of voter registration could serve to mobilize commitment and to measure the progress of the project. What must now be added is that when such concrete goals are not realized or lose their urgency, the malaise may be especially pronounced.

A good many volunteers seem to have directed their disappointment not merely at their fellow workers and local projects but also at SCOPE as a whole and at SCLC. "A lot of it is SCOPE's fault. We ought to be educating the Negroes as to their needs and the nature of the government they have now. But this isn't SCOPE's purpose. SCOPE's concern is to register one more voter, one more statistic. It just kills me that we're not allowed to organize demonstrations. You need something to shake the town out of its apathy, and you need something to make them think. Things are *not* going smoothly." "Our greatest difficulty was with SCLC rather than with white power structures or Negro apathy. Needless to say, this was somewhat disillusioning. I will never be able to accept such total disorganization in any 'organization.' I cannot see any progress and neither can SCLC (though they will never admit it)." Ironically, we now seem to have come full-circle. At the end of the summer, many of the volunteers seemed to take issue with SCOPE for reasons that are in remarkable agreement with the admonitions of the SCOPE director at the beginning of the summer.

Still, the organization may have been more a victim of the volunteers' aspirations than of its own failure to live up to realistic possibilities. As much as the SCOPE workers articulated disdain for bureaucracies, they wanted promises and appointments to be kept, planning to be incisive and well in advance, money to be available, advanced groundwork laid, and field commanders well-chosen from among the small group working out of Atlanta. When anything went wrong, the organization was a convenient scapegoat. It could be damned for being either too bureaucratic or too inefficient, too concerned with procedure or too willing to break schedules to fit its own needs. And headquarters were far enough away from most local communities that those on the local scene could develop a detached feeling of being jointly wronged and jointly blameless.

RELATIVE SUCCESS OF SCOPE ACTIVITIES

So far we have seen that voter registration was the principal SCOPE activity and that it faced a number of problems, some of which were internal to the SCOPE projects themselves. But to describe the contingencies of success is not to reach an ultimate verdict. Now we want to pursue an answer not in terms of the numerical talleys of SCOPE but rather in the judgment of the volunteers themselves.

A number of items on the second questionnaire are relevant. First, of course, is the direct question. Thirty-nine per cent of the volunteers judged voter registration as "highly successful"; another 51 per cent deemed it either reasonably or somewhat successful; and only a combined 10 per cent felt that the program had been either fairly unsuccessful or very unsuccessful. Thus, nine out of ten were willing to judge the voter registration drive as successful in some sense, but the question remains in what sense?

Several other items help provide an answer. In both the first and second questionnaires we asked the volunteers to express agreement or disagreement with the following statement: "This summer's voter registration campaign will produce (produced) a politically momentous increase in registered voters in the Deep South." At the end of the summer, the volunteers expressed less agreement than at the beginning (a significant shift in mean response from 2.82 to 3.22 on a scale of increasing pessimism from one to six). Or consider another item. We have already mentioned that 79 per cent of the workers spent all or most of their time on registration. Against this backdrop, the respondents were asked after the summer how much time they would have *personally preferred* to spend on registration, and only 61 per cent said all or most of the time. Finally, we also asked the volunteers to judge the strategic value of voter registration to the southern Negro and to the movement, and only 56 per cent opted for the topmost category, "crucial."

Taken as a whole, this evidence suggests a paradox. On the one hand, the volunteers were relatively successful in the sheer number of potential voters registered—that is, in actually persuading people to go to the courthouse and fill out the appropriate forms. On the other hand, some of the volunteers seem to have had second thoughts about the ultimate significance of registration by itself. This is what they were equipped to do, but was it what was needed most? In this discrepancy and its festering doubts part of the disenchantment with the daily routine may have been rooted. Also, in this discrepancy voter registration is distinctive when compared to other tasks.

Table 8 makes the point empirically. The four criteria of success

Table 8. EVALUATION OF SCOPE ACTIVITIES

	Spent "all" or "most of time" in activity	Would have preferred to have spent "all" or "most of time" in activity	Felt activity was "crucial" for civil rights	Felt activity was "highly successful"
	Per Cent			
Voter Registration	79	61	56	39
Political Education	19	43	58	4
Community Organization	26	52	66	18
Tutoring and Remedial Education	8	31	28	8
Seeking Negro Employment and Economic Benefits	4	27	41	2
Integrating Public Accommodations	1	10	9	11
Protest Activities	5	17	6	a
General Medical Care	2	6	7	a
Birth Control Education and Assistance	1	8	11	a

a This question was not asked concerning these activities.

are presented for voter registration and for eight other SCOPE activities, including community organization and political education. Let us focus on these two specifically for their contrast with voter registration.

The far right-hand column reveals that 39 per cent of the volunteers judged the registration effort to be highly successful, but this same judgment is true of only 4 per cent and 18 per cent for political education and community organization respectively. In part, of course, this difference is due to the small amount of time devoted to these latter activities, as revealed in the far left-hand column, although the results on the right are partially controlled for this in restricting the evaluation to those who actually attempted each activity. But consider the two middle columns of the table. We have already commented on the declining percentages who would have preferred to spend time on registration and who regarded it as crucial when compared with the percentages of actual time expended. This pattern is reversed for political education and community organization, and for most of the remaining activities as well. That is, the volunteers spent less time than they would have preferred, and their time allocations seemed to under-represent the extent to which they judged the activities as crucial.

It appears that the earlier paradox has a mirror-image. Registration was something they did well but with reservations about its importance; organization and education were not done well but were ranked slightly higher in strategic value and the volunteers' personal preferences. Once again we are reminded of the SCOPE director's admonitions at the beginning of the summer: registration without organization may lead to a poorly mobilized electorate with low voting turnouts; registration without education may produce political activity that is unresponsive to the issues and vulnerable to prior identifications and manipulated stereotypes. As one volunteer put it, "The most important thing to many of the kids is getting so and so many people registered per day, and this is what their whole lives are dedicated to. Now I see registration as important, but I don't see it as *that* important. I don't see that it does any good unless you educate the people so you can get them out to vote intelligently. Some of these guys get mad at us because we're not out on the streets every minute pushing drunks in to register. To me this is just a futile waste of time."

And yet community organization and political education were every bit as difficult as the director had promised. Lack of success was not simply a function of the relatively small amount of time invested. For many the reasoning could be reversed; that is, they invested relatively little time because the pay-off seemed so elusive and remote despite its importance. Two volunteers express the sentiments of many in the following quotations. Note in particular the theme of black dependency and the consequent difficulty of instilling a sense of critical outspokenness.

Everybody here, wherever we go, they say, "Gosh, I'm glad you're here, glad you're doing something for the colored people here, we're all 100 per cent for you." I'm getting so I don't like to hear that any more. We're not here to do anything *for* them, first of all—we can't, it's impossible. We're here to do something *with* them, and if we can, to get them to do something for themselves. This is something we've finally come around to do. Up until now, people didn't go down to the courthouse themselves, we had to take them; up until now, people didn't volunteer their services for tutoring, we had to go around and find them. But now, things are changing I think. And I think this is the way it is everywhere; you've got to stay around for a while before they realize what's coming off. I think things are changing and by the end of the summer we should have some very active local groups who are glad we were here and glad they finally did something.

One of the most frustrating things for me was knowing, because I got to know some adults and many teenagers well, how much dissent, criticism, questioning, etc. there was that was *never* voiced at a meeting, never voiced in public and since I (and the other volunteers) were all white, we *couldn't* be spokesmen for the dissent. A Negro volunteer, even a northern one, could have, I believe. But not the white man. So even though the kids, for example, trusted me and believed I was really their friend, they still recognized that I couldn't speak for them at a V.L. meeting. And they, along with the adults, were just *too* well trained into keeping quiet to speak out. (Even with my encouragement.) Marching in large groups takes a lot of courage, but it takes a different kind to stand up and debate policy at a large meeting. It's the latter which I feel is tragically missing in SCLC-dominated organizations. I would not work for SCLC again precisely because I do not believe they are interested in developing that kind of courage and therefore are not really bringing self-government to anyone.

Here is the essence of the black power position with its emphasis on participatory democracy at the grass roots. In Chapter Three, we commented on this as a major dilemma for the Civil Rights Movement and perhaps for any political movement that seeks to turn apathy into activism. We noted the tendency to alternate in cyclical fashion between periods of elitism and thorough democracy. There is no formula to provide the optimal combination of autonomy and authority in any educational or maturational process, and one would hardly expect to find it in the context of a stressful social movement. The dilemma was often so salient and so frustrating that it produced considerable despair. One volunteer said, "I worry, as well as others, that they will lose hope before they get anywhere. I just have a tenuous feeling about the movement. Talking to some of the parents, seeing how frightened they are, how timid they are, and seeing how many little things are engrained in them from the time they're born to keep them down, to put them apart. How deep it goes. I never realized what a tremendous thing they are rebelling against. It seems so difficult. I fear for their ability to go on, not because they're faltering, but because there is so much to be done."

Let us now consider several other activities listed in Table 8 in addition to registration, organization, and education. Clearly none of these other activities commanded as much time. However, as with organization and education, many volunteers would have preferred to spend more time on these matters than they actually did, particularly with tutoring and economic issues. Moreover, these two issues seem to be judged strategically most "crucial" in comparison to protest, public accommodations integration, medical care, and birth control.

Turning to estimates of success, we find again the double paradox noted with the major activities above. Even though integrating public places was not judged a crucial activity, it still received high estimates of success; even though the economic and employment cluster ranked fourth of nine in terms of its importance, it ranked sixth in its perceived success. Again there is not only a gap between what the volunteers actually did and what they preferred to do, but there is also a tendency for success to occur in areas judged less rather than more crucial.

None of this is unique to civil rights activities. Social movements often fix a routine quickly without insuring that it will maximize either organizational stability or ultimate objectives.[2] To be sure, we have stressed the problems rather than the triumphs of SCOPE. At the same time, these problems are not artificially contrived for research purposes. They were salient and widely felt. Indeed, the confusion, discrepancies, and frustrations that occurred with respect to the formal objectives of the summer all help to explain why the volunteers' estimates of overall project success depended less on specific accomplishments than on certain informal contingencies not necessarily related to the formal goals of SCOPE, as we will see in the next section.

    [2] See N. J. Smelser's discussion of "norm-oriented movements" in his masterful *Theory of Collective Behavior* (New York: Free Press, 1963), pp. 296–301. See also the distinction between the "organizational" and the "stable" phase in C. W. King, *Social Movements in the United States* (New York: Random House, 1956), pp. 40–49. For a case study that is especially relevant to the civil rights movement, see J. H. Laue, "Direct Action and Desegregation: A Study in Social Spontaneity and Institutionalization," Ph.D. Dissertation, Dept. of Social Relations, Harvard University, 1965, quoted in W. B. Cameron, *Modern Social Movements* (New York: Random House, 1966), pp. 111–120.

CORRELATES AND CONTINGENCIES OF OVERALL PROJECT SUCCESS

This section marks several departures from its predecessors. For one thing, instead of assessing success with reference to specific and stipulated objectives, we now examine success in broader terms so as to note other factors that may be relevant to the volunteers' overall evaluation. A second difference involves the level of analysis. Heretofore we have focused on the responses from individual volunteers; now we consider the local project as the basic unit. After all, we are really more concerned with the success of a movement than with single individuals. The question is what distinguishes between those local movements or projects that are judged successful by their members. The object is to learn not only about the difficulties of achieving social change in a resistant context but also about the dynamics and contingencies of a movement under stress.

Recall that there were forty-nine projects scattered through six states averaging roughly four of our respondents each. Although a sample size of forty-nine is hardly grounds for statistical complacency it is a broader data base than for most studies of social movements, which typically treat only one or two case studies at a time. As for the data themselves, some variables concern characteristics of the groups that are not reducible to individuals, and many others have been transformed from individual responses by taking the mean position of the project members. Despite more differences of opinion among members of the same projects than we would like,[3] the results are surprisingly instructive.

The key question for the present analysis was asked simply enough in the second questionnaire: "How would you rate your local project as a whole?" Response categories followed the same scale of success used previously, ranging from one to five. Although no project had a mean rating of five ("very unsuccessful") no project was unequivocally evaluated as "highly successful" either. The aggregate mean of all forty-nine local projects was 2.39—midway between "reasonably" and "somewhat" successful. And yet there was ample variance around this figure to encourage an examination of its sources.

---

[3] Of course, this is a standard collectivity problem in contextual analysis. Whenever one tries to represent a collectivity by aggregating individual characteristics, there is necessarily a blurring of individual detail and nuance. The problem is pronounced here only in that the sizes of our groups are smaller and hence are vulnerable to many idiosyncrasies. Since the local projects averaged only four members apiece, one or two individuals who had discrepant perceptions would have more impact than the others on the mean. However, if it is true that our groups are smaller than most, we have more groups to deal with than is common in the literature, and errors may cancel out over the forty-nine local projects at issue.

We explored a number of variables as possible correlates of project success. Table 9 shows the results which are significantly different from

Table 9. CLUSTERED CORRELATES OF OVERALL PROJECT SUCCESS

.64	High opinion of own contribution to project
.47	Small discrepancy between preferred and actual activities
.36	Personally benefited from experience
.35	High opinion of importance of voter registration
.31	Prefer to engage in voter registration
.52	No friction over sex
.49	Happy with coworkers of project
.38	High opinion of SCLC
.38	No friction over dishonesty
.36	Project was cohesive
.36	No friction over race
.30	Lack of cynicism about project personnel and organization
.52	Success in community organization
.51	Success in building Negro self-confidence
.40	Success in achieving voter registration
.38	Amount of local Negro support
.30	Success in changing Negro attitudes toward whites
.28	Amount of time spent protesting

zero. The variables are clustered in terms of their substantive import, and the clusters seem to confirm our prior speculation that four key types of variables would be important. Let us consider each in turn.

INDIVIDUAL FULFILLMENT

It took no great foresight or theoretical acumen to prophesy a correlation between individual and project accomplishment. The two should go together, and indeed they do. Thus, the highest single correlate of overall project success is the extent to which the individual members of the project felt they had personally contributed to the goals of the project. Another strong correlate was a low discrepancy between what the individual volunteers actually did and what they preferred to do—an aggregate scale constructed from data summarized in Table 8 (see Appendix). The theme is further substantiated in that the most successful projects were those in which the volunteers actually preferred doing voter registration, the dominant activity in most settings. Finally, it is important to note that project success was related to the extent to which the project members claimed to have derived important personal benefits from the experience.

But if these are the statistical correlates, the question of their causal direction remains unanswered. Unfortunately there are no reliable statistical techniques for deciding between one causal interpretation and another with the available data. Perhaps the most obvious interpretation is that the success of the project often caused the extent of individual self-fulfillment, of the feeling of meaningful contribution or preference for performed activities, and of general personal benefit. We have already cited testimony from volunteers who attributed their lack of individual fulfillment to the lack of project success. Surely it is not farfetched to attribute much of the fulfillment that did occur to participation in projects which actually accomplished a good deal.

Without disparaging this inference, let us suggest another that runs in the opposite direction but is not mutually exclusive. Just as project accomplishments may have influenced self-fulfillments, so may have self-fulfillments been an important cause of both actual project accomplishment and a subjective estimate of overall project success. Without dipping too far into the mysterious mores of management science, it is axiomatic among administrators and organizational theorists that the successful organization is one that both harnesses and maximizes its participants' energies and morale.[4] This means that the participants should have a sense of both contributing and benefiting in their own right; it also requires that participants act out of preference rather than coercion.

There is ample illustration, if not evidence, for this interpretation. Unfortunately the material makes the negative rather than the positive case, since the volunteers rarely reported on smooth organizational process, saving their comments for the disruptive and the dysfunctional. But the following quotation represents the views of others who also reported that when the project members felt personally stifled, the project as a whole floundered:

I hope there will not be general knowledge of the results of this study outside civil rights groups, for although I have much criticism I feel civil rights organizations are necessary. I was frustrated in my work

---

[4] This point has been long-established in a literature recently well-summarized by P. Blumberg, *Industrial Democracy: The Sociology of Participation* (New York: Schocken Books, 1969).

this summer, partly through my own fault. I sincerely wanted to do wonderful things, but by the end of the summer I had almost lapsed into pseudoapathy. I think our project would have been far more successful if we had understood more about what sort of things we should be doing (e.g., our canvassing was once-over-quickly—after that we feared going back for we had nothing concrete to say and couldn't remember whether we had met people before or not). We had virtually no transportation and this was a terrible problem, for most of the country is rural. Much of our time (most of it) was spent in the office waiting for cars or people, or unable to canvass because there were only us two white SCOPE workers, who were forbidden to go canvassing alone (with good reason). Much was our own fault, but we lacked unity and our two staff members had drastic personality problems. The one who led did not like canvassing and many times we ended up talking among ourselves, not canvassing, or talking on and on to one person because he didn't want to move on.

Actually this remark illustrates several problems in relying upon such materials in the first place. Quotations of this sort can be manipulated by a researcher picking and choosing from among the statements available. And this quotation really adds support to *both* of the causal interpretations that are possible for the data. That is, the volunteer is saying not only that the inability of individuals to contribute leads to reduced project success, but also that the lack of project success produced an overall feeling of futile resignation by the end of the summer.

Without denying that both interpretations may apply, there is one bit of empirical support for the view that unfulfilled volunteers sometimes caused low project morale and hence low overall success. To repeat a finding cited earlier, both questionnaires asked the respondents' reaction to the following statement: "Under no circumstances whatsoever should a participant place his judgment above the policy of the project leaders in determining how to act." Prior to the field experience, 56 per cent expressed agreement; afterwards, this figure had dropped substantially to only 22 per cent. It is clear that the volunteers often chafed under project control. Indeed, this leads to the second cluster of correlations in Table 9.

SOLIDARITY

Earlier we suggested that overall success was related less to overt accomplishments than to such covert matters as the mood and tone of a project. One example involves project solidarity, a cluster which claims more significant correlates (7) in Table 9 than any of the other three. The successful project was apparently one which experienced little internal friction over sex, dishonesty, or race; whose members were happy with each other and cohesive; and in which there was a sustaining faith in project personnel and efficiency, accompanied by a high evaluation of SCLC when compared to other civil rights organizations.

Again, however, the causal directions of these relationships may be two-way. One can infer that success made for smoother relationships both in the local project and in its dealings with SCLC-SCOPE headquarters. In this sense, it was undoubtedly true that both success and solidarity were at the mercy of forces beyond the control of the volunteers, forces such as the number of days in which the local courthouse was open for voter registration. It is also plausible to posit that the quality of cohesion was an important precondition to success itself. Lack of cohesion would make it difficult to coordinate diverse personalities toward common goals, and where faith was wanting in the larger SCOPE project and SCLC, there was likely to be considerable tension.

A number of the specific correlates in this category are self-explanatory; for example, happiness with coworkers, project cohesiveness, and faith in project personnel and efficiency. The matter of sex may be more surprising. The correlation intimates that sex may be almost as important to political as to marital success, although cynics may reply that marriages and radical movements both tend to generate more heat than light. In any event, sex *was* a divisive force within many of the projects. As one volunteer put it, "We came down with an expectancy of dynamic action taking place most of the time, and this carried over into our social life." In fact, the social life for most was anything but dynamic. Not only were there early curfews to minimize the possibility of volunteer harassment on dark streets, but there were also very few to socialize with since the projects were typically small. "The fact that we had to be in about five . . . every afternoon became upsetting. As far as the two of us girls living in a house outside town were concerned, there was little threat of 'immorality.' The boredom was very bad—I can see why there are such problems as emotional breakdowns, drinking, and sexual immorality, for there is unrelieved tension for weeks and, as our occasional would-be seducers told us, 'You're just frustrated.' I think if we'd worked from 6 am to midnight on important matters it would have been different. But a four-hour or less work day was common for us." Such situations tend to produce a result that is well-known to students of small social movements; minor interpersonal abrasions are often irritated to the point of becoming major interpersonal wounds.[5]

[5] See M. N. Zald and R. Ash, "Social Movement Organizations: Growth, Decay, and Change," *Social Forces,* 1966, *44,* 327–341; see also H. Toch, *The Social Psychology of Social Movements* (Indianapolis, Bobbs-Merrill, 1965), especially pp. 157–181. For a discussion of the problem from the standpoint of social

But it was not just sexual relations among the volunteers themselves that produced frictions; the tension stemmed more often from
actual or potential sexual relations between the volunteers and the local
blacks. As we saw in Chapter Three some of the workers found poignant
meaning here, while others found the meanings overlaid with problems.

> I don't know how much you've heard about the sex thing, but that is
> a problem. The thing is that maybe the Negro people here haven't ever
> had a white person, you know, on an equal relationship. And just for
> the sake of it being a little different and a new experience, well, they're
> very attracted to civil rights workers. This was a great problem . . .
> and it was also very important because it could cause great difficulties.
> First of all, the White Citizens Council's whole main phobia of race-
> mixing. This can also cause great problems in the Negro community
> because the white man has always exploited the Negro woman and if
> they now see the civil rights workers doing the same thing, as far as
> they are concerned, that can start a lot of problems and people will be
> trying to discredit us whenever they can. If we give them an inch
> they'll try to go a mile anyway.

Sexual relations then were both an ultimate expression of togetherness
and a threat to the system of separatism. Alas, it may be characteristic of
sex that it should elicit opposite reactions for expressing both the loftiest
and lustiest emotions. The point is that it elicited these reactions from the
volunteers themselves, many of whom differed sharply and openly on the
propriety and danger of sexual intimacy with local Negroes.

In any case, the high correlation between the lack of sexual friction
and project success is probably related to the correlation between the lack
of *racial friction* and project success. We have already explored the volunteers' difficulties in communicating with the blacks in the community at
large; the finding here indicates that there were also difficulties with other
black volunteers and with local Negroes working within the projects. Of
course, such interpersonal problems were not only a function of cultural
differences and covert prejudices; they were also political and ideological
as the abstract issues of participatory democracy and black power became
increasingly relevant and acute. Once again the dilemma of elite versus
grassroots control is at issue. One volunteer expressed his own ambivalence
by saying that, "One thing I learned from the summer experience was that
I became more of an elitist when it comes to social action. There is a very
strong need for a leader; the eighteen of us suffered from internal bicker-
ing which led to increasing conflict; there was a need for one or two

---

movement itself, see the analysis of Bolshevism by P. Selznick, *The Organizational
Weapon* (New York: The Free Press, 1960), especially pp. 17–74.

persons to emerge as strong leaders. It's not that I don't believe in participatory democracy; it's just that I don't think that it's feasible right now in America." It is true that this smacks of the segregationists' ploy that the "nigras just aren't ready for integration." But the substance is different, despite the similarity in form, and the dilemma is not easily dismissed by the activist or by his sideline observers.

One of the surprises among these correlates of overall success is *dishonesty* as a source of friction. Throughout we have used qualitative quotes to interpret empirical results, but here the quotes fail to provide much light. There is nothing in the material we have combed or in our personal experiences to indicate that dishonesty with regard to money was significant. What is probably alluded to in the correlation has more to do with violations of confidence and the failure to fulfill commitments and to discharge responsibilities. The last chapter mentioned several volunteers' suspicions that their local project leaders were in fact in clandestine league with local white authorities. Although such clear subversion was no doubt very much the exception rather than the rule, suspicions of it were more common as were the underlying strains which produced it in the first place.

There is, however, another level at which dishonesty was an issue on occasion. This level involves the relationships between the local projects and SCOPE headquarters. A number of volunteers noted instances in which they had been promised manpower or support which never materialized. Others also commented somewhat bitterly on the actions of SCOPE field supervisors, some of whom seemed hypocritical to the volunteers. Consider, for example one volunteer's summary judgment of the SCOPE leadership. "I think the SCOPE director is excellent, just excellent. . . . Most of the rest of the leadership from Atlanta touring around are pretty much incapable. They work for nothing, and that's about what they're worth. One of them came down and gave us a lecture on the women, and then propositioned one of our girls. So they're not too honest." It has never been claimed, least of all by SCLC itself, that social movements are manned by anything but mortals. Granted this much, such stories were inevitable.

Finally, if dishonesty was surprising as a negative correlate of success, this is hardly true of the importance of holding a high opinion of SCLC relative to other civil rights organizations. Not only is it likely that success sustained such a high evaluation, but it is also reasonable that continued high evaluations were important to success in that they supported commitments to specific goals and coordination between local projects and headquarters.

Earlier in this chapter we presented data and interpretation concerning several specific objectives of the SCOPE project, including the three principal goals of voter registration, community organization, and political education. Table 9 offered evidence on the extent to which the volunteers had been successful with regard to these and several other objectives. Here the question is the extent to which such specific success is related to the volunteers' sense of overall success at the end of the summer. For purposes of this analysis, we included not only success with respect to those variables mentioned in Table 9 but also several others on which information was available from the second questionnaire.

Actually only five such items yield significant correlations with the global success measure. One of these is voter registration, and yet registration has a lower correlation than two others. Success in community organization and increasing Negro self-confidence both outrank registration as a correlate. Further down the list we note two other variables that embellish the same theme: the extent of local Negro support and success in changing Negro attitudes toward whites. These results are consistent with our earlier analysis of volunteer reactions to the specific programs. As central as voter registration was to the formally stated program, the volunteers felt that registration was insufficient without the ultimately more important step of developing black community pride and organization. Certainly this message is communicated here as well. Once again we get a glimpse of what was later to become the black power shibboleth.

But there is perhaps another less obvious reason for the strong correlation between success in community organization and overall success. One of the criteria of personal success for many of the volunteers was their ability to relate effectively and meaningfully to local blacks on an individual basis. This ability is almost necessarily entailed in community organizing, but not necessarily in public accommodations integration, employment, or even classes in political education. For this reason, community organization may represent more than a mere tactical achievement. It may also represent the very intimate personal triumphs that meant so much to so many volunteers who had discovered that the objective gains of the summer were not as radical or as overwhelming as they had hoped. In this regard, it is particularly instructive to note one of the correlates in this cluster—success in changing Negro attitudes toward whites. As we remarked in Chapter Three, a good many of the volunteers commented on both the difficulties and the triumphs of establishing relationships with Negroes. It was frequently a pivotal experience because of the change it required in black and white alike. Here there is an abundance of testi-

mony, of which the following are representative. The first puts the sentiment most succinctly, and the second indicates the kind of seemingly trivial
incident that often came to mean so much: "I think the biggest success
was being able to relate to people there as a fellow human being." "We
were relatively ineffective, being able to register only one hundred Negroes
since the literacy test obstructed our efforts. On the other hand there were
a lot of intangible rewards. By the last few days of the project, the Negro
kids began to trust us. It used to be that when we'd buy a Coke from the
machine in the church where our office was and we'd offer to let them
drink from our Coke bottle, they would refuse; that was probably a carry
over from the separate drinking facilities. Near the end, however, we were
able to break that barrier, and we felt that we had accomplished something with these thirty or forty high school volunteers."

By now we have commented on very nearly all of the significant
correlates of overall project success; in fact, all but one, and the weakest
at that. We were able to describe each project according to the amount
of time spent on a variety of activities ranging from voter registration to
tutoring and medical care. But only one of these seems related to the sense
of project success at the end of the summer: the amount of time spent
on protest activity and demonstrations. It is true that the correlation is
hardly overwhelming. At the same time, it would be foolish to dismiss it
on statistical grounds alone, partly because the correlation is artificially
attenuated in that so few of the volunteers spent any time at all in the
activity. Indeed, because of its particular theoretical and substantive importance, we shall consider the item in some depth.

FUNCTIONS AND VULNERABILITIES OF MILITANCY

It is incongruent that of all activities in Table 8 protesting should
be the most highly related to success. Registration, community organization, and political education were supposed to be the central tasks. Tutoring and increasing employment opportunities attracted many who were
oriented toward long-range effectiveness. In fact, of the nine activities in
Table 8, protesting was the *least* likely to be judged "crucial" to the civil
rights movement. Why then its relation to success?

One possibility is that time spent protesting reflected better than
any other variable the difference between militant and nonmilitant, dynamic and cautious, projects. Militance, dynamism, and protest all had
symbolic as well as real consequences. These consequences were related
less to the actual accomplishments of a project than to the feelings about
the projects held by the individual volunteers, feelings which would make
the projects seem more highly valued.

To probe further into the matter, let us consider the significant correlates of protest itself in Table 10. Some of the correlates are highly predictable. It would be odd if protesting was not related to both a preference for protest and a high evaluation of its importance. It is not surprising that protest activity is related to a preference for and high

Table 10. CORRELATES OF AMOUNT OF TIME SPENT PROTESTING

Pearsonian Correlation Coefficient	Item
.53	Preference for protest
.46	Success in community organization
.45	Expected success (before summer)
.43	Amount of time spent on economic issues
.43	Amount of harassment
.41	Lack of time spent on voter registration
.38	Number of local Negroes involved in project
.37	Preference for integrating public accommodations
.36	Amount of local Negro support
.35	Lack of cynicism about project personnel and organization
.35	Success in building Negro self-confidence
.33	Lack of concern with public image of volunteers
.32	Success in changing Negro attitudes toward whites
.31	Project was cohesive
.31	Importance of protest
.31	Amount of time spent in community organization
.31	Importance of integration
.28	High opinion of SNCC

evaluation of integrating public accommodations, and the amount of time spent on economic issues. These are after all the goals which most protest was calculated to achieve. In turn, these goals often ran counter to the routine of voter registration, which suggests why protesting was related to a *lack* of time in registration activities.

The remainder of the correlates are more illuminating. Indeed, if one were to summarize their collective message it might be that protest activity seems a part of the very model of a proper project, according to the volunteers' own specifications. We have already noted that developing local black power took on increasing importance during the summer, and this finding is positively related to protest activity along with such specific related items as the degree of success and the amount of time spent on community organization, the number of local Negroes involved in the project, the amount of local Negro support, success in building Negro self-confidence, and success in changing Negro attitudes toward whites—presumably including white activists.

Just as interesting is the correlation between protest and harassment. The relationship is predictable, but its existence alongside the correlates concerning community organization recalls a consistent theme in the sociology of conflict running from Karl Marx through Georg Simmel to the work of Lewis Coser in our day.[6] Overt conflict often serves to galvanize conflicting parties. It converts loose and even fractionated alliances of formality and convenience into tightly-knit solidarities. Put less abstractly, those projects which engaged in militant protest to the point of provoking reactions from the local white community may have been especially successful in using the polarization to cement their relations with the local blacks.

At the same time, militancy had apparently similar consequences among the volunteers themselves. Not only was protest activity related to cohesion among the volunteer personnel, it was also related to a faith in the efficacy of the volunteers and of the SCOPE project as a whole. This is true despite the added correlation between protest and a high evaluation of SNCC. As the latter intimates, there was a substantial contingent of SCOPE workers who viewed SCLC as a second-best affiliation. To these people, SNCC represented both the soul and the muscle of the movement by virtue of its more militant grassroots credentials when compared to SCLC. Not only did these volunteers constantly assess SCLC and SCOPE in the light of SNCC criteria, but some of them even jumped affiliations during the summer. Occasionally this involved a formal shift in loyalty. More often, it involved simply spending more time with SNCC workers who were frequently close by and sometimes in the same community, although even these informal shifts of allegiance were the exception rather than the rule. It was common for the volunteers to regard the SCOPE experience as more successful the closer it cleaved to the SNCC image.

[6] See L. Coser, *The Functions of Social Conflict* (New York: The Free Press, 1956), which leans heavily on Georg Simmel's classic insights.

This, of course, returns us to the importance of militant confrontation as an expectation held by the volunteers at the beginning of the summer. If it is true that reality is frequently a chameleon in the eyes of the beholder, it follows that assessments of reality are vulnerable to prior expectations of it.

THE ORGANIZATIONAL UNDERBELLY OF THE MILITANT MOVEMENT

Clearly militancy has positive consequences as indicated among the correlates in Table 10. But it is important not to neglect some of its possible negative consequences as well. The point is not to offer an ultimate judgment of militancy in general, but rather to point out that it has costs as well as benefits. Because many of these costs pertain to the group rather than to the individual and to the long-haul rather than to a summer, they are not clearly reflected in the individual questionnaire responses. Instead, most of what follows will draw upon our own experiences and conversations with the volunteers, as well as on our understanding of social movements at large.

Once again the distinction between SNCC and SCLC offers a convenient focus. At one point during the June orientation session, one of us asked a prominent young member of the SCLC staff why he had opted for SCLC rather than SNCC as an organizational base. His response was instructive on several counts. "Basically I like to be in a position where I can be creative in developing new ideas and new programs. The problem with SNCC is that they put so much importance on consensus with whatever their crash program happens to be at the moment that they get uneasy if someone starts to challenge that program or comes up with something new. In SCLC, on the other hand, you have a real organization that doesn't depend so much on consensus because it has a kind of stability that it gets from Dr. King's leadership and the various other officers and administrative posts in the chain of command. Therefore SCLC can afford someone like me to swing out and say what's on my mind because the organization is going to continue no matter what I say and because it just doesn't have to rely on a full consensus." This remark contains a good deal of sociological insight and in fact offers one perspective for a comparative analysis of organizations generally. In suggesting a distinction between those organizations which provide for their stability, cohesion, and coordination through *ideological consensus* rather than *administrative structure*, the insight applies not only to SNCC as opposed to SCLC, but also to sects as opposed to churches, political cells as opposed to political parties, traditional firms as opposed to large-scale economic corporations, and indeed to premodern societies as opposed to complex societies as a whole. For our limited purposes here, the distinction leads to some further remarks on the vulnerabilities of the more militant and ideologically focused projects within SCLC-SCOPE itself.

As a beginning, one volunteer, a rare southerner, commented explicitly on the extent to which he chafed under the ideological demands placed on him.

> One thing which bothered me greatly this summer was the tendency within our group to pigeon-hole and categorize other workers into convenient niches if their opinions differed from the "liberal norms." This caused some hostility, and led me to question much that professes to be "liberal" and to understand for the first time how my fellow southerners react (as does anyone) to being stereotyped before being met by those vocal few who have little acquaintance with the South and who seem to be there only partially out of a deep and pervasive LIBERAL LOVE. In this same connection, I think the summer made me realize just how important it is to ask the *right* questions when trying to explain the environment in which one lives—not, "How COULD they . . ." (full of indignation), but rather, "What complex factors contributed to this situation?"

Of course, one important characteristic of the militant pursuit of ideologically determined goals is that these goals are frequently more idealistic than realistic since they derive from considerations of ultimate value rather than penultimate strategy. This is no intrinsic defect. Societies depend upon such groups to serve as moral entrepreneurs, focusing attention on what is best in the long-run rather than practical in the short-run, and reminding us all of the gap between our ideals and our accomplishments. And yet such groups are vulnerable to several internal problems that make their own organizational lives more difficult.

It is true virtually by definition that ideological as opposed to structural groups will experience problems with leadership and coordination. Although leadership difficulties did not emerge as a significant correlate of the success of these summer projects (perhaps because leadership rarely crystallized in any of these small and short-lived groups), the leadership dilemma has been especially acute in some of the enduring militant parties under the civil rights umbrella. SNCC is a case in point. Changes in leadership tended to coincide with changes in ideology—although there was more continuity than was seen by the public press. And the COFO organization of 1964 witnessed one of the most bizarre symptoms of leadership strain when its very charismatic prophet suddenly left the scene and even changed his name in his search for a less conspicuous niche elsewhere in the movement.[7] As this instance indicates, such leaders are not

---

[7] This was Robert Moses, a man whose stature is recognized in every ac-

only subject to strain in having to embody an ideology which is by definition unrealistic, but the strain is compounded since in the absence of more
developed organizational structure the leader must assume responsibility
as an individual rather than as a mere role-occupant—hence the importance of charisma.[8]

Another vulnerability of militancy, however, stems from the ideo-
logically-rooted goals themselves. Precisely because such goals tend to be
exceedingly ambitious and difficult to approach, let alone fulfill, groups
often fall prey to the process of *goal displacement,* or the tendency for
means to become ends in their own right.[9] Some would argue that protest
itself sometimes fits under this rubric. Thus, project members begin to
regard protest as good regardless of what it might do to jeopardize some
goals without achieving others. It is clear that some of the SCOPE volunteers regarded protest as an end in itself, partly because it served to
publicize the local problems if not solve them. On the other hand, there
were other volunteers who felt that protest was too often called for where
inappropriate. This feeling is the implicit debate between the two quotations which follow. "One of the things the summer did for me was to
give me some adventures to talk about. Being gassed was great." "Demonstrations here are pretty silly. We did one at Warner-Robbins. I was there,

---

count of the formation of SNCC and the events of the COFO Mississippi Summer
Project in 1965. See H. Zinn, *SNCC: The New Abolitionists* (Boston: Beacon
Press, 1965), and W. McCord, *Mississippi: The Long, Hot Summer* (New York:
Norton, 1965). For a fascinating interview with Moses, in addition to many others
involved in the movement, see R. P. Warren, *Who Speaks for the Negro?* (New
York: Random House, 1965), especially pp. 87–100.

[8] In light of these strains, it is no wonder that charisma is an important
aspect of leadership in any social movement under stress. While Max Weber's
classic analysis of charisma emphasizes its importance in the minds of the followers,
it is well not to underestimate the feedback to the leader himself, who needs to
believe in his own gifts sufficiently to withstand the difficulties inherent in his
position.

[9] The phenomenon of goal-displacement is well known and often described
in the context of formal organizations and bureaucracies, but there is also a relevant
literature with respect to social movements. See, for example, S. Messinger, "Organizational Transformation: A Case Study of a Declining Social Movement,"
American Sociological Review, 1955, *20,* 3–10; N. J. Demerath III and V. Thies-
sen, "On Spitting Against the Wind: Organizational Precariousness and American
Irreligion," *American Journal of Sociology,* 1966, *71,* 674–687; and Zald and Ash,
op. cit. The latter article is especially pertinent in two senses. First, it argues that
neither goal displacement specifically nor increasing conservatism in general is inevitable for social movements. Second, it points out that some civil rights organizations, such as CORE and SNCC, were structured in ways which minimize these
tendencies. Thus, they generally recruited members who were somewhat marginal
to the existing kin and occupational structures of society; they rewarded them in
nonmonetary terms; and they were involved in a competition for members which
forced them to maintain some of their radical objectives as a measure of their
distinctive appeal. Some of these points are applicable to SCOPE as well and help
to explain not why no goal displacement occurred, but rather why the displacement
went no further than it did.

only to protect the lives of the innocent. But it was ridiculous. Totally ridiculous. We went to a place that had nearly all-white patronage; business got better and better as we picketed. One man asked the cop, 'Why you lettin' those kids do that?' and he said, 'Good advertisement.' This is really silly." Actually this same debate was often waged between the volunteers in the field and SCOPE headquarters. The headquarters staff often urged the local projects to stick to voter registration and more routine activities, but local projects sometimes went ahead to launch protest and confrontations over the specific objections of the Atlanta leaders. The point is not that SCLC was categorically opposed to protest and demonstrations. Ironically, SCLC was often criticized for being too anxious to demonstrate in order to capture national attention without doing the tedious but crucial work at the local level. And yet it is one thing to engage in protest activities in a calculated effort to attract national attention and promote national legislation; it is quite another to engage in protest with no articulated end in view. The latter is goal displacement in the sociological sense. And if such displacement is common to militant movements generally, it may be especially common when a movement is depending on outside volunteers who are strangers to the scene and have only a summer to manifest their worth and allegiance.

In such circumstances, it may also be appropriate to refer to the pathology of *over-commitment,* as opposed to the more common problem of under-commitment that afflicts most conventional organizations and voluntary associations. Over-commitment is more likely when a project coheres around an ideology rather than a structure. It is especially likely when that ideology seems to demand not only lip-service but also actual deeds as a sign of adherence. The fact is that many volunteers felt compelled to do the spectacular rather than the strategic. Here protest was particularly important. And beyond the staging of demonstrations and confrontations, violence itself was sometimes regarded as a test of loyalty and a badge of identity. Not only did some look forward to violence, but others actually seem to have courted it to earn the sorts of battle-ribbons that had distinguished their predecessors during the celebrated summer of 1964.

Here again the volunteers' personal recollections are germane. For example, one recalled a day when his registration team had been taunted by whites in a given neighborhood; later that evening the volunteer went out of his way to return home through the same neighborhood alone. "Nothing at all happened but the important thing here is that I had a sort of 'secret desire' to be in a dangerous situation, or maybe a desire to be a real 'freedom fighter,' i.e., to have experienced violent physical action or maybe to be the first in our chapter to undergo an 'attack' by segregationists." In the same vein, consider the following remarks:

> Last night was a big night for John. He was arrested for driving with-
> out a license (actually he was stopped because we have a loudspeaker
> on top of the car). . . . The arrest affected us favorably: there was
> more spirit and determination than usual, as expressed in our singing
> at the mass meeting. But a problem also arose: several SCOPE mem-
> bers began to express desires to be arrested also (the "spirit of the
> movement"). This is a case in point of the excitement, adventure idea.
> . . . It seems to me that some (or too many) students have too much
> of an expectation of violence. I think one of the reasons that students
> come south is because of the excitement and the status gained when
> we go back to our friends at home. For example, I become a "man"
> when I go to jail or march to Montgomery. I probably realize this
> motivation in myself and am ashamed of it. . . . However, I too favor
> the idea of my being arrested some time this summer because I would
> have more status back at school.

The theme of violent adventure was a leitmotif that ran through the entire
experience for many of the volunteers. And sometimes it was more than
a subtle undertone. For example, one volunteer articulated a rumor that
she had heard during the early part of the summer: "The main theory
going around is that SCOPE would like to have another white martyr,
preferably a white girl, so that the Voting Rights Bill will get passed
earlier. You see before you a prospective martyr. It's so easy to be objective about it when it's not you they're thinking of assassinating." It is important to emphasize that this was only a rumor born of the sort of
hysteria that social movements often foster in their early disarray. There
was no truth to it whatsoever to our knowledge, but it does indicate again
the importance of violence as a focal theme. A more typical sentiment,
however, concerns violence as a criterion of success. Many of the volunteers felt that they could gauge their own success as individuals, and their
project success as a team, according to the amount of reaction it elicited.
One commented after the summer was over, "I would term our efforts
unsuccessful in terms of there being any local movement or the local
blacks being able to have voter registration by themselves. *In fact, we
weren't even successful enough to be harassed,* although we were followed
a couple of times and people took down our license number." [Italics
added.] This is understandable in the context of a movement seeking
radical change with militant tactics. After all, one of the characteristics
of radical change is precisely that first-steps for little feet are spurned as
measures of achievement; the real test is the cry of pain as the feet of the
status quo are stepped upon.

    This characteristic in turn suggests one more possible dysfunction
of ideologically sustained militancy. Because ideologies are purposeful distortions of reality, it is almost inevitable that they should produce some
tactical misperceptions in pursuit of their own goals. We have already seen

that stereotyping was a two-way street: not only did the southerners have erroneous expectations of the volunteers, but the volunteers had erroneous expectations of the local scene. One of these expectations involved the perception of local southern officialdom in terms of an unbridgeable polarization between the movement on the one hand and the monolithic local power structure on the other. There were few phrases that enjoyed more colloquial currency among the volunteers than "the white power structure." But in many communities such a structure was more the consequence than the cause of its ideological reference. That is, prior to the arrival of the volunteers many of these communities were fractionated in their leadership with major divisions between business and political interests, between the moderates who favor change in the interest of stability and the archsegregationists who are willing to go down with a sinking ship so long as the Confederate colors are the last to get wet. Such communities were vulnerable to a movement willing to play one faction against another, but this seldom occurred. Instead, because the movement was generally disposed to treating the situation as monolithic, it became so in response. Thus, natural sore spots among the leaders were temporarily healed in order to produce a common defense against the radical intruders. Although some of the business interests could have been forced to make economic and employment changes by the injunction of federal law, this course was often spurned as a token maneuver that would leave the fictional power structure intact. Although some of the political interests might have been willing to make substantial concessions in voter registration, this course was ruled out by the escalation of polarized conflict. Ironically then, as Norton Long has pointed out, some of the effort to do ultimate battle with that structure may have helped to give it reality.[10]

Finally, the emphasis on ideological commitment to militant objectives raises one more dilemma that is common to social movements outside of the mainstream of society and continues to be conspicuous within the Civil Rights Movement itself. This concerns the relation between the *commitment* of existing members of the movement and the *recruitment* of new members to the movement.[11] In one sense, the two are mutually exclusive priorities for any movement under duress. That is, once a movement is launched it may be necessary to smooth some of its rougher edges if it is to appeal to outsiders, but this may betray the insiders and

---

[10] For a discussion of this point under the subheading "The Misfortune of Marx," see N. E. Long, "Political Science and the City," in L. F. Schnore and H. Fagin, *Urban Research and Policy Planning*, Vol. 1 (Beverly Hills, Calif.: Sage Publications, 1967), pp. 252–254.

[11] This dilemma is especially apparent in the religious context, particularly as sects evolve into churches. See N. J. Demerath III and P. E. Hammond, *Religion in Social Context* (New York: Random House, 1969), especially pp. 180–185.

lead to a decline in commitment as a consequence. The reverse is also possible, of course. In order to maintain the commitment of the original members, it may be necessary to steadily increase militancy and thereby forego opportunities to broaden the base of the movement through recruitment.

Actually the whole history of the American civil rights struggle can be read from this perspective. There have been times when its leaders sought sweet reasonableness to recruit the sympathies of the majority of American whites only to discover that many Negroes lost interest or felt conspired-against in the process. There have certainly been phases, such as the summer of 1965, when the movement sought to recruit a minority of strategic whites to a somewhat more radical perspective, thus hoping to galvanize white and black together. And with the current emphasis on black power, the recruitment of whites has lost favor altogether in order to cement the commitment of blacks. As William Gamson has suggested, black power may be more important for consolidating the inner ranks than as a strategy of confrontation.[12] Of course, the question remains whether consolidation is likely to occur on these terms or whether the ultimate success of the movement may not still depend on a mass coalition of blacks and whites. However, our objective is not to choose a direction but to indicate some of the problematics in the choice itself.

Certainly this tension was manifest among the SCOPE volunteers at a time when the strains of black power were becoming audible and tension-provoking. The volunteers were frequently caught in the middle of a dilemma with both personal and organizational consequences. Such dilemmas are apt to be especially acute in the midst of militancy. But, of course, militancy must often be pursued in spite of its agonies. And, in this respect, we have more sympathy than agreement with the following sigh from one of the volunteers: "I now think that there should be no movements. Things should be on a more personal level. With love we will help without causes. The trouble with causes is that the people involved forget about love." This may say too little for expressing so much. Still, in discussing such matters as ideology as opposed to structure, goal displacement, the problems of over-commitment, the distortions of tactical stereotyping, and the dilemma of recruitment as opposed to commitment, our object is to clarify rather than to pass judgment.

SUMMARY

This chapter has been as much a chronicle of frustration as a saga of achievement. In part, this is because we have sought to burrow beneath the layer of accomplishments so as to grasp obstacles and contingencies

[12] W. A. Gamson, *Power and Discontent* (Homewood, Ill.: Dorsey, 1968), pp. 98–99.

that are less apparent. But more important, we feel that frustration was a key to the volunteers' mood at the end of the summer. Certainly that mood was not triumphant, even though victories had been won. Rather it was a deepened realization of the immense job that remained and of the volunteers' own inadequacies for accomplishing it. What had begun as an intoxicating adventure grew sobering to most and left others with an acute hangover.

If this is the general theme, it has its specific counterparts. During the course of the summer, the primary objective of voter registration was eclipsed and upstaged in the minds of many of the volunteers. As they grew intimately acquainted with the local scene, many began to realize that registration was no panacea for the racial agonies so grotesquely conspicuous. Many began to appreciate the greater importance of community organization and the efforts of local blacks to mount a sustained effort in their own behalf. Ironically, this involved a shift away from a more achievable goal. It meant shifting priorities from the routine of registration to the vagaries and ambivalencies of organization. It involved putting oneself in a position where symbolic advances were the primary evidences of accomplishment. Thus, many of the volunteers who went south with the objective of producing a political revolution at the polls soon began to clutch at fulfillments arising from the heady excitement of a protest demonstration or the more subtle rewards of developing relationships of trust and confidence with local Negroes. However, the most fitting conclusion may lie in the remark of a volunteer who was able to see the optimistic potential in frustration itself. "One of the SCLC leaders said that frustration is good for you. And I suppose maybe he's got a point. In fact, he said that the whole SCOPE summer was going to be frustrating and that was its most useful thing, since it would send all those SCOPE workers home so frustrated at not having been able to do anything that they'd all go home and do something in a context where they could really be effective."

CHAPTER V

The Changers Changed

> We were so idealistic. We really thought we were going to change the world. We would sing, "We Shall Overcome," and we really thought we would. But in retrospect, we thought we would do more than we could.
>
> A SCOPE volunteer

One of the traditional conceits of higher education is that it exerts a strong and lasting liberalizing influence on its students. Recently, however, evidence has begun to mount that like many conceits this one has endured only for lack of evidence.[1] Most students are well-molded before they arrive on the college scene. Perhaps only an extraordinary experience can affect values and behavior patterns established during a youth's crucial first twenty years. If so, work in the civil rights movement might qualify. In this chapter we look not at the volunteers' effects upon the South but rather at the South's effects upon the volunteers.

At the end of Chapter Two we offered an over-all portrait of the typical SCOPE volunteer on the eve of his summer experience. Based on that description, we might expect considerable change as a result of the summer. Strangers to both the South and the movement, they arrived with predictable stereotypes and naïveté. Because they were at the vanguard of an era that seemed to promise sweeping reform, they were optimistic concerning their own contributions and the success of the project. Of course, stereotypes, naïveté, and optimism do not inevitably portend change. In this instance, however, the likelihood must be weighed on the balance of the volunteers' actual experiences. Frustration was a common theme of the summer as the experience did not live up to all expectations. It is precisely because of this gap between the anticipated and the actual that one might expect the summer to exert a major impact.

We examine the impact in three major areas. First, to what extent did the summer disabuse the volunteers of preconceived views of the South and the movement? Second, what were the effects on the volunteers' wider ideological and particularly their political predilections? Finally, what about the volunteers' views of their lives at home, their education, and their career aspirations?

Before turning to the results two brief methodological notes are in order.[2] The first concerns the sample. Since we compare answers before

---

[1] See P. Jacob, *Changing Values in College* (New York: Harper and Row, 1957). See also K. A. Feldman and T. M. Newcomb, *The Impact of College on Students* (San Francisco: Jossey-Bass, 1969).

[2] Panel analysis has never become the panacea for our analytic woes that it once promised to be. While researchers customarily defer to a "needed" panel analysis to be certain of their conclusions, such analyses are scarce indeed. Political sociologists are among the few who have used them to any great extent, along with several interested in evaluating the impact of specific programs. See, for example, H. H. Hyman, C. R. Wright, and T. K. Hopkins, *Applications of Methods of Evaluation: Four Studies of the Encampment for Citizenship* (Berkeley: University of California Press, 1962). Factors stifling use are largely methodological. It is not easy to make elegant inference from even two measurements over time, let alone a series of three or more. Not only do the data mount at an alarming rate, but

137

and after the summer, only the questionnaires of the 166 white volunteers who responded to *both* questionnaires are included here. A second note concerns the form of the data to be presented. For most of the analysis we rely on two measures of change—*net aggregate change* and *proportion changing*. The net aggregate change reflects any shifts in the average response for all volunteers from the beginning to the end of the summer. These shifts are tested for statistical significance to see if the changes differ from what one expects by chance. But the proportion changing is also reported for each measure, and tells us the number of volunteers who accounted for these shifts in the over-all average, as well as indicates the stability of individual opinions on attitudes for which there was little net shift. Theoretically it is possible to have considerable proportions changing on a given item but little net change, since the individual changes may cancel each other in the net total. On the other hand, it is not possible to have considerable net change without a reasonably high proportion of volunteers changing. In measuring the proportion changing we compare the scores of individuals before and after the summer and divide the sample into those whose scores increased, decreased, or remained the same. On the constructed scales, however, "increase" and "decrease" are defined in a conservative manner. Each scale distribution was divided into fourths, and only those individuals who pass from one quarter of the scale to the next are considered as having changed. This simplifies the analysis. Although it means that some changers can move only slightly and still pass a boundary while others must move quite far, these should balance out.

---

there are very real problems of interpretation. Errors of a wide variety tend to multiply, and only the most sanguine can assume that these are random in any ultimate reckoning. One particular source of error requires special attention—namely, the regression effect, or the tendency for repeated measurements to converge upon the overall statistical mean. How does one know whether apparent attitude change which approaches a mean is substantive change in its own right or "merely" an artifact of the regression tendency? This is no less a problem here, though we have tried to cope with it by analyzing both net and proportional change, as elaborated in the text. To mention another problem that we have confronted somewhat differently, there is a difficulty in panel analyses of contriving aggregate scales out of individual items. While one can use such techniques as conventional factor analysis in the ordinary study, these techniques depend upon the correlation between items, and such correlations may change from one wave of the panel to the next. How, then, does one construct scales that remain constant with relatively constant validity and reliability across panels? We have relied on a new variant of factor analysis termed interbattery and described in the Appendix. The relevant literature for all these problems is summarized by B. Levinson, "Panel Studies," in D. L. Sills (Ed.), *The International Encyclopedia of the Social Sciences*, Vol. 11 (New York: Macmillan and Free Press, 1968), pp. 371–379. For recent treatment, see G. W. Bohrnstedt, "On the Measurement of Change," in E. F. Borgatta (Ed.), *Sociological Methodology 1969* (San Francisco: Jossey-Bass, 1969), pp. 113–133. Beyond this literature, we are indebted to James A. Davis for the loan of some instructive unpublished work.

OPTIMISM RECONSIDERED

If one were to predict the attitudinal domain most vulnerable to change it would probably concern those matters with which the volunteers were initially least experienced—in short, their conceptions of the South generally and the southern civil rights movement in particular. In fact, it may be misleading to refer to this as attitude change when it can also be represented as an increase in knowledge or the replacement of stereotypes with more informed opinion.

Table 11 presents fourteen major variables in this area on which we expected change. Because the form of the table will recur, a word of explanation is appropriate. Each variable is described in the far-left hand column and if an index is described in the Appendix. We also provide the range of the variable from low to high, although this is the theoretical range and the empirical responses are seldom distributed so widely. The actual data for each variable are organized according to our two basic measures of change, net and proportional. The former is represented by two figures providing the mean scores before and after the summer and then by an indication of whether the difference is statistically significant at the .05 level, that is, whether the difference would have occurred by chance in more than five cases out of one hundred. Turning to the right-hand side of the table and the analysis of proportions, we provide four figures for each variable. The first three represent the percentages of the volunteers who had moved at least one theoretical quarter of the scale toward an increasing disagreement with the sentiment at issue; had remained within the same quarter for both waves; or had moved at least one quarter toward an increased agreement with the sentiment. Finally, the figures in parenthesis in the extreme right-hand column indicate the numbers of respondents on which the percentages are based in all of the tables. Although the two-wave sample is 166, as noted earlier, there are almost always a few respondents who fail to answer any given item.

Without putting all of the numbers into words, it is clear that change did occur; in fact, the net change is statistically significant for eleven of the fourteen variables, and there is a substantial proportion changing for two of the three exceptions. On the other hand, for four of the variables with significant net change (items 1, 3, 12, and 14), the proportion changing is quite low. In fact, there are only two cases (items 7 and 8) in which a majority of the volunteers shifted in the direction of the net change. All of this suggests once again that what may have been most remarkable about the volunteers was their heterogeneity, and what may have been most remarkable about their southern experience was its

Table 11. Changing Views of the South and of the Movement

	Net Aggregate Change			Proportion Changing (Change across quartile boundaries)			
	Mean Score Before	Mean Score After	Verdict of T-test at .05 level	Increasing Disagreement	Same	Increasing Agreement	(N)
				Per Cent			
1. Index of antipathy toward white southerners. (Range from 3 = low antipathy to 18 = high antipathy.)	10.398	11.305	(significant)	15	50	35	(164)
2. Index of unfavorable image of southern courts and police. (Range from 3 = favorable to 18 = unfavorable.)	6.699	6.548	(not significant)	21	55	24	(164)
3. Index of favoring outside intervention in the South. (Range from 3 = unfavorable to 18 = favorable.)	12.000	12.777	(significant)	19	49	32	(166)
4. "The racial problem will only be solved when all lower-class groups, white and Negro, combine in a common struggle." (Range from 1 = strongly agree to 6 = strongly disagree.)	2.460	2.818	(significant)	40	34	27	(162)

Item							
5. "I expect to have some difficulty relating to fellow workers not of my race." (Range from 1 = strongly agree to 6 = strongly disagree.)	3.976	4.756	(significant)	47	33	20	(163)
6. "I expect most Negroes in the Deep South will be afraid to be associated with the summer project." (Range from 1 = strongly agree to 6 = strongly disagree.)	3.741	3.733	(not significant)	37	24	39	(161)
7. "A major obstacle to the summer project will be a lack of cooperation from local Negroes." (Range from 1 = strongly agree to 6 = strongly disagree.)	3.826	3.232	(significant)	28	20	52	(159)
8. "Most of the permanent field workers in the South probably have developed extraordinary sensitivity to the needs and wants of other people." (Range from 1 = strongly agree to 6 = strongly disagree.)	2.401	3.296	(significant)	59	27	14	(155)
9. Index of concern with worker's public image. (Range from 3 = high concern to 18 = low concern	10.337	11.861	(significant)	46	40	14	(166)
10. "I expect to find the summer project a highly efficient and well-coordinated organization." (Range from 1 = strongly agree to 6 = strongly disagree.)	4.585	4.861	(not significant)	40	39	21	(164)

Table 11. CHANGING VIEWS OF THE SOUTH AND OF THE MOVEMENT (cont.)

	Net Aggregate Change			Proportion Changing (Change across quartile boundaries)			
	Mean Score Before	Mean Score After	Verdict of T-test at .05 level	Per Cent			(N)
				Increasing Disagreement	Same	Increasing Agreement	
11. "The selection process for this summer's program means that those of us who are here are the best possible people for the job." (Range from 1 = strongly agree to 6 = strongly disagree.)	4.685	4.988	(significant)	39	39	23	(156)
12. Index of expected project success. (Range from 3 = high success to 18 = low success.)	10.524	11.179	(significant)	32	48	20	(162)
13. "Almost nothing that can happen in the South this summer would make me feel my summer's work was not a success." (Range from 1 = strongly agree to 6 = strongly disagree.)	3.384	3.788	(significant)	46	27	27	(150)
14. Index of belief in nonviolence. (Range from 4 = low nonviolence to 24 = high nonviolence.)	16.970	16.108	(significant)	26	58	16	(164)

variability from one town and project to another. This variation makes any analysis simultaneously difficult and intriguing.

Most of the change that did occur is predictable and self-explanatory. Many of the volunteers were disabused of an initial optimism concerning the willingness of southern whites to see an end to segregation. That the volunteers did not change as much in their attitudes towards the southern courts and police is due largely to the almost unanimously hostile view with which they began the summer. But apparently the summer did convince many that an end to southern segregation would require further intervention by outside influences and authorities. And 40 per cent suffered an eclipse of faith in the Marxian view of a united lower-class movement in which black and white together pursue a redress of their shared grievances.

It is tempting to see these changes as simply a faithful reflection of southern reality. But we must be cautious, since the volunteers' reactions to southern whites and their institutions were based on a considerably biased sample of events and acquaintances. The volunteers had limited contact with the whites in the southern mainstream and their relations were mostly confined to instances of confrontation and enmity. It remains possible that many southern whites could indeed be persuaded somehow and sometime to join with the blacks in a mass movement, and that the courts and police are no worse than their northern counterparts. The point is not to offer a counter-assertion but rather to offer a caveat with which to restrain our inferences.

Presumably the volunteers were better informants about the blacks. They spent the preponderance of their time with Negroes, and insofar as a crucial question involves the black view of the movement the volunteers should have an informed assessment. With this in mind, consider variables 5 through 7 in Table 11. The SCOPE volunteers had less difficulty than expected in interacting with black fellow-workers in their projects. But note that they found more problems than anticipated with local blacks in general. Although the net change in evaluating the Negroes' fear of associating with the project was not significant, the largest of the three categories of proportion changing (39 per cent) involved more fear than expected. Moreover, there was both a significant net shift and a considerable proportionate shift with regard to the lack of Negro cooperation; more than half of the volunteers found less cooperation than they had expected. Once again the frustrations of the summer surface.

One of the persistent themes in our earlier analysis of the volunteers' motivations involved the romance of protest conceived in a mood of enthusiastic idealism. By predictable contrast, the theme of variables 10 through 14 in Table 11 is one of disillusionment. Although it is important not to overstate the matter and imply that all of the volunteers were abruptly changed from starry-eyed to cynical, the summer did corrode the innocence of many. For example, there was disillusionment with the permanent field staff and the veterans of the movement (another way of putting this is that the volunteers discovered the veterans to be human as well as heroic). Certainly the volunteers came to put less emphasis on the public face of the project and on matters of political and moral decorum. Perhaps this finding reflects the increasing awareness that the project was unlikely to produce momentous change anyway; surely it speaks of the strain of saintliness under stress. It may be surprising that there was no significant net change with regard to estimates of organizational efficiency within the project. But recall that the volunteers had expected little efficiency in the first place, and despite their preparedness the largest group of volunteers found more inefficiency than anticipated. And yet the volunteers did not place all of the blame for the project shortcomings on the shoulders of others. Many of the white SCOPE workers were humbled by the summer, and in reassessing their own capabilities there was a marked tendency to feel more strongly that they were not the best people for the job.

We noted in Chapter Four that the volunteers achieved less than they had expected. Item 12 in Table 11 indicates some further aspects of the issue which deserve mention. For example, although many agreed at the beginning of the summer that they would feel successful regardless of what happened, considerably fewer felt this way at the end of the summer. What began for many as a personal act which could be privately meaningful in its own right became increasingly defined as a tack to be measured in terms of concrete achievements for others. Lacking some of these achievements, the act itself lost some of its lustre.

ATTITUDES TOWARD NONVIOLENCE

In the wake of this disappointment, the last variable in Table 11, which concerns nonviolence, is especially interesting. We see a large net change, although only 26 per cent crossed a quartile boundary in the dominant direction of a change *away from nonviolence*. This may be a fair approximation of the mood of recent activists, only a minority of whom have moved explicitly in the direction of violence. Certainly there were few issues debated more widely among the volunteers during the summer of 1965. If only a few abandoned nonviolence, many considered the possibility.

But what does it mean to "abandon" nonviolence? What are the alternatives? Much of the answer depends on one's concept of nonviolence in the first place, and again there was heterogeneity. Some of the volunteers regarded nonviolence as a philosophy extending to all situations and to all living things; others looked upon it as a tactical weapon for the undermanned and outgunned. To some it required a deep-seated love for one's enemies; to others it necessitated only a willingness to act as if such love were possible. Whereas some regarded a life of nonviolence as governing both means and ends, others considered it merely as an end to be sought but not an inhibitor on the means to be employed. To get a more immediate sense of the range of opinions here, let us consider some of the volunteers' own remarks on the subject—and there was no subject on which more remarks were penned into the questionnaires.

I do not see nonviolence in a moral vacuum, but as a sacrament of love. Amoral (not immoral) history continues among the innocents. *Etiam Peccata!*

One problem with nonviolence is that it may lead to too much tolerance. I feel there is a great danger in tolerance. Put like that, it sounds bad. But tolerance can turn into acceptance and no wish to change the established order. And sometimes this has to be done.

I have a lot of respect for Dr. King as a symbol of the movement, but I am not really satisfied with his degree of militancy. I believe in nonviolence as a weapon, not as a philosophy of life. I cannot love Governor Wallace in my heart. Nonviolence is practical, good publicity, and something you use because you can't fight back and because *they* have the weapons and the power.

In Freedom School we were talking about nonviolence with the kids. One kid says the Bible tells you to turn the other cheek if someone slaps you, but it does not tell you what to do if they slap the other cheek. And I think that maybe that's my position. Ideally nonviolence is a beautiful way of life. But the American Revolution could not have happened nonviolently or pacifistically. And I am not a pacifist.

I had an argument with [an SCLC staff member] about nonviolence. . . . He said a civil rights worker that's being attacked should stand there and take it. . . . Even if you get killed. My nonviolence is to go into a nonviolent position if you can't run, and if you can run to get the heck out of there so you can come back the next day and do what you're supposed to do. My nonviolence is not to fight back, . . . it's to protect yourself and to protect the people with you and to protect the movement.

A friend of mine, a Mississippi Negro, . . . said that he felt that the problem with the movement was that none of us came down with guns, that if each and every one of us came down with guns, this would be a better movement. And I said . . . that if every white northerner who came down had a gun, you'd see a lot more dead white northerners.

Unfortunately, our questions on nonviolence were worded more to elicit agreement or disagreement with nonviolence than to explore the alternatives and their nuances. But it would be illegitimate to infer that the volunteers moved en masse to a position in favor of initiating violence as an offensive tactic or accepting violence as the appropriate response to a summer of frustrations. The postsummer mean of 16.108 is still closer to the nonviolent than to the violent extreme of the scale (14.5 is the midpoint on the scale). To give a few specifics, only 32 per cent indicated any agreement with the notion that "it is morally correct to use the threat of violence as a strategy to avoid violent attacks from others," and only half of these could muster more than the most tentative agreement. Much the same is true of the statement, "violence is proper when it is the only way of defending yourself or others," where 39 per cent indicated assent and 30 per cent showed strong agreement. Eighty-eight per cent disagreed that "the civil rights movement may have to abandon the policy of nonviolence if long established southern customs are to be changed," perhaps because 95 per cent felt that to abandon nonviolence would make the country "much more antagonistic" to the movement. At the same time, only 17 per cent expressed any agreement with the proposition, "it would be better for the Negro to remain in his current position if violence were the only way to change that position." The last item suggests that although most of the white SCOPE workers could *conceive* of an ultimate stalemate that would justify violence, most did not believe that such a situation had yet materialized.

In sum, these statistics do not reflect a trend in favor of explicit violence in its own right. Rather, there was a withdrawal from some of the stringent philosophical requirements of nonviolence and a move toward militancy in general. This shift is in keeping with the mood of 1965, when the issue was not whether violence should be used to demand change but whether it was proper as a means of protection. Clearly the movement has changed since then, at least in some of its segments and in some of its members. Any movement that has had to suffer the kinds of frustrations sampled here can hardly be expected to avoid easily an escalation of militancy, even to the point of violence.

WHITE POWERLESSNESS AND BLACK POWER?

If nonviolence had been the byword of the civil rights campaign up to 1965, black power became the shibboleth shortly thereafter, marking a major change in the nature of the movement itself. To what extent did our volunteers sense this change and agree with it after their return from the South?

We saw in Chapter Four that by the end of the summer many volunteers began to feel that community organization was more important in the long run than the immediate task of voter registration. To this extent, they were already in stride with the early march of black power. And yet we also noted that the process of community organization was anything but simple. Many volunteers found the local Negroes to be more fearful and less cooperative than they had expected, and their prior image of permanent staff workers within the movement left them unprepared for some of the problems and frictions encountered here. In short, the volunteers realized both the importance and the difficulty of developing black power in the literal sense. But black power today implies blacks going it alone. What about this aspect of the movement's future? What role did these white students see for themselves and others like them in the next stage of the movement?

Conceptions varied. One volunteer said, "The summer was a frustrating experience for us. We started a lot of projects and left them up in the air. I did get the feeling that the most important thing we did was not voter registration or community organization, but helping make some Negro feel good, to give him a sense of dignity. That's the sort of things that was most valuable. The summer led me to understand and believe in black power. I realized that most of the things we were doing was not the best way to solve the problem. We didn't have the answers; they can help themselves better, and doing it themselves gives them an important sense." This kind of sentiment is commonplace now, after black power has been widely preached and institutionalized. But it was not the dominant mood of the volunteers in the fall of 1965. As if in debate with the above, several others defended their presence in the South and conveyed indignation at their treatment as whites. "Well, as far as this white middle-class business goes, I think that if they are going to canvass eastern colleges, all colleges, they are just going to have to face the fact that that is the kind of people that they are going to get, and they're going to have to reconcile themselves to the fact that that's the way the majority of the people are going to be and not keep throwing it back in their faces. . . . It irritated me, it irritated a lot of the people down there, that they'd asked for us, and once they'd asked for us, they started damning us. It irritated me also, because I hate being categorized that way." This statement begs the question of whether whites belonged in the movement in the first place, but other volunteers answered in the affirmative for several different reasons. For example, in a taped radio interview, a white SCOPE worker said,

The need for whites in the movement will decrease, but it won't disappear. The reason they can never dispense with whites in the movement—I say never, I shouldn't say never, but for a good deal of time —is because there's one thing that nobody here can overcome without going north, and that is the point of view that's preached down here. The newspapers simply do not print the truth, the education is abominable, and there are just some things that people can't do here, points of view that they can never hold, they just never will be able to, especially the older people, just simply ideas that are automatic to a northerner which just aren't automatic to a southerner at all. You know, the ability to rebel in certain ways, and the ability to think of certain things. Just the education, I mean, our education has included methods of rebellion. When you learn history in the North, you learn about revolutions; in the South, in the Negro schools in the South, you simply don't learn this. . . . Negroes can use the educations . . . that the whites have until their education is improved, to help teach their kids.

Presumably blacks educated in the North could serve the same function in the South as whites. But consider the remarks of another volunteer who offered a somewhat different reason for white inclusion. He said,

As a white civil rights worker, I encountered hostility from fellow staff workers who feel that white people are generally speaking ineffective civil rights workers. I agree with them that whites are generally ineffective in organizing a Negro community; however, I think the white volunteers gain a great deal from living within the Negro community and take back to their native culture an awareness both of Negro culture and of much of the poverty and Nazi-like oppression that is taking place. I feel it is important that whites be able to become involved in the movement, but I think there should be a more effective screening and training program for summer projects (such as that set up by the American Friends' Service Committee) ; I also think that a few people with really creative ability should try and work out some sort of effective program to channel the energies of the many middle- and upper-class white young people, like myself, who are sincerely and seriously interested in eliminating racial discrimination not only so that the Negro has a fair share of our country's riches, but also because we believe that *each segment of America's melting pot has something to contribute to the whole, and that the white community is being deprived, spiritually, by setting up artificial barriers.* [Italics added.]

Unfortunately we were not perspicacious enough to ask about black power on the first questionnaire. However, the second included several relevant items. The data leave no doubt that the dominant mood of the volunteers after their experience did not support an exclusively black movement, even though they were quite sensitive to the black-white tensions involved. Thus, although three-fourths of the volunteers expressed agreement with the statement, "there is a tendency for most experienced Negro civil rights workers not to have strong trust in white middle-class summer participants," two-thirds also gave assent to the statement, "white summer civil rights workers will be needed even more in the years to come. Their importance is just beginning." The white volunteers all were not prepared to accept limitations on their roles and possible effectiveness. Although 40 per cent tended to agree that "white summer volunteers should be restricted to limited areas and limited kinds of projects," apparently much of the reason was their *summer* status rather than their color—only 10 per cent expressed agreement with the statement, "white civil rights workers will never be able to really do anything in the South precisely because they are white." And this is clearly the crux of the matter. Despite their troubles across racial lines and despite their own failures to contribute maximally as individuals, the overwhelming majority of the white volunteers felt that there was still a place for whites in the movement. And very few felt that the southern movement had begun to realize its goals. Only 5 per cent agreed with the sentiment that "the battle for southern civil rights is basically over. The local Negroes need no further help to reap the benefits; they can and should do it alone." In fact, that only a few agreed is somewhat surprising since the statement paraphrases a much publicized remark by a charismatic SCLC staff-member during the summer itself.

These data and observations concerning both nonviolence and black power help to provide a rounded summary of the volunteers' reactions to the southern experience. They remind us that even though significant attitude change did occur among the SCOPE workers, it was seldom drastic or wrenching for either the individuals or the group. In spite of the disappointment, the disillusionment, and even the occasional despair, the overwhelming majority retained a faith in a more militant but nonviolent movement with white participants.

IMPACT OF THE SUMMER ON OTHER ISSUES

In addition to the effects of the experience on the volunteers' views of the South and the southern movement, it is worth probing the effect of the experience on the volunteers' broad perceptions and beliefs. Table 12 presents several variables of this general sort using the same format as in Table 11. For example, the first item concerns preferential treatment for Negroes and offers a measure of the extent to which one is willing to bend theoretical democracy to accommodate the exceptional severity of the racial problem. Many volunteers became willing to condone preferential treatment; the net shift is significant, with a plurality of 45 per cent changing in this direction. Importantly, most white workers had not approved of the idea at the start of the summer, and their average score in the fall was still on the side of disagreement. Thus, although they had changed somewhat as a group, even this activist white vanguard still

Table 12. CHANGING VIEWS ON WIDE POLITICAL AND IDEOLOGICAL ISSUES

	Net Aggregate Change			Proportion Changing (change across quartile boundaries)			
	Mean Score Before	Mean Score After	Verdict of T-test at .05 level	Increasing Disagreement	Same	Increasing Agreement	(N)
					Per Cent		
1. "In view of past discrimination, Negroes should now be given jobs ahead of whites." (Range from 1 = agree to 6 = disagree.)	4.264	3.614	(significant)	15	40	45	(160)
2. Index of attachment to American political institutions. (Range from 3 = low attachment to 24 = high attachment.)	17.253	16.939	(not significant)	26	57	17	(166)
3. "American culture is sick and moving along the road to destruction." (Range from 1 = agree to 6 = disagree.)	3.677	3.524	(not significant)	26	43	31	(162)
4. Index of moral concentration. (Range on index from 0 = all							

(more important to 8 = none more important; range on each issue from 1 = much more important to 5 = much less important.)ᵃ						
	4.540	3.759	(significant)	25	16	59	(159)
a) ending war in Vietnam	2.588	2.287	(significant)	26	32	42	(159)
b) reducing poverty	2.822	2.564	(significant)	16	52	32	(162)
c) world nuclear disarmament	2.049	1.842	(significant)	14	59	26	(162)
d) ending capital punishment	3.722	3.884	(significant)	32	50	18	(160)
e) increasing student rights	4.185	4.200	(not significant)	23	51	26	(161)
f) reducing juvenile delinquency	3.595	3.736	(not significant)	33	46	21	(160)
g) halting House Un-American Activities Committee	3.770	3.762	(not significant)	20	58	22	(160)
h) aid to foreign countries through Peace Corps	3.525	3.539	(not significant)	28	45	27	(159)
5. Index of religious conservatism. (Range from 1 = low religiosity to 21 = high religiosity.)	7.301	6.325	(significant)	17	77	6	(163)

ᵃ For this index and its items, this column includes percentage who assigned *more* importance to noncivil rights issue after the summer.

tended to view preferential treatment as discrimination and hence incompatible with the dictates of equality.

FRUSTRATION AND RADICALIZATION?

One of our most interesting findings in Table 12 concerns a variable on which there was little change. The Index of Attachment to American Political Institutions has to do with the volunteers' faith in the constituted political system of the nation, particularly its ability to incorporate change in the area of civil rights. At the beginning of the summer, as noted in Chapter One, the volunteers had more faith in the system than one might have predicted. But despite the frustration that the volunteers experienced over the summer, there is little evidence of radicalization in a revolutionary direction. Not only is there no significant net change, but only 26 per cent of the volunteers moved in a radical direction, 17 per cent became less cynical, and fully 57 per cent remained the same in that they crossed no quartile boundaries on the scale. In many ways, this is the single most surprising finding in the study, and yet it is supported by the similar pattern that obtains with reference to the volunteers' opinions regarding the sickness of American culture. Once again there was no significant net change and a proportion changing of less than one-third in the direction of agreement with this shibboleth of the left.

Certainly the hypothesis of frustration producing radicalization has a great deal of currency among psychologists, sociologists, political scientists and activists themselves.[3] Why does it get so little confirmation here? Part of the reason may be the timing of the follow-up questionnaire. The fall of 1965 came on the heels of the Voting Rights Bill, which was considered to be a major national civil rights legislation. The movement was still concentrated in the South. It had not yet encountered the more sophisticated obstacles of the North, or provoked second thoughts from northern consciences. Moreover, as we discussed in the preceding section, most of the volunteers continued to feel that the movement could make substantial gains with a coalition of black and white effort. And insofar as increasing militancy was kept within the bounds of nonviolence, some

---

[3] The theme of frustration leading to radicalization is pedigreed in both psychological and historical literature. As a variant on the frustration-aggression theorem, it has enjoyed long currency in psychology. As related to the historical tendency for revolutions to emerge in response to progress thwarted, it has equal justification there. In both cases militancy emerges not from a mere continuation of frustration but from sudden frustration after a series of seeming triumphs. Perhaps this observation helps to explain why the SCOPE workers were not more radicalized than they were by their summer experiences. While many had gone south with an idealistic expectation of massive change, few experienced any such triumphs, and hence their frustration was not so abrasive. It was not until 1966 and later, when de jure victories began to seem only de facto water-treading, that aggressiveness and radicalization set in in earnest among many blacks and whites who had been involved in the early phases.

volunteers may well have seen it as a part of the American political system itself, a system that is touted by many for its tolerance of dissidents just as it is derogated by others for its slowness to change.

There is perhaps another reason for the lack of radicalization which draws on some earlier conclusions of Chapter One. The volunteers' motivations for participating in the first place included a substantial emphasis on a personal quest for independence and identity. Although the summer moved many to identify directly with the goals of the movement, a substantial number no doubt continued to view the experience in personal as well as political terms. After all, they were white strangers in a black context, and summer participants rather than full-time staff members. All of this has two implications. First, insofar as the experience was less successful than anticipated, some volunteers may have blamed this as much on their individual failures as on the intransigencies of the national political system or on the imperfections of the American democracy. We have already seen that their view of themselves as a group depreciated during the summer. The following remark by a SCOPE volunteer illustrates how frustration may be interpreted in personal terms, leading to alternate forms of personal fulfillment. "I'm afraid the summer sort of contributed *negatively* toward my interest in civil rights. I am less enthused, less hopeful. Sometimes I feel that the summer's experience contributed to my increasing interest in *violin playing,* by making me feel less convinced of any possible personal effectiveness in civil rights. This is an exaggeration—but I have always felt that music and civil rights conflict in that each demands full-time work if you really 'believe' in them. Now I lean toward music as something obviously more achievable." Of course, the tendency to internalize the blame for political shortcomings is longstanding among the Negroes themselves and therefore a major target of the black power movement and of such phrases as "black is beautiful." It may only be the vicariously oppressed volunteer who, when he is not personally effective, finds his interest waning. Thus, there may be an inevitable gap between such individuals and a movement representing those who have little alternative but to participate. (See Chapter Seven.)

But a second and quite different implication of a personalized view of the experience is that regardless of the failure to fulfill objective goals many white workers found enormous personal meaning in the life and in its people. Indeed, many waxed particularly rhapsodic on this note, and remarks like the following represent an aftertaste that was more poignant than political, more nostalgic than revolutionary.

What this summer did to my life I still do not fully comprehend—I was ready in myself to grasp the meaning that was added. People in the movement and the people in local communities are so advanced in sensitivity to others that I may never be able to leave the movement. The movement with all its many, many faults and defects is one of the most beautiful things I have ever been a part of.

I loved my entire summer in the South. It was often frustrating, but then something nice would happen (one of my adult pupils would suddenly really understand what I was teaching) and things would be great again. I met the first man I've ever known with my hopes, dreams, and ideals. One of the major results of the summer, for me, was a disgust with the American social system. Clothes, money, and education, and good looks— ugh! I met too many people who lacked all these things but who were absolutely wonderful to ever think material things are important again. I will always be willing to fight them and make real values realized.

It is true that this last quotation speaks of a "disgust with the American social system" and a willingness "to fight and make real values realized." But this is somewhat different from a revolutionary reaction to the American political structure. The objection is not to a conventional structure, at all, but rather to a system of values at a more abstract level. And insofar as this volunteer is determined to take issue with these values, one senses that the battle will be waged more by personal example than by political action. But one also wonders how long such a mood can be sustained once the volunteer returns to his normal context. Indeed, one of the problems of a movement that depends on upper-middle-class workers in temporary roles is that once the context changes, the cause may lose much of its urgency. Certainly such movements must be prepared for the continuing crisis of a high turnover rate and for the loss of ideological thrust that may result. (See Chapter Seven.)

DIFFUSION OF CONCERNS

To say that the volunteers were not generally radicalized in their attitudes toward the American political system is not to say that they underwent no political changes whatsoever. Surely there are other possible changes worth exploring; there are even other possible consequences of frustration. For example, one consequence involves diffusion of concern according to a hypothesis derivable from the psychological tradition of "cognitive dissonance."[4] Thus, if one wishes to do something and is unsuccessful at it, a dissonance develops for which one resolution may involve turning to other goals and concerns. Surely 1965 suffered no paucity of potential concerns for the activist on the left. Table 12 checks the supposition by presenting the data for our Index of Moral Concentration and the various causes which are its ingredients. The results confirm the hy-

---

[4] See L. Festinger, *A Theory of Cognitive Dissonance* (Evanston, Ill.: Row, Peterson, 1957) for a broad statement of the concept. See also L. Festinger, H. W. Riecken, Jr., and S. Schachter, *When Prophecy Fails* (Minneapolis: University of Minnesota Press, 1956).

pothesis through the significant and the substantial shifts away from civil rights as the preeminent issue and toward other issues deemed equally or more important. Fifty-nine per cent of the volunteers crossed a quartile boundary in this direction, one of the largest proportional changes in the study. But it is worth noting that just three of the eight specific issues (ending the war in Vietnam, nuclear disarmament, and reducing poverty) account for almost all of the change in the index. Capital punishment shows a slight but significant shift in the opposite direction, but the rest of the issues remained basically stable, although there was some gross change in counter-balancing directions.

The three issues which captured increasing concern are hardly surprising. The war in Vietnam had been steadily escalating since 1965. In the eyes of many volunteers, what had begun as an isolated error was becoming a long-term international disaster, no doubt helping to account for the increased concern over nuclear war. Surely it is understandable that so many of the volunteers should have escalated their disaffection here. In fact one volunteer reported having chafed throughout the summer because "with few exceptions (a philosopher and a sociologist) the local liberals on civil rights wouldn't touch Vietnam, although that atrocity is perhaps even greater." In this statement he reflected a political dilemma for many of the civil rights organizations during 1965 and early 1966. Although SNCC declared its position on the war very early, CORE, SCLC, and the NAACP waited until later, mostly out of fear of losing support for civil rights.

The volunteers' increasing emphasis on poverty in its own right reinforces the previously noted fact that economic action was something that many volunteers felt was a crucial issue. The volunteers' experiences possibly had led them to a conclusion similar to that of two of the authors during their study of Mississippi school desegregation the following winter.

This leads to a final word on the transition from racial to economic problems in the future of the Delta. One can imagine the day when the South will have achieved the dubious northern par in its race relations. One can even imagine the time when the question of money will supercede that of skin color. Certainly the problems that are most likely to plague the South disproportionately in 1986 are the problems of a depleted economy. The downfall of cotton and the lack of a skilled work force with which to attract industry hang like a pall over the Delta in particular and the South generally. Manpower retraining programs are admirable and important, but hardly equal to the task. Unionization is necessary to bring wages up to a meaningful standard, but unionization creates difficulties in attracting industry in the first place. While a moratorium on state and local taxes has served to woo some industry, it is precisely the taxes that are necessary if the region is to benefit from the industry it has seduced. . . . It is within this framework that school desegregation and indeed desegregation of any sort must be seen. Talk of equal opportunity in education, employment, and even at the polls is idle rhetoric addressed to people ensnared by poverty. Equal opportunity means increasingly an opportunity to share in the problems rather than the benefits of the region. Equal schooling will be poor schooling. Equal employment will be equal *un*employment. And equal voting will be an equal chance to make decisions of little impact. There is no doubt that there are immediate problems that can and must be solved quickly. But the effectiveness of federal legislation only points to the necessity of massive federal funds. The tragedies of Mississippi have yet to reach their climax.[5]

As important as the economic fate of the South is, the point at issue is the diffusion of political concerns among the volunteers over the summer. One way to refer to issue-diffusion is with the word *sophistication,* and up to a point, any movement depends on the increasing sophistication of its members in such terms. But there is also danger involved. Once the members of the movement become aware that problems are more complex than the movement's own goals would suggest, crises may develop and both motivation and coordination become difficult to sustain for the day-to-day routine of pursuing one single-minded objective at a time. It is perhaps for this reason that students and intellectuals have often made poor revolutionaries. Because they have a tendency to see issues in complex rather than simple terms, they tend to lack an ability to channel their energies over the long haul. This is not news to the current radical leadership of the civil rights movement. Indeed, this may be a reason the movement has increasingly spurned the campus for the ghetto in its recruiting. In this sense, the organizational success of any movement may depend on its ability to desophisticate its members so as to develop and maintain a distinct focus on limited but achievable objectives.

ATTITUDE CHANGE VERSUS CRYSTALLIZATION

So far we have seen that the volunteers were not as radicalized as we expected, and this was at least partly because of a tendency to react to the summer in personal terms and to diffuse their political concerns. But in studying the interviews and comments of the volunteers, it appears that the questionnaire missed a particularly important type of impact of the summer on their beliefs. A number of the volunteers reported that the summer's primary effect on their political views was to sharpen them, clarify them, and perhaps give them a greater sense of urgency. This is a kind of impact that is difficult to measure with a conventional question-

---

[5] M. Aiken and N. J. Demerath III, "Tokenism in the Delta: Two Mississippi Cases," in R. W. Mack (Ed.), *Our Children's Burden* (New York: Random House, 1968), pp. 105–106.

naire because it does not necessarily require substantive change at all. Instead, many workers found that the experience breathed life into what had been a series of abstractions. Without actually changing their values, it made them considerably more meaningful. Some representative comments illustrate this point.

During the summer I was converted from a position of not knowing what I thought about anything. I'm a Quaker, and I am nonviolent theoretically, only I never really believed it, you know, or I did believe it, but I didn't know why, or I didn't feel solid about it, you know. I was against violence but I wasn't for nonviolence. I was against hatred but I wasn't for love.

I gained tremendous depth and grassroots insight and affirmation for many of my preconceived ideas.

I don't think I changed, but I strengthened some of my own attitudes. For example, I don't think I had ever really resolved the question of interracial marriage for myself, but I think I've discovered in this situation that it doesn't make any difference to me either. After the close day-to-day relationships with the people here, I know that I don't even think of them as Negroes any more, and I know that if a person I wanted to marry were a Negro, it wouldn't make any difference to me if I really wanted to marry him. I'm sure of this because of this real lack of comprehending color now. This was well on its way out before I came, I think, but this has strengthened the attitude.

Even when values are as much under siege as they are today, they do not change as rapidly or as commonly as the popular rhetoric would have it.[6] Very few of these volunteers went through a major reorientation of personality or social perception in the few months of the summer of 1965. Instead, most found that the experience enriched the qualities and views they had brought with them initially. To generalize the point, new situations or moments of stress tend to accentuate old qualities rather than produce new ones.

RELIGIOUS CONSEQUENCES

The effect of the summer on the volunteers' religious views provides a particularly apt illustration of this process. We have noted previously that the volunteers harbored at the outset two almost distinct religious groups. First, there were some who saw their civil rights work as a religious witness, and who came with a deep conviction in the efficacy of the church and traditional doctrine. A second and larger group held less conventional views. These ranged from strict atheism through an indif-

---

[6] W. J. McGuire, "The Nature of Attitudes and Attitude Change," in G. Lindzey and E. Aronson (Eds.), *The Handbook of Social Psychology*, 2nd Edition, Vol. 3 (Reading, Mass.: Addison-Wesley, 1969), pp. 136–314.

ferent agnosticism to a position which esteems religious ethics but finds doctrinal orthodoxy and the church to be at best irrelevant and at worst hindrances. Looking again at Table 12, we see that by the fall there had been a significant net shift away from conventional religion as measured by a scale combining four items central to Christion orthodoxy. But two qualifications are important. First, despite the net change in the aggregate, there is very little change across the quartile boundaries on the Index of Religious Conservatism; 77 per cent remained within the same quarter of the scale before and after the summer. Second, further analysis[7] indicates that the best predictor of a decline in religious conservatism over the summer is low religious influence at the beginning of the summer. Conversely of course, the best predictor of increasing conservatism over the summer is high reported religious influence at the beginning. In both instances the summer served to accentuate rather than alter religious proclivities present from the outset—a common pattern for the other types of change as well.

But it would be an oversight to dismiss the religious relevance of the summer by considering only its impact on formal orthodoxy. The fact is that the experiences of some of the most formally irreligious volunteers could only be described in religious terms, using the term broadly. In part, this is because many were deeply impressed with what religion meant to the local Negroes, and found that Negro church services were highly moving despite their own nonreligious bent.

Another sense in which the summer was religiously significant recalls the distinction between the religious institution and the religious quest as sources of frequently incompatible types of spiritual experiences. Once religion becomes institutionalized and codified as a set of answers it tends to stifle the sort of questioning which is responsible for launching religious movements in the first place.[8] Hence, those who are least religious

---

[7] It is one thing to describe attitude change but quite another to explain or predict it. This chapter is devoted almost entirely to description, though only after we tried and failed to produce empirically grounded explanation. Using a regression model, we analyzed change with reference to a host of possible independent variables, representing the dominant themes of each of the foregoing chapters. None of these produced consistent statistical significance, except for the finding that prior attitudes go hand in hand with later attitudes, as illustrated by religion. Why is it so difficult to produce explanatory relationships? A large part of the reason may be that insofar as change occurred, it occurred with respect to opinions about the southern scene in general. Since all of the volunteers were exposed to that scene in a very basic sense, this was the major factor in change and it was not variant among them. There was some degree of change in other areas as well. But many of these changes were either idiosyncratic or dependent upon interacting sets of factors impossible to capture with such a small sample and without additional information on the situations to which the volunteers had returned for three to four months during the subsequent fall before answering our second questionnaire.

[8] See T. Luckmann, *The Invisible Religion* (New York: Macmillan, 1967).

in form may be most religious in pursuit and vice versa. To many observers, there are few people more alert to ethics, morality, and the discovery of new meaning beneath old veneers than the new left. Many participated in the Civil Rights Movement in much the same way that a convert participates in a sect. Qualities of love, self-transcendence, and grasping for the ultimate were all present in the recollections of most of the white SCOPE workers. Here are a few examples in addition to those we have already seen:

I think I've come to understand my own feelings a great deal. . . . I've come to understand the mechanics of what is involved in the movement. I've learned who the people are and can identify a little bit with what they have done because I've heard them say it, and my religious belief becoming quite a bit stronger has coincided with it. I've come to believe that any kind of God there is, this is the kind of thing that he would believe in too. This is the kind of thing that man should do and this is the kind of world that we should work for. All these kinds of new situations in the South, the new people I've met, the white people, the Negro people —I wouldn't be able to understand them and to be able to look back at them. Right now it's all inside doing what they're doing and it's very hard to look and say this did that and that did that because it's still working and will be working until I leave and some time afterwards.

I wish I could capture for you, for myself I guess, really, even a part of what the summer meant. We miss being there. It doesn't seem quite right that we were one day there and one day gone, leaving behind a life filled every minute with giving, taking, learning, and teaching. A distant dream.

I am optimistic—I've seen pure subjective faith work, and felt its impact within me. This is not civil rights but human rights; not a social movement, but a psychological one; it is a spiritual revolution that sweeps the blind before it and makes the light evident in the dark; this is a "movement" into the essence of man.

This is eloquent testimony of a sort that statistics cannot provide. Perhaps all lasting change entails a religious element of the type so apparent among these young moral entrepreneurs. Their experience simply cannot be described without noting the fellowship of the elect, the vigor of the crusade, and the spiritual aftertaste that lingers on. Indeed, the summer was enacted, sustained, and concluded as part of an on-going political consecration of a religious vision.

RETURN TO NORMALCY

One of the important ingredients of any successful organization is a continuing membership, but one of the obvious characteristics of SCOPE and perhaps social movements in general is its reliance on temporary workers. The leaders had hoped that many would stay in the South and extend the summer activity into the fall and perhaps indefinitely. But by the fall most had returned to the lives they had led before. Seventy-five per cent were doing in the fall what they had been doing the previous spring or what they had planned to do all along. Another 18 per cent were no longer working on civil rights, although the summer had caused a change in their plans; 2 per cent were still working on civil rights as they had planned all along; but only 5 per cent were still working on civil rights as a result of changes caused by their summer experiences. Although 58 per cent reported that they had given some consideration to remaining in the South at the end of the summer, less than 10 per cent of the volunteers actually did so. It is worth exploring some of the reasons why the volunteers left and some of their feelings about the departure.

We asked them to list the most important reasons for not staying in the South. By far the most common was to return to school, cited by 60 per cent as the most important factor and reminding us again that these were students rather than permanent activists, and volunteers rather than professionals. Some reported other considerations in the decision, but not more than 8 per cent cited as the primary factor disillusionment with the movement, the needs of family and loved ones, or the draft (at a time when college enrollment virtualy guaranteed deferment).

The volunteers did not report much guilt about leaving the South. Indeed, 40 per cent of those who left said that they felt no guilt at all, and 24 per cent said not very much; only 9 per cent indicated a good deal or extreme guilt. One wonders why there were so few compunctions? A few may have felt rejected by the initial phases of black power. Some may have felt that leaving the South was not really leaving the action, since the movement was already broadening its protest against many other aspects of society, including the war in Vietnam. To others, the summer project was a way of expiating guilt in the first place, and having participated once they could return to their original pursuits.

CHANGING VIEWS OF THE UNIVERSITY

Certainly there were many volunteers with high ambitions and high promise in conventional terms, and it is striking to note how little change occurred in career aspirations over the summer. Of course, this is partly because most were already planning to enter such directly relevant occupations as social work, the clergy, or education as opposed to such careers as business, medicine, or engineering. Still, one might have expected far more flux than actually occurred and perhaps more of a shift away from those careers that required the delaying pedigree of professional training. This did not happen, although there was an increase from 10 per cent to 17 per cent in the proportion undecided on their future careers, a statistic that could presage greater change to come.

Indeed, the possibility of greater change to come is worth exploring further. Although surface indications suggest that the overwhelming number of the volunteers returned to school and its conventionalities, this answer may be too simple. For one thing, returning to school is not strictly analogous to returning to a business occupation or to a standard niche in the community. For many students, college is a kind of legitimized limbo, one of the very few places where one may safely tread water while deciding in which direction to swim, or whether to swim at all. Not all the volunteers who answered the call of the next semester were simply reimmersing themselves in the lives they had left behind. For example, 23 per cent of those who were in college in the fall had changed their major, and more than four out of five claimed that this was a direct result of the summer experience. Predictably, the bulk of these changes were into fields that were presumably more directly involved with problems encountered during the project. Sociology was the leading recipient of new majors, attracting 25 per cent of those who changed; political science claimed 14 per cent; and history, law, social work, psychology, and education all received slightly less than 10 per cent each. One surprising fact was that 14 per cent changed not into a directly applied field but into religion and theology. As we have seen, religion was not irrelevant to the summer project, and of course the clergyman's role is increasingly identified with social action as suggested by the Southern *Christian* Leadership Conference.

But in addition to changes in curriculum, many experienced changes in their perceptions of the university. A return to college not only preserved their options but also involved a new awareness of some of the options available to the colleges themselves. Here, for example, is the testimony of one student concerning the transition from Alabama back to UCLA: "In Alabama every white folk is an enemy and every car spells danger and all this business. . . . To go from that to a tree-shaded UCLA campus . . . is a very hard adjustment to make especially with all the problems of the multiversity and the . . . questions I have as to just what the hell is going on over there. Is it worth it and the whole value system behind it, . . . the whole set-up? You know, I'm not against education but what that education is designed to accomplish, which is as Clark Kerr said . . . a factory to produce minds for business, the military, and government. . . . To make that jump, to see the other side of the coin, . . . all these people who you couldn't explain Selma to, . . . it's very difficult to adjust to that." General student animus against the university has obviously escalated since 1965. On the one hand higher education is *too* relevant to the status quo as a "factory to produce minds for business, the military, and government. . . ." On the other hand the uni-

Table 13. CHANGING VIEWS OF THE RELEVANCE OF COLLEGE

	Net Aggregate Change			Proportion Changing (change across quartile boundaries)			
	Mean Score Before	Mean Score After	Verdict of T-test at .05 level	Increasing Relevance	Same	Decreasing Relevance	(N)
					Per Cent		
Index of relevance of college. (Range from 3 = low relevance to 18 = high relevance.)	12.595	11.591	(significant)	12	48	40	(147)

versity is not relevant enough to the need for social change and to what *should* be the real values and interests of society. Using relevance in the latter sense, we find another point at which a major shift in volunteer attitudes is empirically discernible, according to Table 13. Earlier, in Chapter One, we noted that the students who went south had found their college experience quite relevant to their own concerns and to the concerns of society. Table 13 shows that by the end of the summer the perceived relevance has decreased considerably. In fact, this change is one of the largest net shifts in attitude, as is the proportion of changers (40 per cent).

The volunteers were not prepared to accept this situation passively. In returning to school, many were bringing their activism closer to home, to the university itself. The second questionnaire included several questions on student politics that had not been included in the first. Although it is impossible to demonstrate shifts in opinion since we have only attitudes at the end of the summer, it seems inconceivable that sentiment in favor of campus activism could have been any higher at the start of the summer. Only 16 per cent expressed any disagreement at all with the statement, "I would consider supporting a student strike or sit-in to protest against some aspect of educational policy, such as a particular faculty member or particular courses, etc.," and 35 per cent indicated strong agreement. In the same vein, only 9 per cent expressed disagreement with the statement, "The Free Speech Movement among the students at the University of California, Berkeley, was both desirable and important," and 45 per cent agreed strongly. These data are prophetic of more recent events on campus. They support the view that the civil rights movement may ultimately have an impact on higher education that is every bit as profound as its impact on civil rights.

WRONG-WAY CULTURE SHOCK

Finally, we should consider the effects of the summer on the volunteers' relations with friends and relatives, and the sociopsychological import of the transition from the South back home. We asked the volunteers specifically about the reception they received from those who knew about their summer in the South. While 39 per cent reported that they were treated no differently now than before, 40 per cent answered that they seemed to have increased stature among the people they cared about. Many volunteers found that just being back among friends was gratifying after the interpersonal strains of the summer. For example, the diary of one white volunteer provides a contrast between the initial enthusiasm of the movement and the later return to a predominantly Negro fraternity context: "June 28: An early thought: the feelings of 'fraternity' that

I have felt in Kappa Alpha Sigma seems so superficial as compared to how I felt when I saw again James Greenlee and Willie Jones, the SCOPE recruiting team that visited the university in May. I worked with them for only four days in May, but when I saw them here it was like seeing a real brother again. Oct 5: The 'fraternity' feeling does not seem superficial now."

For some volunteers, however, the return home provided as much culture shock as the southern experience. In this respect the white SCOPE workers may have a good deal in common with Peace Corps volunteers who report similar problems.[9] Although the Peace Corps workers may seem subject to far greater shock for traveling far greater cultural distances, one must be careful not to minimize the gap between the world of the lower-class southern black and the upper-middle-class northern white. One SCOPE worker said,

There is an area you didn't treat as extensively as you might have (perhaps it would be a study in itself): The psychological impact of returning home to your predominantly white homes in the north. In my case: While living the summer totally within the Negro community, it seems that I completely internalized their norms, hopes, fears, anxieties: I "became" Negro (down to the same speech patterns). When I returned home, white people looked "funny"; I had difficulty relating to them; and I didn't trust them. My skin was white—but I was not a white man. Attitudes and views that white acquaintances had now seemed to "reek of" bias and prejudice. I seemed to have developed a more acute ability to sense bigoted individuals. And I was slightly paranoid. I was bitter. As if my whole value scheme, learned from infancy, was a lie. The contradiction between ideology and practice became acutely apparent—apparent to a degree I would not have been aware of if I had remained a "northern-white-liberal." We're a sick people with a system fabricated on lies.

As this suggests, there were probably many volunteers for whom the summer experience only really crystallized after returning home. That is, the contrast between the movement and the home context stimulated many to sort out the issues for the first time. A lengthy statement from a volunteer describes the perhaps predictable anguish of readjusting to Orange County, California, an area vaunted for its conservatism.

It was a very startling experience for me to return to my home town and find people sympathetic with my stories of problems concerning the South and yet terribly, violently, against the Negro in the North. Some said they were really beginning to believe in the Negro cause until the Watts riot. Somehow they could not see the problems where they lived and resented

---

[9] Here is another similarity between the SCOPE volunteers and the Peace Corps workers, as well as others who have spent time abroad. For a good summary of this literature, see R. C. Angell, *Peace on the March: Transnational Participation* (New York: Van Nostrand Reinhold, 1969), especially Chapter Five.

any suggestions of mine. They seemed to want me to think that I had been taken in by the Communists or (if not that strongly) to a highly emotionalized situation without understanding the whole problem. I was weary when I returned. I was frustrated, disappointed and hurt to hear the bigoted attitudes of well-liked acquaintances. I was constantly attacked verbally by numbers of people everywhere I went. I never wished that I had not gone south, and I constantly wanted to share my experience, but I was suddenly identified with civil rights and civil rights alone. It seemed that they forgot I had grown up with them and had much in common with them. Had I remained . . . longer, perhaps my experience would be set aside in their minds—although I would have intended to try to show them my views beginning at their level. I guess the main impact this action had on me (besides making me tired from the threatening letters my parents got which emphasized the feelings of the conservative area) was that it made me realize just how lackadaisical I had been toward the cause of humanity in the hub-bub of my life. I noticed how little communication media offers at all. . . . I noticed how people who did not have *facts* made up their own. I noticed how people were unconcerned with what did not directly involve them. I noticed how people could shift blame to some obscure person or circumstance. I remember how, in the past, I had accepted my father's answers and then dropped my questions as he seemed to do when he could not find answers. My father is conservative in that he never claims to know answers; he is not conservative in that he does not (in the political sense) condemn or label movements or people, but rather looks for good. I like this latter aspect of my father, although this is not enough for me. While he is a peace maker and a mediator. . . I now realize that upset is of vital importance if I find a truth my contemporaries are ignoring or suppressing. I am able to understand why some people sacrifice themselves, why some excommunicate themselves from the white race, and why some become hermits. At times, I have thought of doing the same. However, I prefer the direction of challenging my society; this is slow but more exciting and real.

Of course, not all volunteers suffered so, and this is only partly because so few returned to Orange County. Most were genuinely relieved to be back home, and some began to turn away from the disparities and hypocrisies that so agonized their colleagues. This after all is the dominant response for most of us, and it is important to recall that the volunteers were products of the very political culture they sought to change.

SUMMARY

Any treatment of changes in the volunteers based on data collected only a few months after their experience must necessarily be incomplete. It is useful to know something of the immediate impact of the summer, but we dare not confuse this with its impact over the long run. Trends that seemed apparent in the fall of 1965 may have altered considerably with intervening events. Thus, although the summer experience alone may not have had an immediate radicalizing influence, the experience could have had such an influence when coupled with more recent happenings. Most of the volunteers appear to have undergone a diffusion of political concerns rather than a redoubling of commitment to civil rights alone, but this too could change. And although it would appear that most returned to school and to "normalcy" in order to pursue their original aspirations, there are hints that the aspirations could sour and the pursuits go awry as the students continue to confront the contrast between the lives they left and the live they lead.

For all of these reasons, we need more information before hazarding a denouement. While we have no third questionnaire to rely upon for this purpose, we did interview a small subsample of volunteers four years later to provide some suggestive leads. The result of these interviews are the substance of Chapter Six.

CHAPTER VI

Four Years Later: A Gap Within a Generation

I wonder where the place for old revolutionaries is. There's so many, probably, who feel the same way I do. Right now, there's plenty of things to do. But can you tell me, if you were an activist with lots of organizational experience, who you'd want to join?

Remark reported at 1969 SDS convention[1]

[1] Quoted in B. Kalb, "Parting of the Ways for S.D.S.," *The New Republic,* 1969, *161,* 12.

To a student of student activism, the interval since 1965 seems nearly an epoch. The spotlight of publicity has shifted from SCLC, CORE, and even SNCC to SDS, the Third World Liberation Front, and the Black Panthers, all within a period of four years. As the action has shifted from south to north, sophisticated urban centers have been stripped of their veneers to serve as scarred battlegrounds for the most searing confrontations. Perhaps nowhere are the changes more pronounced than on the campuses of the nation. No longer are universities merely recruitment strongholds for groups that would move out into society. Now the universities themselves are under siege as the movement has turned back upon its source, trying to revolutionize the campus as a first step in revolutionizing society as a whole. For many, the object is no longer to use political movements as a means to societal ends; there are now those who see the political movement as an end in its own right and as a model for the future of society itself. Indeed, it is difficult to conjure up those bygone days of 1965 when liberals were united in their admiration for radicals who did, in fact, differ only in their means and not in their ends. In a society witnessing a strong conservative reaction, it is no longer possible to bask in the political optimism that sees progress as the inevitable wave of the future. Clearly a great deal has happened to affect our vision of the future as well as of the past. It is just such change of which epochs are made.

We have been almost painfully aware of these events throughout the writing of this book. Our treatment of materials in previous chapters has been influenced by the actions swirling around us at the moment. In fact, if this book had been finished in December 1965, immediately after receiving the second wave of questionnaires, it would have been far different for lack of such hindsight. Throughout we have been seeking not merely to understand the facts of the past but to make sense of them in light of the present. Events begat perspective, shadows became foreshadows, and the differences between June and September of 1965 became merely the first steps on a political escalator.

But the lapse of time does more than inform; it becomes a goad. Knowing that the story of the volunteers had continued to evolve, we wanted to know how and in what directions. Who and where are these people now? Are they still student activists but with shifts in emphases? Or have they withdrawn from activism, either in retreat from society or in pursuit of more conventional careers and interests? What has become of their energies, their ideals, and their frustrations? What is likely to become of anyone who exposes himself to such stern commitments with such equivocal results?

Our scholarly inclination was to design a third questionnaire and to administer a third wave in the panel design. The temptation was stifled primarily because our research funds were nearly depleted, but also because we wanted to wait perhaps a decade before such a follow-up, and because we felt considerable pressure to get the already available materials into print. Throughout we have been aware that our sociology-of-the-moment could become a mere period piece.

With all this in mind, we settled for a series of brief telephone interviews. At first we intended to call only ten or fifteen volunteers. But our interest eventually led us to contact forty, or roughly one in four of the white SCOPE workers who had previously completed both the first and second questionnaires. Unfortunately, the forty respondents do not represent a systematic sample. The volunteers are an especially mobile group in a particularly mobile society and were therefore often difficult to reach. Because we wanted to capture something of the full range of post-project experiences, we sometimes tried to insure diversity of respondents based on our earlier information, although this was never a rigorous operating principle.

These were not depth interviews, even in the often diluted sense of that phrase. At long distance rates with a quickly diminishing budget, we were unable to talk at the length we would have preferred. Instead, the interviews ranged from ten minutes to over thirty, with twenty as a rough average. The interviews were kept informal in order to allow the volunteers to tell their stories. But we did follow a general list of questions, including the following: How do you evaluate the SCOPE summer from your current perspective? What have you done in each of the succeeding years? Have you engaged in further civil rights activity and, if so, of what sort? Have you been involved in other forms of political activity? Can you trace any long-term changes in yourself, your attitudes, beliefs, or personality to the summer of 1965? Have you kept in touch with people encountered during the summer, whether members of the local communities or other volunteers? (This last query gave us data on several additional volunteers who were not reached by phone.)

Two of the authors did all of the interviewing, mostly in the evenings and on weekends. This plan not only saved money, but it had the advantage of breeding direct familiarity with the nuances and connotations of the responses. This is especially important because the discussion to follow rests heavily on qualitative rather than quantitative evidence. Although we rely somewhat on our respondents' earlier questionnaires for basic background data, the bulk of our analysis focuses on the interviews alone.

FOUR POLITICAL LIFE STYLES

Although there are a few characteristics shared by virtually all of the volunteers four years after their return (for example, opposition to the war in Vietnam) there is considerable diversity as well. The volunteers were heterogeneous when they began the SCOPE project, and the summer did little to homogenize them. No two of their subsequent stories are the same, despite similarities that appear at first glance. For instance, two former volunteers who were Catholic seminarians before SCOPE have left the seminary and the priesthood—but for somewhat different reasons and with somewhat different concomitants. For one, leaving the seminary was part of leaving his religion altogether; for the other, religion remained highly salient even though he felt that he had become too political to settle for the constrained role of the clergyman.

Of course, we cannot tell each of the forty stories in detail, capturing the individuality of each life history. This demands more than the resources available, and it would make it difficult to appreciate the common variables and shared experiences. Instead we concentrate on some basic themes which reveal the larger psychological and sociological patterns resulting from a fusion of previous histories, current situations, and of course the summer in the South. Because we work backward from the kinds of persons the respondents are today, we begin by distinguishing four kinds of political life styles into which the volunteers may now be sorted.

Instead of simply positing four categories on a purely intuitive or inductive basis, we tried to derive them more theoretically. The types are specified by the intersection of two dimensions, both of which enjoy colloquial status among students of students as well as among students themselves. The first of these is *alienation,* a concept with a list of interpretive nuances and debated subtleties that is perhaps longer than for any other term in the sociological vocabulary.[2] But this is not the place for a thorough exegesis. For the moment, we merely use the term in its most basic sense as it has come to connote an estrangement from and rejection of existing society and its institutions. If then the dimension of alienation refers to a state of mind, our second dimension refers to actual behavior.

---

[2] For a classic delineation of the various meanings of the term, see M. Seeman, "On the Meaning of Alienation," *American Sociological Review,* 1960, *24,* 783–791. Note, however, that not all alienation refers to estrangement from the society. A recent article relies on a content analysis of popular fiction to show that social alienation has tended to give way to self-alienation during this century. See I. Taviss, "Changes in the Form of Alienation: The 1900s Vs. the 1950s," *American Sociological Review,* 1969, *34,* 46–57. For an extended treatment of the concept as it applies to today's youth, see the special issue on "Alienated Youth," A. J. Tannenbaum (Ed.), *Journal of Social Issues,* Spring 1969, *25.*

Clearly one can be highly alienated and do either a great deal or very little as a result, just as those who are not alienated may vary widely in their political roles. The dimension at issue here is *activism,* or the extent to which one works beyond the bounds of political propriety to achieve some change in society or in the lives of others in keeping with one's own political ideals. All of our respondents were at least temporary activists during the summer of 1965, but even then some were more alienated than others.

Unlike Keniston, who treats the alienated and the activists as two distinct types in their own right,[3] we use them as two variables whose interactions define the types indicated in Table 14. Of course, it is an

Table 14. POLITICAL STYLES FOUR YEARS LATER

	Alienated	Nonalienated
Active	Radicals	Reformists
Nonactive	Drop-outs	Disengaged

oversimplification to collapse the two variables into crude dichotomies. Moreover, the labels are relative to the population at issue; for example, when we speak of *nonalienated* former civil rights workers, it should be understood that they are likely to be more critical of society than most of the nonalienated majority among the seven million college students in this country. With these caveats in mind, let us briefly introduce the four categories before placing our respondents within them.

In the upper left-hand corner, the *radicals* are not only alienated but activist in their determination to do something about it. Moving clockwise to the right, we come to the *reformists,* who are actively seeking changes in society, although their malaise has not reached the point of alienation. In the lower right-hand corner, are those *disengaged* from the

---

[3] K. Keniston, *The Young Radicals* (New York: Harcourt Brace Jovanovich, 1969), especially Appendix B, "The Sources of Student Dissent." This latest volume of Keniston's analysis of the student scene focuses on activists, and his earlier book, *The Uncommitted* (New York: Harcourt Brace Jovanovich, 1967), focuses particularly on what he terms the alienated. Indeed, one reason we prefer to use the concepts of activism and alienation as cross-cutting variables rather than as discrete types is because it is difficult for us to imagine the alienated as uncommitted in Keniston's sense. This is largely a semantic problem. But, from our perspective, alienation involves a high commitment to the values and standards that are being violated, though not necessarily a commitment to action in their behalf.

movement who are neither alienated nor active and have made at least an uneasy peace with their society. Finally, the *drop-outs* are so afflicted by their alienation that they withdraw from society altogether, whether into hippiedom, drugs, or a host of competing alternatives.

Using impressionistic judgments, we placed each of the forty follow-up respondents into one of the four categories and succeeded to our own satisfaction in all but three instances. Each of the three had overlapping characteristics of the reformer and the disengaged, and they will be discussed as a special group. Finally, it is worth noting that our categorizations apply only at the time of our interview, since some volunteers had moved through several of our categories since 1965 and had recent pasts which were at wide variance with their current behavior. For example, one girl now classified as disengaged had remained in the South with the movement until Christmas of 1965, after which she went to Chicago to work with an SCLC staff group. At the end of 1966, she abruptly stopped her activity and entered law school. "I'm not marching anymore. I am for [Senator Eugene] McCarthy but I'm not going to get involved in any political activity. . . . Demonstrations are kind of worthless. I resent the fact that people melt away when there is real work to do. When there are demonstrations you can get any number of people. People come for the excitement. But they won't do the hard long-term work." Three years earlier she would probably have been classified as a radical. Three years from now . . . who knows?

RADICALS

Ten of the forty respondents appear to be radicals. Perhaps the clearest case is a self-described "radical socialist" who was a member of the Students for a Democratic Society three years before going south, and who helped to seize Fayerweather Hall during the celebrated student siege at Columbia University in 1968. Less clearly radical was a young volunteer who was working out two years of alternate service to the army because he was a conscientious objector. He has persistently if not spectacularly engaged in opposing the war in Vietnam, and organized peace groups wherever he has been. He also continued an interest in organizing educational experiences in interracial communication and contact. He spoke of his alienation in terms characteristic of all the radicals in mentioning that he has "come to some disturbing conclusions about our society." But his is a gentle activism, eschewing the large demonstrations and public confrontations. Indeed, he is one of only two radicals in our group who campaigned for Eugene McCarthy in the 1968 presidential primaries, and he apparently did not share the attitude of the other former SCOPE worker who said, "I worked for McCarthy not because

I liked him but because I wanted to radicalize all those people who liked him."

The rest of the radicals fall between the extremes of the Columbia SDS member and the conscientious objector who worked loyally for McCarthy. One is an ex-Vista worker who was fired for his radicalism; another is a full-time SDS organizer; still others include a member of a guerilla theater group, one of the resigned seminarians, a teacher in Harlem, and a worker at a black cultural revolution center.

Perhaps this statement from the SDS organizer most nearly summarizes the position of the group as a whole: "The struggle against racism and capitalism are intimately interlinked. . . . These problems can only be solved by altering the economic and political system of the United States." Although the others shared the view, most did not (and possibly could not) articulate it so clearly. Their positions were grounded not in a rationalized view of the world but rather in an inchoate emotional feeling that somehow "things are wrong and there must be major changes."

By and large, these are not wholly new feelings for these respondents. Six of the ten were socialists of one variety or another before the summer of 1965, whereas only four of the remaining thirty respondents had shared this political identification, or indeed anything else to the left of "liberal Democrat," before SCOPE. The prior socialists agreed that the experience of the summer had moved them somewhat further to the left and had sharpened their sense of disenchantment, but the impact was obviously stronger for those who had not been as radical to begin with. For example, one indicated, "Before I had been a liberal in the classic sense; now I'm more of a radical." Another put it this way: "[The summer in the South] made me realize that Vietnam simply fits in with the general trend of American society and American politics. . . . I now see interrelations between issues such as the draft, the war, and various policies concerning the treatment of minority groups and other economic issues." And yet for many the impact of the summer was gradual rather than sudden, often requiring comparison with conditions at home for the full measure of its significance to emerge. Two volunteers commented in this vein:

[The summer] gave me an awareness that I could no longer believe in the liberal myth in America. My political opinions moved to the left, although the process was a slow one. That is, it didn't happen right away, but it gave me a perspective that later led me to a much more leftist point of view.

The impact of the summer wasn't immediate. But as I thought about what I had seen, I came to grips with my own views on race, poverty, and the general social climate. This pushed me strongly to the left.

Interestingly, all ten of the current radicals are males, a character-istic which distinguishes the group from the other three categories, since only half of the reformists are males and almost none of the drop-outs or disengaged. This is not to say that the female respondents had not been or will never be radicals. One of them described herself as a radical in 1966, although the label no longer applies, and at least two noninterviewed female volunteers were described as radicals by people who had kept in touch with them. Nevertheless, radicalism may generally be a male pre-dilection. Males are more directly confronted with the society that alien-ates them. Not only are they vulnerable to the draft, but they are under pressure to make difficult career decisions in a society in which more and more careers are losing their luster.

All ten of the radical respondents made it clear that they do not intend to serve in the military. This decision may be both a cause and a consequence of a larger series of choices, each of which takes the individ-ual further away from conventionality. Of course, resisting the draft in 1970 has some characteristics of joining the southern civil rights move-ment in 1965; both are specific actions which appear to place the in-dividual's present and future identity on the line. Although the radicals were unanimous in their sentiments concerning the draft, not all had had to put their sentiments into effect. Two had not yet been contacted by their draft boards (for idiosyncratic reasons); two were still being de-ferred as graduate students; one was yet too young to face the issue directly, although he was "very strong in opposing the draft and will not go" and like others had led and participated in numerous antidraft demonstrations. Four of the radicals applied for conscientious objector status. Two were successful as long-time members of religious groups with histories of conscientious objection, the Mennonites and the Quakers. Two others were refused deferments. One refused induction and expected to be arrested. The other appealed the decision of his board, although he felt that he had no chance as a Catholic of obtaining conscientious ob-jector status. In his words, his religion gave his draft board "the oppor-tunity to wash their hands of my appeal like Pontius Pilate." Finally, the tenth radical was teaching high school mathematics specifically "in order to avoid the draft."

But if the radicals were unanimous in what they did *not* want to do, they were highly uncertain in their aspirations. Again the summer seems to have had an effect, at least when coupled with their subsequent experiences and perceptions. Looking at their responses to the first ques-tionnaire in the study, we find that eight of the ten had mentioned college teaching as a possible or probable career, as compared with only four of the remaining thirty respondents. By 1969, however, only four of the radicals (and one of the nonradicals) still had designs on an academic future —and even they were unsure. For one, this change reflected personal failures in attempting to achieve an advanced degree. But for the rest, it was the result of cumulative events which had tainted the last institution which had seemed exempt from the corruption of society. It is true that six of the ten were still in school at least part-time. But the majority of these were taking advantage of the campus as a place to bide their time while generating new political perspectives. Even the one who was most definite about his long-term plans (he wanted to be a sociologist) was now having second thoughts after his involvement in the Columbia University crisis. More typical responses were:

I have no real long-term plans. I intend to keep working where I am [black cultural revolution center] or go to Chicago and do similar work, unless I'm in jail.

I am currently seriously thinking over my long-term plans. Do I really want to be a college professor [he is currently working as a computer programmer]? I just don't know.

I still might possibly teach or do something related to publishing. . . . Or I might go back to [Africa] or a similar place if I can get an interesting position. Or I might try to write some fiction.

Three of the radicals flatly stated that they had no idea whatsoever of what they might do in the long-run.

Of course, it is possible that many will return to the academic fold after the shock of academic fallibility subsides and the pressure for a career decision mounts. Meanwhile, most of these radicals share in a sense of drift and rootlessness. Certainly they move around more than our other respondents; three of them had been abroad, and all but one had lived in at least two different communities since 1965. This drifting was not confined to geography. Four had mentioned potential fiancées at the beginning of the SCOPE summer, but none of them mentioned being married or even engaged four years later. Withal, it is difficult to predict any sort of specific future for these young men. Meanwhile their sense of drift both feeds and feeds on their vision of a society adrift in polluted seas.

REFORMISTS

In an age of confrontation politics and violent tension, scholar and public alike tend to divide the world into radicals and nonradicals, thereby neglecting some important intervening types. Among these are the reformists, those nonalienated activists who care without bitterness. Here are the committed ameliorators, the part-time shoulders for full-time burdens, those who, perhaps naively, act with faith in a better future.

Among the respondents, the reformists include a girl who worked with neighborhood legal aid centers in poverty areas, two members of church-related service organizations, a Headstart teacher, three other teachers who were committed to working in ghetto schools, and a part-time politician who spent his off-hours lecturing to churches and other groups on civil rights and the black revolution. In all, this category embraces thirteen of the forty respondents and is the largest of the four groups. But this should not be surprising. This is a group that had to change least, since SCOPE was itself more of a reformist than a radical venture. These are the volunteers who kept going despite frustration and without turning against the society itself. One indication that these respondents continued in the spirit of the SCOPE experience is that four of the thirteen, but only one of the other twenty-seven, stayed in the South at the end of the summer and went on the Meredith march in Mississippi during the summer of 1966. Of those who left the South, four felt guilty about it. Three (including one who was returning to a wife and child he had not seen for two months) commented almost identically that they had left only to "continue my education so that I can be of more worth to similar projects in the future."

Most of these reformists share the general characteristic of stability. Many mentioned that the summer had had no basic effect on their values. "I felt that my political attitudes and beliefs were fairly well crystallized by the time I got to Atlanta. The experiences with SCLC had the impact of giving me a considerable amount of political experience and understanding." Even the youngest of the reformists, who had just graduated from high school in 1965, said, "My parents and environment gave me my values regardless of whether or not I went south, . . . but the summer was good personal contact with the meaning of poverty and discrimination."

On the other hand, a few of the reformists did report substantial change, although not of a sort that led to radicalism. Consider for example the note of practicality in the recollections of one: "The summer had quite an effect on me. I know now that I'll always be involved in politics. I realized there in the South how important practical action is. I realized how important a poverty program was. I kind of began to realize what was important and what wasn't. I had never done anything before. I had known only about ten blacks before, and not really *known* them. I got to know them as people during the summer. I let down some of the barriers. I now have black friends. The summer opened my mind to the fact that there was more than Catholicism. I had been engaged to a Catholic and that kind of broke off. I came to realize that many intelligent people had other religions besides Catholicism." Clearly this respondent was influenced by the summer to continue as an activist. And yet this is an activism without alienation, perhaps because the respondent is too new to activism for its setbacks to produce the bitterness from which alienation may develop.

Turning to aspirations for the future, the reformists are more likely to have well-crystallized career conceptions than the radicals. Indeed, reformists are also more likely to be conventionally employed. Ten of the thirteen held full-time jobs at the time of the interview, although one of these was in the army and another was serving alternatively in the Public Health Service. All but one of the remaining employed were working in jobs related to their long-term career plans. The exception was also the only reformist who indicated uncertainty concerning his career plans. However, the uncertainty is understandable in light of his recent change from a novitiate priest to a nonreligious graduate student and campaign manager for a legislative candidate. This former volunteer described his recent life with masterly understatement: "I discarded some old values and picked up some new." Like many, he reports having undergone "a confused kind of time" after the assassination of Martin Luther King, Jr. In many ways, in fact, this respondent seems much like the radical students described previously, and it is worth repeating that the boundary between the categories is more impressionistic than concrete. Still, despite his wrenching changes, he did not seem alienated. He retained a faith in society, if not in religion. He was confident of his future, although he would probably take more time than most to get there.

We have noted that the reformists had a more stable life style than the radicals. But stability can be a cause as well as a consequence of reformism. Those people who are more stable to begin with may be less inclined and less able to develop the kind of studied unrootedness that characterizes the radical. And one prior factor that helps account for the reformists' stability is their age. Seven of the thirteen reformists were twenty-two or older when they went south in 1965, whereas only six of the other twenty-seven respondents were that old. There is some justification for the radicals' suspicion of those over thirty and for the waggish definition of the liberal as simply a radical with a wife and two children. After all, age generally involves increased pressures and responsibilities, and it is possible that full-time career pursuits are not so much the results of reformism as a factor which inhibits a less conventional political posture. Describing what may prove a common syndrome for many others, one current reformist said, "When I first came back [from SCOPE], I was a real radical about everything, participating in demonstrations and sit-ins. But I've changed a lot since then; I've mellowed considerably."

One particularly strong stabilizing influence on the reformists was their religiosity. As of 1965, ten of the thirteen reported that religion was quite influential in their lives, whereas this was true of only four of the remaining respondents. Eleven of the thirteen reformists came from homes which were either Roman Catholic or Conservative Protestant, while the remaining two were Jewish, including one who was Orthodox. By contrast, seven of the ten radicals came from homes in which there was comparatively little religious influence, including two who had no religious affiliation, three who were Unitarians or Universalists, and two who were only nominally Jewish. In all, only ten of the twenty-seven nonreformists came from basically religious backgrounds. The comparative importance of religion to the reformists was also evidenced in another way. On the prequestionnaire, the volunteers were asked several questions concerning "the three persons closest to you, other than your parents." Seven of the thirteen reformists selected a religious figure among the three, as compared to only three of our other twenty-seven respondents. Of the religious figures mentioned by the reformists, six of the seven had themselves participated in civil rights demonstrations, including Father James Groppi who was to become famous as leader and advisor to the Milwaukee Youth Commandos of the NAACP.

Finally, it is worth remarking on the social class backgrounds of the reformists (and of the disengaged) as opposed to the class backgrounds of the radicals (and of the drop-outs). The critical issue is the relation between social class and alienation. If one were to follow a strict economic formulation, one would predict that alienation should increase the lower one goes in the class hierarchy. But here we find evidence for the opposite. Of the forty respondents interviewed, only eleven were from working- or lower-class homes. Of these eleven, nine were either reformists or disengaged, both of which are categories defined by a lack of alienation. Of course, this is a precarious sample from which to generalize to other civil rights volunteers, let alone the population at large. At the same time, the finding complements increasing evidence with better methodological pedigree as cited in Chapter One. The fact is that the alienated radicals and drop-outs of today are disproportionately middle-class among students at large. Even among blacks, alienation seems to be more pronounced in leaders from the middle-class than in followers from the ghetto. Apparently, there is something about high status in a society of affluence that is conducive to alienation. Indeed, it may be precisely here that our simplified conception of alienation is convergent with more intricate interpretations, including the Marxian. To Marx, the alienated individual is first and foremost estranged from self so that he sees himself as an unacceptable outsider.[4] In order to be alienated from society as a whole it may be necessary to identify one's self with that society. Insofar as high status is more likely to facilitate that identification than is low status, high status may indeed produce alienation under accentuated conditions of guilt. This is not to equate high status with alienation. Rather it is to suggest that high status is one of a number of predisposing factors to this complex sociopsychological reaction—a reaction more complex than hostility itself.

THE DISENGAGED

For every student who responded to the challenge of the southern civil rights movement in the 1960s, there were hundreds with similar beliefs who remained behind to tend to other business. And many of those who did volunteer returned to other business once the experience was over. These are the people we call the disengaged. We refer to disengagement not from society but rather from the movement. Neither activists nor alienated, these are often people who have been one or both and moved away. Like most of us, they remain interested and generally informed; they may even sign a petition now and then or give money to local political candidates or perhaps spend time in distributing leaflets and canvassing neighborhoods. For the most part, however, their political beliefs and activities have become submerged beneath the conventional concerns of family, career, education, and recreation.

Ten of the respondents qualify as disengaged. For many, participation in the movement was a kind of ultimate test of their public efficacy, and having failed it, they turned inward to more personal pursuits. For example, one described his current feelings by saying, "I'm not greatly interested in political organizations, and marches or protests now. I'm more interested in improving myself, in my spiritual development, in the way I reach and handle other people." Another made a similar point, but identified the transition as part of her growing maturity: "I'm not sure that I could get involved again politically. It's not that I'm disenchanted with politics, it's just that personally I couldn't do that sort of thing now. I've studied the problem a lot since that summer, gone deeper into it, and now I feel that these sorts of things affect people personally, so there are other aspects of the problem that are important besides politics. My personal interests have changed; I'm very interested in literature and philosophy now, and I guess I've matured since then." These remarks describe

---

[4] For a sample of Marx's writings on alienation, see T. D. Bottomore and M. Rubel (Eds.), *Karl Marx: Selected Writings in Sociology and Social Philosophy* (London: Watts, 1956), especially pp. 167–177.

the end point of the disengagement process, but some reached it more quickly than others. In fact, a few had almost reached this point before the SCOPE summer began. These were volunteers who thought of the summer all along as only an episode in their lives, an interesting and noble experience, but one defined as temporary from the start. These people fully expected to disengage at the end of the summer and did so.

On the other hand, most of the respondents in this group phased out of their activism more gradually. We mentioned one of these at the beginning of the chapter to illustrate how a few volunteers had shifted among the four types since 1965. This was the girl who stayed in the South until the end of that year and then returned to Chicago where she "had a job during the day, and at night . . . worked for SCLC." At that time, hers was still a full-blown activism; SCLC was her primary commitment, and she lived in a house with the local SCLC staff. This period lasted roughly a year, but the frustrations began to accumulate in the North much as they had in the South. Finally, she left SCLC and enrolled in law school, and was learning to fly an airplane. She was enjoying them both, although she was not particularly committed to becoming a lawyer either.

This is the sort of political decompression typical of the disengaged. For one, it involved working as a social worker for a year after her SCOPE experience. Another organized a SCOPE group for the summer of 1966 and took it south before returning to school and leaving the movement. Several reported participating in 1965 in campus activities and demonstrations concerning the war in Vietnam. Two were briefly involved in tutoring projects after they returned from SCOPE.

The disengaged have one obvious distinguishing characteristic in that eight of the ten are females. Indeed, we see shortly that three of our four drop-outs are also females, indicating that women may not be good bets for sustained activism of any sort. Twentieth century suffragism notwithstanding, we noted that males are more exposed to social pressures and societal follies. They are also expected to achieve masculine mastery over their contexts, alienating or otherwise. The feminine role continues to be more passive, and normative conventions quite naturally channel feminine energies into the life of the family. In fact, the disengaged were the most marriage-oriented group of all. Four were married at the time of the reinterview, including one who had been engaged and two who had mentioned potential fiancees before going south in 1965. Two more of the girls mentioned getting married as an element in their *career* plans. One of the males in this category had had a potential fiancee before going south but indicated somewhat plaintively on the second questionnaire that the summer had "cost him his girl friend."

In sum, the disengaged are those who have returned not only to school and to career, but also to close interpersonal relationships, many of which had been established before the summer of 1965. Although we have no further information on the matter, it is possible that these volunteers returned to such conventionalities precisely because they had a niche awaiting them. In any event, the point is not so much that they are different from the rest of the volunteers, but that they are so similar to the rest of their generation. For all of the talk and agony surrounding both activism and alienation, those without either remain by far the most common.

As a postscript, however, it is worth mentioning again that the boundaries between the four categories are somewhat diaphanous, and it was sometimes difficult to decide where to place a respondent. For example, we mentioned that three persons fell between the categories of reformist and disengaged. In one case, the army put at least a temporary quietus on his political activities, although he planned to become a lawyer specializing in civil liberties cases. A second former volunteer was teaching in a small midwestern college. In his spare time—and it was clearly not his principal commitment—he led discussion groups on Vietnam and advised the eighteen black students at the college. As for the third enigma, he was also teaching but in a school located in a predominantly black community. He was teaching partly in order to avoid the draft but also because he had designs on a teaching career. His comments on the SCOPE summer are very similar to those of the disengaged. "The summer was very upsetting. I had no political sense before. I was kind of a do-gooder, but I had no idea how to get things done. By the end of summer I was sour and bitter about the chances of much change. The bitterness hasn't lasted permanently, but the tone of how hard it is, a kind of resignation, has lasted." And yet this respondent had helped to organize a group of welfare mothers, worked a little for McCarthy, and tried to stop a superhighway from displacing the heart of the black community in which he was teaching. Withal, he is a difficult man to categorize, which may say more about our categories than about him.

DROP-OUTS

From the standpoint of the traditional liberal, the most mystifying reaction to social injustice is that of the drop-out. "Why," asks the liberal, "if you feel so strongly about what is wrong and hypocritical in our society, don't you try to do something about it instead of simply turning your back?" The drop-out's answer may take the form of another question: "Well, what about doing the following—and will you help me?" But the liberal is apt to respond, as he has in the past, "Perhaps that's too much for now; in any event, I don't think I could become involved in anything quite so drastic." To this, of course, the drop-out may reply in turn, "You see. You want me to do something, but you don't want me to do what really has to be done and you won't help me. Go away and come back when your back is against the wall too." And so the liberal retreats; in fact he may effectively drop-out in his own more comfortable fashion.

Dropping-out in the face of real or incipient alienation is a long-established response, one to which religion is very much in debt as an obvious case in point. In this study, however, we are *not* dealing with people who learned to drop-out from the very beginning as a part of a fatalistic subculture. Our respondents withdraw much later and only after a great deal of frustration in attempting to change the society.

Although only four of forty qualified as drop-outs, the proportion is no doubt an underestimate for former SCOPE workers as a whole. After all, one characteristic of drop-outs is that they live more commonly in out-of-the-way places and are not easily accessible by long-distance telephone. In fact, during the interviews there were frequent allusions to others who might also fit the description. For example: "Many of the SCOPE workers I know are doing the hippie drug bit in California." "The girl I worked with moved into the East Village in New York, copped out altogether, went out only with blacks, was antiestablishment, and the like." "One of the girls on the project quit school and worked. She lived north of San Francisco in the mountains someplace. Then she quit work and just lived there." Of the four we did manage to locate, two would be quickly labeled hippies, and the others are more accurately described as drifters who manifested their alienated malaise through an almost studied rejection of the usual modes of life.

The two hippies were among the most cooperative and eager interviewees of the entire forty, although their alienation was quite clear. One who lived in the Haight-Ashbury district of San Francisco described her life by saying, "We don't have a radio, or television, or read newspapers. No commitments of any kind. Just a drop-out. This summer we [she and her boyfriend] are planning to go to India to try life in a different culture. I hope that it will let me change emotionally and socially. . . . The power structure in this country is such that no activism makes a difference." The other, who had been using various drugs over an extended period of time and "wants to use the insights that come from drugs," said, "I now think there should be no movements. Things should be on a more personal basis. With love we will help without causes. The trouble with causes is that the people involved forget about love."

The two drifters were somewhat different. One is a girl who had originally planned a career in social work but had been plagued by self-doubts. In fact, at the beginning of SCOPE she listed as one of her most important worries an "inability to accept myself and hence others." After she left the South, she "visited around" for a time and then lived with her parents for four months while seeking a job somewhat half-heartedly. Although a college graduate, she finally accepted employment as a clerical worker and moved into the North Beach section of Los Angeles. Two years later she quit, and at the time of the interview she had not worked for four months. This did not concern her. In fact, she had lost interest in working, was absolutely (almost resolutely) without long-term plans, and anticipated only "playing it by ear." Her sole political activity during this period had been "a couple of peace marches" in 1967. She no longer felt that projects should be oriented to specific goals, but rather that they should operate on a people-to-people level. Even so, she could generate little enthusiasm or hope.

Finally, the one male classified as a drop-out was also a wanderer and seemingly unconcerned with the usual standards of achievement. He played the guitar "badly," but spent his time "bumming" from Mexico to the East Coast washing dishes, playing for little or no money, and thinking vaguely about the possibility of returning to school. He had been one of the youngest volunteers in 1965, still in high school. After graduation he entered college, but not for long. Eventually he may go back to school, "I guess." "I'm not married, so I work when I want to or need money or something. I like freedom from responsibility."

This phrase, "freedom from responsibility," characterizes the drop-outs in a broad, political sense as well. As compared to the similarly alienated but activist radicals, most of the drop-outs are trying to shuck the burden of caring, having found it so heavy in the past. And yet it is not easy to discard a commitment once felt so deeply. In fact, it may be so difficult that drugs and total isolation are the only way for them to achieve nirvana. In this sense the drop-outs are rarely successful in achieving the kind of personal catharsis and disaffiliation they seek. Old hopes and ideologies continue to prowl about in their lives, however unwanted. Many attempt to manifest their freedom by "doing their thing," but this is sometimes a grim and desperate charade.

NOTES ON THE DYNAMICS OF POLITICAL DISILLUSIONMENT

Throughout this chapter we have played on the differences among the SCOPE volunteers some four years after the summer of 1965. In using the twin dimensions of alienation and activism to define the four distinct categories of radicals, reformists, disengaged, and drop-outs, we tried to show some of the variegated after-effects of a shared episode in the continuing saga of political protest. Because the volunteers were heterogeneous when they arrived in the South initially, they were almost sure to be heterogeneous later. Not only did their experiences vary in the South itself, but the impact of these experiences was filtered through a host of other differences in backgrounds, abilities, aspirations, and the interpersonal contexts to which they returned.

But there are similarities as well. Despite their individual reactions to the summer and its problems, all of the volunteers continue to *think* about the issues, although in some cases against their wishes. Formally, all are either liberal or further to the left, and most retain an emotional involvement as well. Confront them with political questions, trigger again their memories of the summer, and much of their interest returns along with at least some of the passion and a host of ideas concerning what will work and what will not. There is, however, a tone of disillusionment that has persisted and even intensified in the intervening four years. Of course, they are disillusioned to various degrees—the drop-outs and the radicals more than the disengaged, and all three more than the reformists. At the same time, only a few with whom we spoke could muster quite the same zeal that had been so apparent in June of 1965. Most now agree, as they did not immediately after the experience of the summer, with the basic thrust of black power and with the peripheral utility of white activism in behalf of the black.[5] A number are haunted by the blatant contrast between their own lives and the lives they left behind. Many still feel that the intimacies they shared with one or two local Negroes are among their most beautiful and poignant experiences, but for most these intimacies have blurred into a dream-like past and are no longer an on-going reality. Thus, although many wrote letters for awhile, this quickly tapered off to a Christmas card, and finally to nothing at all. Of the forty volunteers interviewed, only six (all classified as reformists) still maintained communication. Others are perhaps too embarrassed at how little was done despite the enthusiasm of the moment. Although none feel that their original objectives were false, all have been sobered by the obstacles to fulfillment.

In light of this common disillusionment, it is hardly surprising that only one-fourth of our respondents were radicals after an intervening four years. In fact several other studies of student activists report similar conclusions after follow-ups. For example, Solomon and Fishman[6] find

---

[5] It is worth repeating here a point noted earlier. Volunteers may have been slow to admit limitations on the role of whites in the movement as part of the cognitive dissonance syndrome. That is, such admissions were quite dissonant with the idealism originally taken south. Hence, it may have taken a while for the mix to mellow and for support of black power to become acknowledgeable.

[6] F. Solomon and J. R. Fishman, "Youth and Social Action: II. Action and Identity Formation in the First Student Sit-in Demonstration," *The Journal of Social Issues*, 1964, 20 (2), 36–45.

that the black students involved in the initial sit-ins of 1960 faced an identity crisis all over again in pondering where to go from there in their personal careers. On the one hand, many despaired over the lack of success in the movement itself and were led back to more conventional pursuits; on the other hand, the prospects of returning to the mainstream also elicited despair in its own terms. Or consider Keniston's psychological study of fourteen radicals involved in the 1967 Vietnam Summer project.[7] Keniston notes that only a fraction of those who had participated in the movement came to think of themselves as radicals. Indeed, Keniston uses the term *radical* far more selectively than most in reserving it for those who, having participated in an activist episode, continue to think of themselves as radicals. The point is that participation within a movement does not insure a long-term radical career. Participation may be viewed as more of an intervening test than an ultimate criterion.

Even now it is difficult to predict how our respondents will see the world and themselves after another four years. As with Keniston's group, "psychological change, the movement for social change, and the changing modern world are linked in them. This linkage means that predictions about their futures are extraordinarily difficult."[8] At a chronological age which often fosters a kind of floating suspension between statuses, and in an age undergoing agonizing problems, the volunteers face a problematic future.

[7] Keniston, *The Young Radicals, op. cit.*
[8] *Ibid.,* p. 217.

CHAPTER VII

Politics and Studentry in a Post-Idealistic Phase

$\mathbb{I}$t is said that no man lives in a vacuum, and only the scholar-scientist is licensed to pretend so. But any such pretensions here would be fatuous. This is a book about a series of events and emotions which continue to haunt us like the spirit of a world that might-have-been. It is a volume about idealism, but also about a less than ideal denouement. Although the data pertain only to one small group involved in one specific program, they can hardly be understood without reference to the broad context which we have sought in turn to illumine.

The research and writing have coincided with pivotal periods in two related developments in society. The first concerns the substance and style of national politics. The change from optimism to pessimism between 1960 and 1970 was so great that only prophets with strong masochistic streaks now peer into the decade ahead. A second development involves the general area of students, student activism, and the structure of higher education. Changes which many professors would have regarded as grounds for resignation a decade ago are now being accepted with relief as compromise settlements. Students once chided for apathy have ventured out into society and have taken the university with them.

Without hazarding a definitive treatment of either of these trends, we want to ponder them both. More like crude twine than sparkling ribbon with which to tie the volume off, these remarks serve partly as a disavowal that any single study can capture the capricious essences of a complex society. In hazarding judgments concerning such complexity, we rely on our general perceptions as much as on the data presented in the preceding chapters. We also give vent to personal concerns as well as to sociological considerations. All three of us are roughly of the same political ilk and share similar ego and status pigeonholes. We are too young to identify with the fiftyish men of national and local prominence, whom we discuss in the first part of the chapter; we are too old not to have lost some of our lingering identity with students, whom we consider in the second part. In many ways, we write from a position in the middle — and with an uneasy feeling of being caught there.

NATIONAL POLITICS AND RADICAL CHANGE

At several points during the book, we have contrasted the national civil rights mood of 1965 with that of today. At the time of SCOPE, there was little question that the mass of national public opinion was in favor of major changes—at least in the South. It is true that the number who actually went south as volunteers was but a tiny minority, but it was a minority acting in behalf of a much larger proportion which approved means as well as ends. The South was anything but eager to make concessions, as indicated by its Jim Clarks and its "Bull" Conners. But there was a feeling that these types were shrinking and that the time had come for national medicine for regional cancers. Equal educational opportunity, integrated public accommodations, and full voting rights were constitutionally provided for; surely implementing legislation and enforcement were now at hand.

Obviously there has been some change on these terms. No one who knew the South fifteen, ten, or even five years ago would hold that it is the same today. Over the long run, this society has probably changed more rapidly in response to more social problems than any society with a continuing constituted government in history. By any absolute measure, the United States of 1970 has less poverty, less racism, and even less civil violence than past eras. But of course the past has little relevance to activists looking to the future. And from this perspective it is clear that the millennium has not materialized.

Today the de jure triumphs of the Civil Rights Movement appear to many as de facto defeats. As the movement moved north, its goals grew increasingly diffuse and amorphous and were no longer covered by constitutional provisions. Slums are not easily done away with by political fiat, and poverty is far more complicated and deeply-rooted than most had realized. All of these problems are exacerbated when the nation's attention and its funds are drained by a divisive war. Vietnam has both preempted and fragmented much of the activist effort. Moreover, activism itself has become a major bone of contention, as it has grown strident and desperate in a political context which seems repressive in reaction. In short, we have moved in the short span of five years from a period in which the bloom of the liberal dream was beginning to blossom to a time in which a chill has begun to numb and perhaps to deaden.

It is against this general backdrop that the current mood of activism must be assessed, for activists are responding to the society around them as well as to their individual needs. And yet the status of the society and the prospects for change are too important to be left to quick assertions or facile assumptions. Before we consider the activists' reactions, we need to delve into detail concerning the political scene at issue. To what extent is their pessimism for the future really justified? In our view, it is difficult to defend anything other than pessimism from the perspective of those who seek not simply change but radical change today rather than tomorrow. Although sociology and the activist ideology may disagree on some crucial particulars, they do concur in their estimates of how difficult it is to effect such change. Many would disagree that radical change is necessarily desirable, but given some inevitable unhappy by-products and few assurances of ultimate success, the issue before us concerns not so much the desirability of radical change but its feasibility.

If one asks what the possible sources of change in American society are, the answer is plausibly four-fold, according to both accredited political theoreticians and activist perceptions. The four categories emerge from the intersection of two distinctions. On the one hand there is a distinction between change manipulated from the top (*power elite, power structure*) and change in response to pressure from the mass (*grass roots, participatory democracy*). On the other hand one can distinguish between change originating at the national level and change which accumulates from the local scene. Let us examine the resulting combinations.

POWER: STRUCTURES, ELITES, AND VACUUMS

In listening to the contemporary left, one infers that the devil is incarnate not in a man but in some supraindividual named, interchangeably, Power Elite or Power Structure. Both refer to some small group of *haves* who sit at the top manipulating situations in accord with their own interests. But although the two terms have been blurred, they should not be regarded as synonymous.[1] Indeed, there is a sense in which they are mutually exclusive. A true elite may be defined by its ability to transcend the structures which hobble lesser influentials; a power structure, on the other hand, may be onerous because it lacks the wherewithal to act at all. Structure can be strangulating as well as expediting.

What is new in the area of civil rights is that this dilatory aspect of the national power network has become more and more dominant. The progress of the late fifties and early sixties, although sparked and spurred by the Civil Rights Movement, was clearly the result of actions by national elites. The Supreme Court decisions, the various legislative actions, and the stance of the national media all supported change. These actions were particularly effective in securing constitutional rights for blacks, especially as the weight of national power was brought to bear primarily on the much weaker communities of the South. As the issues moved from these constitutional and regional issues to broad questions of the life style and life chances of American blacks, national power became less efficacious and national elites less helpful. It is one thing to force the opening of public accommodations, schools, or voting booths. It is another to create new lives and to achieve a basic redistribution of goods and services. The implementation of these positive policies relies on an enormously complex

---

[1] For a recent representation of this diversity, see M. Aiken and P. E. Mott, *The Structure of Community Power: An Anthology* (New York: Random House, 1970).

organization, requiring countless decisions and activities over which no one man or small group of men can exert quick control.

In this context, it is useful to distinguish between two types of power, one negative in the sense of preventing change and protecting the status quo; the other positive in the sense of initiating change and producing new programs and priorities. There are certainly a variety of elites with negative power, and these are especially influential because there is no comparable set of elites with respect to positive power. Where initiating change is concerned, the power structure usually resembles a *power vacuum* much more than a power elite. This is the case not only with civil rights but perhaps even more so with national foreign policy, where even the theory of democratic partisanship is foregone in the absence of direct involvement and in the interests of patriotic, bipartisan support.

The issue turns less than many suppose on the political stripe or personal inclination of those nominally in charge. The impotence of the power structure is more a function of an organizational complexity so severe as to sap initiative and perpetuate policies out of inertia rather than conviction.[2] The wielders of negative power seem more personally influential than they actually are, since the weight of organizational conservatism serves as their ally. On the other hand, those seeking positive power are frustrated by factors which seem to defy single-handed intervention and reversal. Bureaucracies are designed to implement policies rather than to change them. Certainly the largest bureaucracy in the world can be expected to tie its leaders to the path of the past rather than to the wave of the future. It is one thing to favor governmental restraint borne out of wisdom, but it is quite another to favor restraint caused by organizational incapacity.

So much for a brief appraisal of the national power scene and its ability to produce rapid change. What of its *local* counterpart? In some situations, the analysis can be applied intact, as in large metropolitan areas whose governments are similarly constipated through bureaucratization. But in thousands of smaller communities, the position of the local power figures is quite different. Traditionally white, these men have been the bane of civil rights radicals everywhere—but perhaps for the wrong

---

[2] The notion of the organization eclipsing the individual is, of course, a leitmotif for the twentieth century, one originally orchestrated by Max Weber among several other European social commentators at the turn of the century. Indeed, this notion can be seen as Weber's principal contribution to sociology and his principal advance over Karl Marx. Far more than simply adding dimensions of status and power to the Marxian construct of individual class stratification, Weber argued that the individual of any class paled increasingly before the onslaught of bureaucratization and the organizational monolith. In this sense, he would have appreciated R. C. Townsend's popular *Up the Organization* (New York: Knopf, 1970).

reasons. Precisely because there is less bureaucratization in these communities than in metropolitan areas, there is more potential flexibility. And insofar as community leaders have been depicted statistically as disproportionately educated, liberal, and amenable to change, this flexibility might well be used to produce the sort of change at issue. After all, community influentials have a considerable stake in the well-being of the community as a whole. They own and run the bus lines which are boycotted; they operate the retail stores which are burned; they control the land to which outside industry could be attracted. Because it is very much in their interests to maintain community stability, many of these influentials have found themselves moderating the disputes between antagonistic white and black communities. And even if stability should be purchased at the price of very severe change, such influentials are in a position to pay a corresponding price to avoid the burden. Thus, if public schools are integrated, private schools are feasible; if neighborhoods are integrated, theirs is likely to be among the last; if taxes are increased to provide greater welfare services, their sacrifice involves a much smaller marginal cost than would apply to the lower-middle and working classes.

And yet there are complicating factors. For one, it makes a difference whether one is talking of elected elites or those elites which gravitate to influence by appointment—self or otherwise. Whereas the appointed often have considerable latitude as a result of their insulation from the political process, the elected are frequently hobbled by a constituency which is far more begrudging in its view of change. For example, an appointed school board has the opportunity to be more progressive than one which is elected, although it obviously matters who is making the appointments. A city manager system may be better able to implement change than a mayoralty system, although again it matters to whom a city manager is responsible. It is probably no accident that most of the change that has already occurred in civil rights has stemmed from the appointed judiciary rather than from elected judges or from the legislative branch of the government.

Obviously this argument points to a position quite the reverse of the radical view: the problem is not the existence of power elites but rather their absence. If only there were indeed a small group of men in control either nationally or locally, one could at least hope to impress on them the grave need for change and know that change might ensue. Lacking such elites, one faces either strangulation through structure at the national, state, and metropolitan level or suffocation through electoral conservatism on the small-town scene. And yet elitism has always been a risky business and at best a gamble with very high stakes. Although elites do have the instrumental capacity to produce change, they are the least *needful* of change. Moreover, they can produce change which is repugnant to their community fellows. This curbs our own elitist sentiments, just as it has curbed the elitism of democratic theorists everywhere.

Returning to the local community, however, there is one more constraint that would operate even with an elite of the most beneficent and foresighted variety. We have indicated repeatedly that the issues have changed since the early sixties and have become more diffuse and more economic. The changes now demanded are frequently beyond the power of local influentials, and require federal money if not federal rulings. Certainly it is difficult to imagine most local communities mobilizing sufficient resources on their own to produce a radical increase in economic benefits to welfare members or to a school system. The mayors of our wealthiest cities argue its impossibility. The fact is that federal aid is crucial, and this returns us to the depressing portrait of the national power structure. In sum, it is little wonder that traditional power sources have done little in the past and are doing little today to produce massive change. But if change cannot be produced from the top, there is a long-standing alternative which has been central to recent radical rhetoric.

GRASS ROOTS AND THE DEMOCRATIC ALTERNATIVES

So far our analytic skepticism would seem to constitute a brief for democracy. If the power structure is unable to produce change, the populace offers a classic source of prodding through the polls.[3] Although few recent studies of policy-formation and change have taken conventional democracy seriously, the radicals have called for a reassessment. What then is the mood at the grass roots?

There was a time when the job of estimating public opinion invited crude and self-serving intuition on the part of pundits who re-

---

[3] Debate over the power elite is now focused upon pluralism as the alternative. Thus, some studies, largely by sociologists, argue that elites do indeed stand athwart the decision-making process at both local and national levels; other studies, largely by political scientists, purport to show that an elite image of decision-making is less apt than a pluralistic model. Such a model is often construed as democratic, but there is nothing inherently democratic about pluralism. It refers simply to a situation in which societal decisions are made primarily by the particular institutional sectors affected by the particular issues at hand. Thus, economic issues tend to be decided in the economic sphere; educational decisions tend to be made by educators; and so on. Within any given sphere, however, the decision-making may be either elitist or democratic. Some decisions may involve participatory democracy of the grassiest variety; others may be quite autocratic; and both may fit into a structure of pluralistic politics for the society at large. For an early round of the continuing debate here, see C. W. Mills, *The Power Elite* (New York: Oxford Press, 1956) and its review by T. Parsons, "The Distribution of Power in American Society," *World Politics*, 1957, *10*, 123–143. For a recent episode of thrust and reaction, see G. W. Domhoff, *Who Rules America?* (Englewood Cliffs, N.J.: Prentice-Hall, 1967) and its review by N. W. Polsby in the *American Sociological Review*, 1968, *33*, 476–477. See also Aiken and Mott, *op. cit.*

sponded like patients to a projective test. Now (for better or for worse) the question is amenable to relative precision. Public opinion polls have become such a routinized feature of American political life that many have begun to cite their efficacy in creating opinion as well as in measuring it. There can be little doubt that politicians are today more mindful of public opinion than ever before and that some of the politicians' own views are self-consciously framed in response to that opinion.[4] At the same time, the public has greater awareness of the role of the political official than ever before, and is likely to be manipulated in turn by his views— the views of one who supposedly knows all the facts. Sociologists may protest that no political official can have a complete or unbiased catalogue of facts when he is enmeshed in organizational structures subject to such common organizational pathologies as communication distortion. Still, public opinion remains highly manipulable, and this fact together with the concerns of the politicians themselves generates an image of an artificial consensus that may involve little independent consideration of the issues at hand. Thus, the politician generates his positions with an ear for the opinions of the electorate on whom he will depend in the next contest; the electorate in turn develops its opinions on cue from the politician himself. The point is two-fold. First, here is another factor which predisposes American government in a conservative direction. Second, whatever the mood of the nation may be at a single point in time, it should not be regarded as the result of autonomous deliberations. This point is most conspicuous with regard to foreign policy, since most Americans have neither direct interest in nor direct knowledge of, say, Vietnam and are accordingly much more vulnerable to presumed expertise. For a president to cite a majority in support of one policy overlooks the nearly plausible possibility that he might have obtained equal support for the reverse. The situation is not quite as blatant with respect to domestic issues, especially those as highly charged as civil rights. Still, the cycle operates sufficiently to recommend substantial salt in any diet of public opinion polls.

Turning to the substance of those polls, there has been a clear change in white opinion of the Civil Rights Movement, as we have noted. During the early 1960s, a substantial majority of national public opinion supported the southern civil rights movement and its demands for the integration of public accommodations, voting rights, and southern school desegregation. Attracted by the articulate nonviolence of King and the idealistic youth working in his shadow, repelled by the violent response of southern whites, civil rights became a national enthusiasm. Alas, much of this enthusiasm has dissipated and the mood has soured. A number of

[4] See G. E. Reedy, *The Twilight of the Presidency* (New York: World, 1970).

surveys, especially those of Louis Harris in 1963 and again in 1966,[5] indicate that white support for civil rights advances in the area of housing,
welfare, employment, and education suffered a steady diminution as the
movement moved north.

However, note that the change has sometimes been misunderstood
and overestimated. Whites are now more sympathetic than ever before to
the issues of the early 1960s, but they are clearly less sympathetic to the
new issues of the 1970s. Put another way, the ideological distance between
the movement and the white mass is very similar in 1970 to what it was
in 1960. What made the middle 1960s so remarkable was a temporary
reduction of that distance. In short, there has been change, but relative
to the new issues now at hand we have returned to an earlier political
alignment. Today it would be risky at best and self-defeating at worst for
a strong civil rights advocate to voice confidence in the will of the national
majority.

But of course civil rights radicals have long sensed this change of
mood, and blacks have turned to blacks in order to generate new kinds
of force. Actually, the tactic has two forms. The liberal version holds that
blacks should mobilize their members so as to have an impact on elections,
whether as a majority in communities like Fayette, Mississippi and Gary,
Indiana or as a crucial swing vote in other communities and in national
contests. This strategy has had some rewards[6] but is limited by the factors
mentioned earlier concerning elected officials. Gains have hardly been
revolutionary in import even where blacks have actually taken office. Not
only are local officials incapable of resolving economic issues without
federal aid, but frequently these local black officials are anything but
revolutionary in their aims. Most black communities have tended to re-
ward old leaders with these long-awaited opportunities, leaders who either
cannot or choose not to rupture the community as a whole. However, this
strategy leads to a second and more radical strategy of change based on
black grass roots participation. The object is to by-pass much of the conventional electoral route on the theory that where an issue primarily concerns the blacks it should be resolved by blacks without having to go
through the white community at all.

---

[5] Compare and contrast two works by W. Brink and L. Harris: *The Negro
Revolution in America* (New York: Simon and Schuster, 1964) and *Black and
White* (New York: Simon and Schuster, 1967). Subsequent soundings of white
opinions concerning civil rights appear to support an extension of the back-lash
trend indicated in these two works.

[6] See D. R. Matthews and J. W. Prothro, *Negroes and the New Southern
Politics* (New York: Harcourt Brace Jovanovich, 1966) and J. Daniel, "Negro
Political Behavior and Community Political and Socioeconomic Factors," *Social
Forces*, 1969, *47*, 247–280.

This by-passing was a fundamental objective of the SCOPE campaign in the summer of 1965. Although the white volunteers did not subscribe to black power in the sense of excluding white participants and aides, they were seeking to mobilize the black community through an emphasis on political education and community organization. It was assumed that the black community, once aroused, could control its own destiny. It was further taken for granted that such an arousal would be rapid. Recalling that the SCOPE workers were frustrated on this score, however, let us examine the prospects with reference to some currently voguish concepts.

Much has been said concerning a culture of poverty or oppression. But this notion carries a full freight of conceptual ambiguities, and two of its connotations tend to war against each other. The first concerns the extent to which poverty and oppression exert massive psychological constraints on efforts to escape through upward mobility and hence produce a self-perpetuating cycle of increasing despair.[7] Thus, the culture militates against aspirations, motivations, and marketable skills. The very adaptations required to make it within this subculture tend to preclude successful adaptation to the parent society. The second implication of the culture of poverty and oppression has assumed increased currency among radical organizers. Rather than maladaptive or dysfunctional, the subculture is viewed as fundamentally more valid than the parent society which spawned it. Moreover, it is often argued that these cultural pockets (particularly in the urban ghetto) are teeming with potential political resources which have only to be released to save the nation from itself.[8]

---

[7] An early classic of this genre is G. Knupfer, "Portrait of the Underdog," *The Public Opinion Quarterly*, 1947, *11*, 103–114. See also H. H. Hyman, "The Value Systems of Different Classes: A Social Psychological Contribution to the Analysis of Stratification," in R. Bendix and S. M. Lipset (Ed.), *Class, Status, and Power* (New York: Free Press, 1953), pp. 426–442; and the more recent ethnographical treatments such as O. Lewis, *La Vida* (New York: Random House, 1966) and U. Hannerz, *Soulside: Inquiries Into Ghetto Culture and Community* (New York: Columbia University Press, 1969). See also K. B. Clark, *Dark Ghetto* (New York: Harper and Row, 1965) and W. McCord et al., *Life Styles in the Black Ghetto* (New York: Norton, 1969).

[8] This theme has been given loud voice in the literature of the New Left, especially in connection with the importance of grass-roots decision-making. For a scholarly treatment, see C. A. Valentine, *Culture and Poverty: Critique and Counter Proposals* (Chicago: University of Chicago Press, 1968). Two other authors deserve mention. Herbert Marcuse recognizes that the culture of poverty—indeed the culture of American society generally—tends to accommodate more to complacent fatalism than to radical optimism, but he argues that it is the intellectual's task to nip any complacency in the bud and to sow the seeds of radicalism wherever possible since men are truly alive only in the midst of purposeful misery rather than of aimless contentment. See, for example, his *One-Dimensional Man* (Boston: Beacon, 1964). Theodore Roszak's *The Making of a Counter Culture* (Garden City, N.Y.: Doubleday, 1969) argues that if the ghetto does not provide such a culture at the moment, youth does, and hope lies in a marriage between the

Given the proper leadership and a properly positive identity, these are the people who can turn it around for themselves and for the rest of us. Skills that have been honed in response to oppression are the skills required to remake society at large.

There are obvious inconsistencies between these two interpretations. Proponents of the former might well charge that proponents of the latter fail to appreciate the real burdens of poverty and oppression as these are manifest in fatalism, frustration, and political apathy. On the other hand, advocates of the radically optimistic view tend to regard the first perspective as unduly patronizing in foreclosing the political destiny of a substantial segment of the society. In large part, the dispute reflects the perpetual political tension between what is and what ought to be.

If the SCOPE volunteers are at all credible as informants, it is instructive to recall that many arrived in the South with idealistic visions of the southern black culture only to leave with less hopeful images. But the point is not to advocate one position to the exclusion of the other. We do not mean to abandon hope. Radical movements might be defined as forces seeking rapid convergence between what is and what ought to be. And as current radicalism continues within the ghetto, it could become a crucial intervening factor in producing a transition from one implication of the culture of oppression to the other.

Some of this transition has already occurred. But it has not been easy in the past and it is not likely to be in the future. Despite efforts to promote black militancy, the general mood of the black community is far from militant, however much its political self-consciousness has been stirred. Whether one examines the findings of survey research[9] or participant observation,[10] Negroes by and large have continued to identify more with aspects of the current white society than with visions of any society of the future, black or otherwise. It is true that events have grown violent and voices shrill over the past several years. Nevertheless, the country is not yet polarized by mass revolutionary sentiment—much to the chagrin of the revolutionaries themselves.

---

ghetto of today and the youth of tomorrow. Roszak illustrates a continuing tendency on the part of radical intellectuals to treat subcultures as if they were on the verge of becoming dominant. This is the element of hope that sustains them.

[9] See G. T. Marx, *Protest and Prejudice* (New York: Harper and Row, 1967). When Marx's book first appeared in 1966 based almost entirely on 1964 data, it was scorned as out of date by many who claimed that major advances in black militancy had occurred since then. For this later edition, however, Marx did a thorough review of more recent data and discovered that his initial conclusions remained justified. As dramatic as national events have been in the interim, changes in public values and attitudes have been far less dramatic. There is no doubt some truth to Whitney Young's oft-cited remark to the effect that the Black Power Movement includes a handful of militants and an army of journalists.

[10] See E. Liebow, *Tally's Corner* (Boston: Little-Brown, 1967).

REVOLUTIONARY ASPIRATIONS AND REALITY

We have considered a number of possible sources of radical change from within the system. Although we have disagreed with the radicals over specifics, we concur with their fundamental pessimism. Is it any wonder that those most impatient for change should think increasingly in terms of revolution and an effort to tear down in order to rebuild? It helps little to document instances in which the society and the structure have already changed in the desired direction. From the radical's perspective, the issue is not so much where we have been but where we are going, and progress at a snail's pace is only adequate for snails. The fact is that poverty, racism, and civil violence all remain, not to mention violence perpetuated abroad. We all suffer increasingly from the one massive revolution that has already occurred; namely, a revolution of knowledge and awareness. Once sensibilities have been aroused, complacency is precluded.

In this light, what are the prospects for political revolution? The social sciences may offer the ultimate in pessimism, since political revolution is one of the *least* likely sources of change in our society.[11] It is one thing to talk of revolution with Marx and Engels in the context of a political structure that was imposed from the top and widely illegitimate in the eyes of the people. It is quite another to talk of revolution in the context of a nominally democratic government affording great legitimacy and deep roots in the presumably participating electorate. In this country the prerequisites to success are imposing; there is little chance of producing the quick coup d'etat or the typical revolution of the past in which the struggle is rapid, geographically confined, and relatively bloodless. And even if a revolution of this sort did occur, the crucial phase of consolidation would be especially problematic. At this point most revolutions become violent; at this point a revolution in the United States could well become a bloodbath. Although the electorate is manipulable, as we have pointed out, it is only easily manipulable within the symbolic context of the present political structure. But this too has little relevance for the revolutionary himself. From his (and her) standpoint, the relevant con-

---

[11] For instructive data pertinent to the historical pattern of civil violence in America, see H. D. Graham and T. R. Gurr (Eds.), *The History of Violence in America* (New York: Bantam, 1969). As for changing patterns of poverty and racism, there is a plethora of relevant works, but it is important to distinguish throughout between relative and absolute trends. In absolute terms, both poverty and racism have declined. But if one compares the poor with the affluent and the nonwhite with the white, the gaps have widened in some crucial respects. Such relative differences have generally been the more politically explosive. For a masterful elaboration of this and other factors related to political rebellion, see Gurr, *Why Men Rebel* (Princeton, N.J.: Princeton University Press, 1970).

sideration is one which involves needs rather than obstacles to fulfillment. All of which only underscores our current agonies.

So much for a broad and dour overview of the current political scene—one that may be even more depressing than the views of the radicals themselves. Our sociology may be laced with a bit of cynicism, but it seems clear to us that far-reaching changes are required but not likely. In this sense, society is laid up with a wasting disease for which few curative resources are immediately available. We are afflicted by a social structure sadly out of phase with a value system undergoing substantial change. Such change is substantial if only because many now insist on taking values seriously and in undiluted form. Regardless of where one looks for massive change within the system, hopes seem to evanesce—not only with official and unofficial power clusters, but also with the democratic alternatives, even as this entails radicalizing the grass roots. And if change *within* the system is likely to be halting at best, changes *of* the system are even less imaginable. In light of such circumstances, let us examine developments in student activism since the salad days of the middle 1960s.

STUDENT ACTIVISM AND HIGHER EDUCATION

If the decade of the sixties accomplished little else, it did produce a major change in the status of students in the eyes of the nation. Previously regarded as adolescents confined to the political nursery, many suddenly began to play a major role in adult political affairs. In fact, this change from apathy to activism, from frivolousness to deep-seated concern, has been underestimated in several respects.

STUDENTS AS A REFLECTION OF SOCIETY

One minimizing argument is that only a small proportion of students are radicals in any sense. It is difficult to obtain precise data on this subject,[12] but estimates indicate that although the observation is accurate, the implication is misleading. In the past five years or so, student radicalism may have increased from perhaps 2 to 5 per cent representation on the nation's campuses (and potentially violent radicals from about $\frac{1}{10}$ to $\frac{1}{2}$ of 1 per cent). But the more important shift has been in the proportion of potential radicals—that is, liberal students who are sensitive to political issues and can be mobilized with regard to a civil rights episode, a foreign policy decision, or an offensive police action. This group may have increased from 5 to 20 per cent. And if the political stimulus is particularly strong, it could elicit response from as many as 50 per cent of the nation's

[12] See J. W. Scott and Mohammed El-Assal, "Multiversity, University Size, University Quality and Student Protest: An Empirical Study," *American Sociological Review*, 1969, *34*, 702–709.

seven million students. Such estimates suggest that students represent a far more critical political mass than the small numbers of violent and non-violent radicals would indicate. The far right wing of student opinion has also increased somewhat in reaction, but the point is that all of these gains in politicization have been at the expense of the apolitical student of the past, and most of the increase has moved in a liberal-radical direction.

None of this change is surprising if one recalls that this cohort of students shaped its political consciousness in response to a decade of events which followed a recurrent pattern generally identified with the birth of revolutionary movements. It has become a historical commonplace that revolutions derive not from oppression alone but from periods of hope followed by sudden despair. And so it was in the 1960s. Certainly civil rights followed such a pattern as early gains were eclipsed by later reevaluations. Much the same could be said of foreign policy where the hopes surrounding the Test Ban Treaty and the Peace Corps gave way to the disillusionment of Cuba, the Dominican Republic, and Vietnam. More salient still, perhaps, was the succession of national leaders whose appeal to youth was punctuated by sudden and grotesque acts of violence: John Kennedy, then Robert Kennedy, Martin Luther King, Jr., even Malcolm X. As a final instance, there were the rising expectations and ultimate defeat involved in the McCarthy campaign of 1968. All of this has left a particular mark on the impressionable youth of yesterday who have become the cynical students of today.

But there is a second argument which would diminish the impact of student politics. It is often alleged that students can be dismissed in their political significance because they are freakish political creatures, vastly unrepresentative of the nation as a whole. There are a number of respects in which the students are indeed peculiar. For example, they tend to over-represent the white middle-class of American society; they also live within the artificial and less constraining structure of the university which affords them greater time and opportunity for self-expression. And yet the concerns which students are expressing today are not those traditionally associated with the white middle-class. Moreover, there is a sense in which the very absence of constraining roles and responsibilities allows the students to give expressive vent to basic tensions and conflicts which the rest of society suppresses or shunts aside. From this perspective, students may provide one of the most accurate reflections of the inner self of society. They may be the contemporary exemplification of Karl Mannheim's "free floating intellectuals"[13] at a time when the intellectuals them-

[13] K. Mannheim, *Ideology and Utopia* (New York: International Library of Psychology, Philosophy, and Scientific Method, 1936), especially pp. 153–164.

selves have made their way into society at the price of some freedom. That students were frivolous and apathetic in times gone by may have been because society itself was in a period of stagnant complacency. If students today are rife with change and turmoil, it is difficult to deny that this characteristic is common to the nation as a whole. In short, students have a tendency to make manifest what is latent in us all.

STUDENT MOVEMENT PAST AND PRESENT

There are obvious parallels between the radical student movement and the movements in society at large. One of the most profound differences between the civil rights movement of the early and middle 1960s and the current mood on the left concerns the degree to which success could be specifically defined and realistically expected. We have mentioned the mood of optimism and the sense of destiny which characterized many of the volunteers going south for the first time. This same mood seemed to characterize the movement as a whole, even though many of its veterans had come to place it in less roseate perspective. Buoyed by a gathering momentum within the ranks and a series of legislative and judicial advances, the southern movement had concrete objectives and concrete reasons to think that for the first time these objectives were realizable.

By the late 1960s, however, the left had seen a change in issues, and increasing frustration not only produced splits within its ranks but a widening gulf between itself and the broader community of liberal opinion. This frustration produced a deepening sense of desperation which led in turn to the belief that even more radical change was needed. No longer was the object to achieve specific changes in the social structure—now the ends were couched in terms of broad changes in the culture. In Neil J. Smelser's terms, student radicalism had changed from a "norm-oriented" to a "value-oriented" movement.[14] In the process it seemed to have lost touch in some instances with the norms themselves and with the reality of the social structure.

This radicalization has had consequences for the changing basis of student participation. The student activist ceased to regard the university as simply a sympathetic springboard for his operations elsewhere. Partly

[14] N. J. Smelser, *Theory of Collective Behavior* (New York: Free Press, 1963), especially pp. 270–381. This work marks a major departure in the analysis of collective behavior, arguing that it is highly organized, even predictable, in its seemingly capricious course. A scholarly classic in the best sense of discerning order in the midst of intellectual chaos, the book nevertheless has a tendency to give short shrift to the internal dynamics of social movements, preferring instead to focus on their relation to the dynamics of the society at large.

because these operations had been so stymied, the university itself became a target for attack as many students sought to begin the revolution at large by revolutionizing the closest institution at hand. And yet the attack on the university is both less and more than a step in a self-conscious revolutionary plan—less because self-conscious planning tends to be lacking generally among the current student left, and more because the university has a singular and immediate significance for many of these students. Without carrying metaphoric parallels too far, the university resembles the parent who suffocates with understanding and forestalls independence with indulgence. Thus, many students are individually guilt-ridden and ambivalent concerning the university. In this regard, it is appropriate to refer to Lewis Feuer's work on student movements and generational conflict.[15] Feuer advanced the view that the main difference between the new and the old left is that the former has traded its banner of materialistic exploitation for a primary preoccupation with individual alienation. Indeed, as Feuer pointed out, the shift from material oppression to an emphasis on psychological malaise reverses the shift that took place in Karl Marx's own thinking so that the students of today are much more like the young Marx than Marx the gnarled political elder. But Feuer goes further: "The alienation of the generations, the mainspring of student movements, involves an immense social tragedy. It brings a resurgence in action of hitherto unconscious impulses of destruction, of oneself and others. Student movements . . . have a propensity to veer from terrorism to suicidalism."[16]

Such tendencies are no doubt discernible, especially from Feuer's standpoint as a former radical turned skeptic. It is undeniable that the student movement is increasingly concerned with its own psychological problems and that some of its tactics are increasingly militant, even destructive. And yet this change is only part of the transformation at issue. In our judgment, it would be a mistake to see a movement that is born out of personal conflicts across generations as simply an exercise in self-indulgence. As Feuer himself indicates, the thrust continues to drive from a well-intentioned idealism that brooks no hypocrisy in forging a link between the students' own deprivations and those who suffer more directly at the hands of society. The fact is that most student activists are alienated in the name of others as well as for themselves. They retain their identification with the classically oppressed, although this remains more of an identification from afar than the sort of immediate self-involvement which characterized the old left acting in its own behalf. The student continues

15 L. S. Feuer, *The Conflict of Generations* (New York: Basic Books, 1969).
16 *Ibid.*, p. 509.

to aspire to a utopia for all, even though the utopia is more vaguely felt than systematically blueprinted.

This analysis is important if we are to understand the difficulty in predicting the uncertain future of the student movement, let alone the uncertain future of its individual members. This uncertainty is not merely a function of the times or of the ambiguities customarily associated with young adulthood. It is also a consequence of the movement itself.

Because the left is no longer so tied to specific goals and concrete eventualities, it has become all the more capricious in an organizational sense. This flightiness has direct ramifications for its ability to recruit new members and maintain old ones. In Chapter Four, we mentioned the difficulty of simultaneously maximizing both recruitment and commitment within a movement that coheres more around an ideology than around an organizational structure. If the problem was apparent within the civil rights movement of the middle 1960s, it is blatant today. The current left continues to vacillate between a militancy which remains true to its existing members and an attempt to play-down its controversial distinctiveness so as to evangelize. As events shift, and as ideology shifts with them, the membership tends to wax and wane, sometimes dramatically. In sum, the movement has become more of a congeries of factions developing in erratic spurts than a coordinated political surge of smooth evolutionary progression.

Given such circumstances, one can understand not only why the New Left has a special appeal for a special group of students, but also why this appeal tends to be of limited duration. Because the ideological core of the movement is based on the dual premise of self-alienation and vicarious identification with oppressed others, it tends to be limited to those who combine affluence and rolelessness—the limbo of middle-class studentry. The affluence affords access to political opportunity structures and mobilizing bases, such as universities; it also serves as a source of guilt on which the alienation rests. The university years in turn provide a temporary respite from conventional social roles and impede the identification with new ones; they also loosen the constraints on political action. The student combines both these characteristics, but the student status is only temporary.

These circumstances create obvious repercussions for any movement. Hence, let us turn the tables and ask not about the consequences of the movement for its membership, but rather about the consequences of the membership for the movement. Because students have a way of becoming alumni, a student movement faces a perpetual, even perennial, crisis as its actual and potential members change with each student cohort. This fact alone accounts for much of the volatility of student movements, a point elaborated by S. M. Lipset and Philip Altbach.

> One of the main attributes of American student organizations—particularly those concerned with politics—has been instability. Not only do the interests of the "nonconformist" students shift quickly from experimentation with drugs to advocacy of complete sexual freedom, from peace to civil rights, from alienation with any aspect of the real world including revolutionary politics to deep political concern—but a "generation" of students lasts only a relatively short time, three or four years at most, thereby making it difficult to have continuing leadership and ongoing programs. The very commitment of student radical movements to generally nonconformist styles of life in terms of attitudes toward sex, drugs, literature, [and] philosophy tends to give each generation of activists a unique style which cuts it off from those which preceded it and those which may come later. One of the major problems faced by student activist groups is that their participation becomes impossible, and groups which appeared to dominate the campus' political life seemingly disappear a year or two later.[17]

This returns us to the recruitment-commitment dilemma. As Lipset and Altbach point out, recruitment is not easy given the ideological and action commitments which are required for membership. Like the SCOPE chapters which we analyzed in Chapter Four, there is a tendency to react to frustration by upping the ante and resorting to increasingly spectacular and shocking acts as a manifestation of continued perseverance. However, this escalation increases the polarization between the movement and many of its potential members. Such polarization may initiate the cycle again since the failure to attract new members is frustrating in its own right.

Unlike conventional political parties, activist movements can have a great deal of impact despite a small membership; they may provoke both consciences and action without becoming a significant electoral factor. Even in this area, however, the New Left sometimes suffers from several disadvantages. If a movement is to radiate influence beyond its membership, it must rely heavily on a peripheral network of informal commitments which provide links to the population at large.

It is true that student activists are not without support among their peers, their parents, and members of the national press who frequently find them to be more than just good copy. Still these contacts are not as extensive as the students might hope.[18] Just as the students

---

[17] S. M. Lipset and P. G. Altbach, "Student Politics and Higher Education in the United States," *Comparative Education Review*, 1966, *10*, 334.

[18] For an analysis of 1968 political behavior which serves as a rebuttal to some of the students' euphoria and ideology concerning bedfellows past and future, see P. E. Converse, W. E. Miller, J. G. Rusk, and A. C. Wolfe, "Continuity and

feel themselves to be set apart from the general population, the population often returns the sentiment and affords them little credibility and a
great deal of hostility. Moreover there is a tendency for former members
of the student left not to maintain the ties and functions expected of
loyal alumni. Some former students who retain their ideological commitments find that the movement has itself changed to such an extent that
it no longer represents their views. The more common problem, however,
is not that the movement deserts its membership, but rather that the membership itself changes, and former devotees lose much of their commitment
and allegiance. This waning of enthusiasm is not simply a function of a
change from student to nonstudent status. It occurs also because much of
the ideology of the New Left rests not on a systematically developed view
of the world, but on emotions which are subject to rapid change. In this
respect, the current left can again be contrasted to its predecessors. In
lacking a systematic counterpart to Marxian theory for the deductive
analysis of almost any event, the present movement depends more on
emotions alone in sustaining its members' alienation and indignation.
And unlike rigorous overarching theories, emotions do not readily survive changes of role, status, and locale.

The fragility of an emotionally-founded ideology is especially the
case when the emotions are somewhat artificially bred to begin with. Thus,
some students actually *learn* their alienation at the pedagogical feet of
veteran campus radicals. Moreover, the alienation syndrome is often dependent on social rewards and feedback from the group structure of the
activist movement. In this regard, it is no accident that political alienation is often more widely represented among freshmen and sophomores
than among the less lonely and more purposeful upperclassmen and graduate students[19]—although it is true that the small number of graduate
students who *are* involved tend to exert disproportionate influence on the
movement. In any event, to the extent that alienation is a learned emo-
tion, it is likely to dissipate quickly once the student leaves the educational
context. Certainly this is the burden of recent research indicating that
education generally has little permanent effect on student values. And
although the notion can be taken to cynical extremes, it is consistent with
the Marxian emphasis on enduring contexts for the development of class
consciousness. From this view, the university now occupies the ideological

Change in American Politics: Parties and Issues in the 1968 Election," *American
Political Science Review*, 1969, *63*, 1083–1105. See also R. Turner, "The Public
Perception of Protest," *American Sociological Review*, 1969, *34*, 815–831.
    [19] Lipset and Altbach (*op. cit.*, p. 341) summarize several studies which
confirm this point, though the evidence suggests a crucial distinction between radical predispositions and radical involvement. Although the former are likely to be
reflected in the attitudes of advanced students, the involvement is disproportionate
among underclassmen.

role once reserved for the industrial work-place. But whereas industrial workers generally spend whole careers in this nexus, students have little time on the campus.

But what are the implications of a high turnover rate for the structure and tone of the movement? The question of leadership turnover is especially important. Within the literature on conventional bureaucratic organizations, Alvin Gouldner's work has rendered it virtually axiomatic that leadership succession involves a return to the bureaucratic book and to codified conventionality as a source of security for the new leader himself.[20] Our observations would suggest the opposite for precarious ideological movements under stress. In this context, new leaders are frequently more militant than their predecessors since they derive their legitimacy from a greater departure from the conventional. This is particularly true when new leaders emerge in the midst of high membership turnovers within the rank and file. Under these common circumstances, few old members are available to serve as constraints. In fact, those who do stay on tend to be the most ardent and militant members in the first place.

Such considerations are important to the dynamics of many social movements of the radical as opposed to the reformist variety. We noted Lewis Feuer's verdict that student movements "have a propensity to veer from terrorism to suicidalism." To the extent that this is true, it is as much a function of organizational factors as of the particular individuals or ideologies involved. Here is one more instance of the sociological irony that the very noblest intentions can be blunted by the most mundane contingencies.

LOOKING AHEAD: A MEMO TO EDUCATIONAL ADMINISTRATORS

These are times which evoke a number of responses from people seeking solace in the midst of confusion. One of the most common is the wistful hope that surely all of this chaos is temporary. Those pursuing change are encouraged by the thought that it is only a matter of time until the change, and perhaps the utopia, is realized. Those frightened by flux derive comfort from assurances that the changers themselves are only a momentary aberration and like locusts will recede of their own accord.

Neither position is realistic. Certainly it is difficult to imagine sufficent change in the next decade to abolish the breach between the ideal and the real. It is equally unlikely that radicals will be placated by anything else. Although there will be ebbs and flows in the surge of

---

[20] A. W. Gouldner, *Patterns of Industrial Bureaucracy* (New York: The Free Press, 1954).

radicalism, we may be witnessing only the beginning rather than the demise of this political phenomenon. Although the radicals of today may become the liberals or even the conservatives of tomorrow, changes underway among high school students suggest that new radical recruits are underway and possibly in far greater numbers, black as well as white.

Much of this prospect results from the explosion of general social awareness that has shaken us all. While adults have wondered about the effects of Saturday morning cartoons on a generation of youth, it appears that a substantial segment of that generation has watched the evening newscasts as well. Shocked by violence rather than inured to it, many have found their fantasies rudely jolted. Youth is no longer insulated from knowledge of the afflictions of society. Indeed, the burden of such knowledge is often great precisely because youth has neither the roles nor the status with which to effect direct action in response.

Within the colleges and universities, the Student Movement of the 1960s initiated major changes far beyond its specific objectives. It is increasingly problematic whether an end to the war in Southeast Asia or even dramatic reductions of poverty, racism, pollution, and population growth would allow the university and its students to return to the halcyon normalcy of the 1950s and before. Unless such changes occur very rapidly, there is a very real possibility that for many students politicization and protest will become institutionalized as part of the informal curriculum of higher education, finding new goals to replace the old. As a way of manifesting adulthood during a lingering adolescence, protest contributes an aura of reality to years which are frequently vexing in their artificiality. This may be the most conspicuous instance of the new-found relevance of the university in society. And it is difficult to imagine how the university can cultivate funded relevance for its faculty without expecting its students to seek relevance in turn.

There is, however, one reply to protest which is gaining an ever-widening audience: repression. Thus, if the students will not retreat voluntarily, and if university faculty and administrators will not exercise proper constraint upon them, many are demanding the use of wide force and legislation. But at what price? In the short run, this course would vastly increase the problems under which educators are currently suffering by exacerbating present grievances and robbing the faculty of its crucial credibility and leverage. In the long run, such a response would simply shift the burden of protest elsewhere in society. Unhappily, the university appears to its students as one of the few institutions remaining which gives any hope of responding to social problems. When students ask the university to serve as a political agency, this is a sad commentary on current political institutions; when the university is asked to dispense massive group therapy, this says much concerning the depleted resources of those institutions which are designed to attend to individual psychological needs; when the university is asked to respond to social values and to the need for value-change, this tends to affirm the heralded crisis in religion.

Of course, there is considerable danger that the university will founder under such added freight. It was designed for special scholarly purposes and not as a panacea for all causes and all seasons. Perhaps in the best of worlds, other institutions would renew their responsibilities and leave the university to its own mission. Meanwhile, society has come to depend on higher education for more than education alone. The university has become a political lightning rod, and without the university in this role, the lightning would be far more diffuse and volatile. The burden of protest would be shifted either to other institutional spheres ill-equipped to cope with it or to an institutional vacuum with no resources to respond to problems before they reach crisis proportions as yet neither experienced nor envisaged. In our judgment, such a massive shift in the location of political protest is unlikely. The university must confront the problem rather than hope for an invisible hand to pluck it from the campus and place it elsewhere. The fact is that universities are in the business of dealing with youth, and youth has been stamped with a desperate sense of the tragedy involved in all societies to some degree but in our society more than most.

What then might a university do to cope? How can it assure its own salvation and contribute to society in the process? These are sobering questions at a time that is hardly heady with successful answers. But because we are professors, we find it impossible to repress a last brief lecture on the topic, a lecture that draws on our research and experiences as middlemen between administrators on the one hand and concerned students on the other. In offering this unsolicited advice to university administrators, we have tried to respond to a hypothetical query which professors are posing less and less these days: what would we do if we were administrators ourselves?

Anyone now entering the ranks of university administration would do well to provide for getting out of the role before he gets into it. This advice is not meant as waggish commentary in the voguish spirit of downgrading one's local deans and president. We are quite serious in suggesting *two* important respects in which provision for getting out of the administrative role may actually help to serve it. The first is that any administrator should have a tenured appointment on the faculty to which he can turn or return without loss of dignity or even of salary. Much has been said of late concerning the reduced half-life of university administrators. What has not been said so often is that many administrators

cling to their posts long after their effectiveness has ceased, simply for
lack of a viable alternative. Not only is it in the best interests of the administrator to have such an alternative, but it is in the best interests of an
institution to provide one so that administrators will feel secure enough
to take the bold steps which administration at its best must entail. Moreover, the time of the long-term university president is past. No longer will
college buildings be named after beloved leaders whose terms of office
outdistance the anticipated life of the building itself. Just as academic
departments have moved increasingly to rotated chairmen who share the
administrative burden, so are universities moving to the notion of a ro-
tating presidency to insure a plentiful supply of new and youthful recruits.
And if youth is a positive criterion for educational administration (as we
believe it must be) then a highly paid, tenured professorship at the end
of the administrative term may be an important seductive factor.

But there is another sense in which getting out of the role is important to fulfilling the role itself. It seems to us that the morality of any
organization can be partially defined in terms of the capacity of its members to maintain their personal identities as distinct from their organizational selves. In this respect, university administration has been flirting
with a peculiarly insidious immorality—administrators have fallen prey
to bureaucratization and have lost their willingness to step outside their
roles to indicate their personal positions on issues of the moment. Too
many have been convinced that there is no distinction between a leader's
personal opinion and the position of his institution. In this sense, many
academic institutions have become prisons rather than enabling devices
to facilitate free thought and expression. As much as students may rail
against the consequences of educational depersonalization for themselves,
the consequences are at least as tragic for professors and administrators
who lose precious credibility when they lose their capacity to act as individuals. If academic freedom is meaningful at all, surely it cannot
require suppression as the price of its perpetuation. Such perpetuation is
hollow indeed and at the ultimate expense of the university itself.

Of course, the mere mention of bureaucratization is enough to set
analytic juices flowing in any student of the current higher educational
apparatus. As sociologists, we must confess to a generally more benign
view of bureaucracy than that of many current societal critics. Still,
bureaucratization has taken a special toll among universities, especially
when teamed with its allies: differentiation, growth, and normative
change. Not to put too fine a point on the matter, the university has
become an apparition in its own time. As an institution badly out of sorts
with its cultural context, the university is buffeted by demands and expectations for which it is simply not prepared. As a structure, its essence

belies its name. Many have pointed out that the concept of a *university* is no longer apt. And although Clark Kerr talks of a *multi*versity united only by a common parking problem, the point is clear that the structure has begun to wallow in its own diversity and has lost its ability to navigate by relying on outdated charts and refusing to recognize that the stars do in fact move.

And yet the shift from a university to a multiversity has too often been seen as a trend to reverse rather than as an opportunity worth seizing. In our judgment, higher education defies monolithic structure, since it requires the sort of flexibility which is only afforded by decentralization. Thus, rather than expect *the* university to be any one thing, it is clear that a multiversity must be many things to many different clients. In addition to its traditional departmental structure, it needs policy oriented institutes at the interface between departments. In addition to degrees in conventional scholarly domains, it must offer nonconventional programs which are more than bastard offspring serving as sops to the activist community. In addition to conducting programs on campus, it must move off campus. Given this perspective, the role of the administrator changes. His job is not to lurch from crisis to crisis in an effort to bind the institution together. His responsibility instead is to articulate and preside over a process of creative diffusion which takes advantage of crisis as a source of clues rather than a threat to be repulsed.

And yet we do not mean to suggest that the university administrator should emulate the gray whale who rolls to his back and volunteers his tongue for the feeding of attacking enemies. Higher education has become a confrontation camp in its own right, and administrative leadership involves the ability to resist demands as well as to comply. Such resistance obviously requires grit, but grit alone will not suffice. We have already mentioned the importance of distinguishing person from role, of creative decentralization, and of articulating visions of one's own as the best response to competing visions from the flank. Indeed, this last point cannot be emphasized too greatly. Bureaucratic administrators are often weak because they insist on abiding by bureaucratic procedures in dealing with those who spurn such procedures as the first step to the future. If there is a battle to be waged it should be between competing programs of change rather than between change on the one hand and mere perseverance on the other. The strongest organizational structure weakens quickly when it has no visions with which to counter vision, no innovations with which to oppose demands.

This theory presumes a community of student activists as the administrator's perceived natural enemy. But need it be so? Certainly not to the extent which is threatened. The real enemy of any traditional institution is on-going events rather than those who react to them. In this sense, administrators are often myopic in reacting to students as if they were the basic cause rather than a symptomatic expression of the underlying disorder. But granted this much, it is clear that students cannot be dismissed either out of hand or with the back of one's hand. Again an examination of educational structures may be helpful, including yet another sense in which the term *university* may be inappropriate and misleading.

Unlike most other societies, the United States has developed its higher education according to a model of the home away from home, producing a total institution which seeks to integrate every facet of the student's life into the campus setting. This situation has been particularly conspicuous in the case of the small liberal arts college. But whereas the small college remains in a relatively favorable position to maintain the model with all its required close contact and interaction, large schools are adhering to the model against increasing odds. It is no surprise that recent research finds disproportionate student disorder on large, heterogenous, and bureaucratically structured campuses. These are precisely the schools which chafe their students in trying to implement an ideal that must be carried off very well or not at all. To *unify* a campus of thirty thousand students according to a familistic image is an almost impossible task. On the theory that an adolescent is better off with no parents rather than poor parents, the universities may be misguided in their zeal.

There are two possible resolutions of the friction that has been generated by the image of *in loco parentis*. The first is to opt for the model of peer culture rather than parental guidance, and to foster the development of small peer communities within the large symbolic campus. Put another way: where are the fraternities and sororities now that we really need them? On most campuses the age of the Greeks is dying in a double sense, and although the old-style fraternities have little place in the educational world today, there is a crying need for meaningful groups to fill the social vacuum. However, such groups can only become meaningful by attaining control over their members and autonomy with respect to the administrative elders of a campus.

A second suggestion is an extension of the first. In a society with a growing housing shortage, the one type of housing that is increasingly empty is the dormitory on the large campus. Students are opting for apartments in the community and a separate life beyond the campus itself. This is merely one of many symptoms of their need to be released from the real and symbolic constraints placed on them by their student status. Thus, the wise administrator should hasten the change for the sake of his students rather than oppose the trend for the sake of his real estate. At the level of knowledge and awareness, students are far more adult than ever before and part of adulthood may be defined as a willingness and capacity to handle role segregation and differentiation. It is too much to expect them to cede all aspects of their lives to an educational institution. Indeed, it is partly because we have demanded this of them that their protest is directed to the schools themselves rather than to the society at large and its directly offending institutions. Students are not novices any more than professors are monks. To apply the total institutional model of the monastery runs the risk of monasteries everywhere; namely, an embittered apostasy by the disaffected and the drop-outs. This risk is especially likely when a university presumes to set up statutes and sanctions which overlap and supplement the normal civil and criminal law. Although every institution requires a normative system tailored to its own particular needs, the university would do well to define these needs in very particular terms while allowing students to pursue separate lives on their own.

So much for a professional primer on educational administration. We have no illusions of waving any magic wand. Even on campuses which have anticipated our advice—and there are many—student activism remains. As this fact suggests, the real objective is not to do away with activism but rather to provide the proper channels to maximize its constructive impact. Student movements are here to stay, and they pose not just problems of social control but also important challenges to social response. Insofar as there has been a petrification of conventional politics in this country, political struggles increasingly take the form of a contest between the mainline government and parties on the one hand and social movements on the other. In this sense, the political movement constitutes the second party in our nominally two-party system. As the source of political dynamics and a prod to social change in a changing context, such movements should be responsibly preserved rather than irresponsibly trampled.

APPENDIX:

Content and Construction of Indices

Many questions were asked of the subjects of this research. A large proportion of these questions was designed to elicit attitudes toward objects and activities such as violence, southern whites, and conventional religion. It is clear to any observer that such attitudes are generally multifaceted. For example, one might ask whether an individual believes in nonviolence as a tactic for himself, for the movement, for whole countries; if nonviolence is a moral principle to be defended regardless of outcomes; if nonviolence involves actual love for one's opponent or simply turning the other cheek; and so on.

For the purposes of many analyses, however, each of these separate aspects is not particularly important. What matters is an overall position toward the activity or object—something more general. Thus, in keeping with contemporary practices of attitude measurement, we have constructed multiquestion indices to measure several of these more general attitudes. These indices, besides reflecting the broader concept, generally have the advantage of being more reliable than the single items from which they are composed. They also provide more extensive scales than the single items, thus allowing finer discriminations among respondents.

The techniques by which items were selected for combination into indices were somewhat unusual. These techniques were primarily selected because of the political currency of some of the terms used in the questions. This currency meant that the actual *meaning* of some of the terms changed between the beginning and the end of the summer of 1965. Consider, for example, the term *black power*. In a short time the meaning of the term for many American whites changed from "blacks should use arms and violence" to "blacks should have more economic strength." Thus, a question like "would you like to see more black power" would receive different answers from the same people with the same attitudes toward violence and economics at two different points of time. The relevant attitudes would not have changed, only semantic usage.

One of the major purposes of index construction in this research was to allow comparisons in attitudes over time, such as the analyses in Chapter Five. Thus, the problem of changes in meaning became crucial for interpretation of changes in attitude. Our solution was to use only those items which retain a similar relationship to other items in *both* questionnaires for constructing the indices. Interbattery factor analysis[1] was performed using *both* questionnaires at the same time. This procedure assures that the factors used are only those common to both questionnaires.

[1] L. R. Tucker, "An inter-battery method of factor analysis," *Psychometrika*, 1958, *23*, 111–136.

A varimax orthogonal rotation procedure was performed. An item was then used in an index only when *both* its pre- and postquestionnaire version loaded above .30 on the factor. Separate pre- and postfactor index scores were then assigned each subject by summing their responses to the relevant items.

The indices constructed in this manner are all from the major battery of attitude questions which appear in both the pre- and postquestionnaires. The specific questions which were combined into indices in this manner are detailed in the first part of Table 15. For a variety of purposes several additional indices were also used in the foregoing analyses. The construction of each of these indices is detailed in the second part of Table 15.

Table 15. INDEX CONSTRUCTION

Part I: *Attitude Indices from Interbattery Factor Analysis*

All indices in this section were constructed using questions of both the pre- and post-questionnaires. Words in parentheses show differences between pre- and post-questionnaires. Response categories for all questions were: (1) Strongly Agree; (2) Moderately Agree; (3) Agree Somewhat; (4) Disagree Somewhat; (5) Moderately Disagree; (6) Strongly Disagree.

Belief in Nonviolence: Sum, but with the answer to item (4) subtracted from seven.

(1) It is morally correct to use the threat of violence as a strategy to avoid violent attacks from others.

(2) Violence is proper when it is the only way of defending yourself or others.

(3) The civil rights movement may have to abandon the policy of non-violence if long-established southern customs are to be changed.

(4) It would be better for the Negro to remain in his current position if violence were the only way to change that position.

Attachment to versus Alienation from American Political Institutions: Sum.

(1) The only progress that can be expected in the Deep South within the next ten years is token integration.

(2) Most northern state and local judges are usually willing to go along with a frame of anyone they consider to have dangerous ideas.

(3) The American political system has proven itself incapable of coping with the problem of discrimination against Negroes.

(4) The continuing plight of American Negroes has caused me to have grave doubts about the superiority of democracy as a political system.

Concern with Workers' Public Image: Sum and subtract from 21.

(1) I would be greatly disturbed if some of my fellow project participants (are) (were) self-declared Communists.

(2) Since civil rights workers are in the public eye, they must abstain from all nonmarital sexual activities in order to maintain high standards of personal decorum.

(3) The same high standards of personal decorum should apply to drinking; alcohol should be avoided in any form.

Outside Intervention versus Local Southern Solution: Sum.

(1) The racial crisis in the United States should be resolved on a local level without the intervention of the federal government.

(2) Any lasting changes in civil rights in the South will have to come from the southerners themselves, rather than from outside pressures.

(3) The United States Justice Department does as much as it possibly can, given the laws on civil rights within which it must work.

Unfavorable Image of Southern Courts and Police: Sum, but with the answers to items (1) and (2) subtracted from seven.

Table 15. INDEX CONSTRUCTION (cont.)

---

(1) Police in Deep South are generally recruited from among the least qualified segments of the population.

(2) Most state and local courts in Deep South tolerate illegal police methods.

(3) When the case does not concern Negro civil rights, the Negro usually receives a fair trial in a state or local court in the Deep South.

Antipathy Toward White Southerners: Sum.

(1) Most whites in the Deep South feel a good deal of shame about segregation and would like an easy way to end it without a loss of pride.

(2) Most whites in the Deep South are willing to integrate in many areas but they are prevented from doing so by the white power structure.

(3) Most whites in the Deep South know that society is changing and that they will have to go along with integration in the end.

Part II: *Additional Indices Constructed*

POST-QUESTIONNAIRE:

Discrepancy Between Actual and Preferred Activities: Constructed by taking the difference between subject's responses to first and second questions, and then summing these absolute differences for all nine activities. The first question asked, "How much time did you spend on this activity?" Responses were: (1) All my time; (2) Most of the time; (3) Several times; (4) Rarely; (5) Never. The second question asked, "How much time would you have preferred to spend on this activity," and used the same response categories.

(a) Voter registration

(b) Political education other than actual registration

(c) Community organization (working with or building local groups)

(d) Tutoring and remedial education

(e) Organizing and participating in protest activities (picketing, marching, etc.)

(f) Seeking Negro employment and economic benefits (including boycotts but not other demonstrations)

(g) General Medical care

(h) Birth control education and assistance

(i) Integrating public accommodations

FROM PREQUESTIONNAIRE:

Expected Involvement with (1) Whites and (2) Negroes: The question was asked, "How probable is it that you will do each of the following this summer," referring to either "white southerners" or "local Negroes." Possible responses for each of the activities listed below were: (1) Very likely; (2) Somewhat likely: (3) 50–50 chance; (4) Somewhat unlikely; (5) Very unlikely. Scores were given by summing responses and subtracting from 35.

(a) Date a local ——— (white southerner or Negro).

Table 15. INDEX CONSTRUCTION (cont.)

(b) Live in the home of a local ———— for at least a few days.

(c) Visit the home of ————.

(d) Attend church with ————.

(e) Have several rational discussions with ————.

(f) Have several honest discussions with ———— about (civil rights for whites, noncivil rights for Negroes) issues.

(g) Have friendly casual conversations with ———— along the streets.

Cynicism-Optimism About Project Personnel and Organization: Sum.

(1) (I expect to find the summer project) (The summer project was) a highly efficient and well-coordinated organization.

(2) The selection process for this summer's program (means) (meant) that those of us who (are here are) (went were) the best possible people for this particular job.

(3) Most of the permanent field workers in the South probably have developed extraordinary sensitivity to the needs and wants of other people.

Low Expectations of Project Success: Sum.

(1) The summer's voter registration campaign (will produce) (produced) a politically momentous increase in registered voters in the Deep South.

(2) As a result of the summer, a very large number of whites in the Deep South (will move) (moved) to more moderate positions on civil rights.

(3) This summer's program (will lead) (led) to a dramatic increase in militancy among southern Negroes by the end of summer.

FROM POST-QUESTIONNAIRE:

Actual Involvement with (1) Whites and (2) Negroes: These two indices parallel the two noted above. Responses refer to either "whites" or "Negroes." The question was, "How often did you do each of the following last summer?" Possible responses for each question were: (1) Never; (2) Once or twice; (3) Several times; (4) Many times; (5) Daily or almost.

(a) Date a local ————.

(b) Spend the night in a local home.

(c) Visit a local ———— home.

(d) Attend church with local ————.

(e) Have a rational discussion with a local ————.

(f) Have an honest discussion with a local ———— about civil rights.

(g) Have a friendly casual conversation with a local ———— along the street.

FROM PREQUESTIONNAIRE:

Self-Confidence: Sum responses and subtract from 26. "How confident are you of your ability to cope with the following situations?" Response categories were: (1) Very confident; (2) Somewhat confident; (3) Unsure; (4) Somewhat unconfident; (5) Very unconfident.

Table 15. Index Construction (cont.)

(a) Averting violence when faced alone by a small group of drunken, hostile southern white youths?

(b) Teaching an unmotivated southern Negro youth?

(c) Communicating with an older southern Negro woman who is afraid to register to vote?

(d) Working with a moderate white minister in a small southern town to avoid violence and improve communication?

(e) Remaining nonviolent in the face of police brutality against a Negro woman whom you have personally persuaded to register for voting?

Expected Harassment: Sum responses and subtract from 16. Categories: (1) Very likely; (2) Somewhat likely; (3) 50–50 chance; (4) Somewhat unlikely; (5) Very unlikely.

(1) How likely is it that you will be arrested at any time during the summer?

(2) How likely spend some time in jail or some other form of confinement?

(3) How likely is it that you personally will become involved in violence during the summer?

FROM POST-QUESTIONNAIRE:

Actual Harassment: Construct by adding one point for each of the three questions below to which the subject answered yes, regardless of the number of times he indicated each form of harassment occurred.

(1) Were you arrested?

(2) Were you jailed?

(3) Was there any occasion this summer when you were physically beaten?

FROM PRE- AND POST-QUESTIONNAIRES:

Moral Concentration: Add one point for each of the following questions which the subject answered *either* "somewhat less important" or "much less important." The question was, "How would you evaluate projects for each of the following goals in comparison with this summer's campaign?"

(a) World nuclear disarmament

(b) End capital punishment in the United States

(c) Halt the House Un-American Activities Committee

(d) Reduction of poverty through political action

(e) End the war in Vietnam

(f) Increase student rights in American colleges and universities

(g) Aid to foreign countries through the Peace Corps

(h) Reduction of juvenile delinquency

FROM PREQUESTIONNAIRE:

Activism in North and *Activism in South:* Two parallel indices using the same questions. One refers to the "North," the other to the "South." The question

Table 15. Index Construction (cont.)

asked was, "Have you done any of the following?" Response categories were "yes" or "no." For the indices add one point each time the answer is yes. "North" and "South" answers were in separate columns rather than different questions.

(a) Picketing

(b) Fund raising

(c) Circulating petitions

(d) Organizing boycotts

(e) Freedom rides

(f) Sit-ins, pray-ins, wade-ins

(g) Working in a civil-rights organization office

FROM POST-QUESTIONNAIRE:

Optimism over Future Role of White Civil Rights Workers: Sum, after subtracting the response to question (1) from seven. Response categories are: (1) Strongly agree; (2) Moderately agree; (3) Agree somewhat; (4) Disagree somewhat; (5) Moderately disagree; (6) Strongly disagree.

(1) White summer civil rights workers will be needed even more in the years to come. Their importance is just beginning.

(2) Summer civil rights volunteers are too inexperienced to really contribute meaningfully. A summer is not long enough to learn to be effective.

(3) No matter how slow the progress, the civil rights campaign should continue to work within existing southern laws, although the movement should seek changes in them.

FROM PRE- AND POST-QUESTIONNAIRES:

The following two indices appear in both the pre- and post-questionnaires in parallel form, and have the same response categories: (1) Strongly agree, (2), (3) Agree, (4) Disagree, (5), (6) Strongly disagree.

Religious Conservatism: Sum and subtract from 25.

(1) I believe in a divine judgment after death where some shall be rewarded and others punished.

(2) The church is holy and not to be equated with other human institutions.

(3) Men cannot fulfill themselves in the world without believing in God.

(4) Jesus was God's only Son, sent into the world by God to redeem me and all mankind.

Political Pessimism: Sum and subtract from 19.

(1) I believe there is at least a 50–50 chance of a nuclear war in the next ten years.

(2) American culture is sick and moving along the road to destruction.

(3) The United States should try to initiate negotiations in an area like Vietnam and should avoid further military participation.

Table 15. Index Construction (cont.)

FROM PRE- AND POST-QUESTIONNAIRES (response categories the same as above):

Relevance of College: Sum, after subtracting the response to item (2) from seven.

  (1) My college courses provided almost no discussion or controversy over basic values or commitments in life.

  (2) My professors seemed very concerned about political issues and social problems.

  (3) The kind of knowledge acquired in most college classes is of doubtful value outside the college doors.

Scholarly Orientation: Sum and subtract from 19.

  (1) Significant learning may take place even if the professor does not know or relate to the student as an individual.

  (2) I think of myself as an "intellectual."

  (3) It is proper to seek knowledge for the improvement of human and public affairs.

FROM POST-QUESTIONNAIRE ONLY (response categories same as above):

Belief in Student Rights: Sum and subtract from 25.

  (1) I would consider supporting a student strike or sit-in to protest against some aspect of educational policy, such as a particular faculty member of particular courses, etc.

  (2) The administration has no responsibilities and duties concerning student morality and behavior.

  (3) Student evaluations of faculty should be an important factor in the hiring and firing of faculty.

  (4) The Free Speech Movement among the students at the University of California, Berkeley, was both desirable and important.

Negative Attitudes Toward College Administration: Sum.

  (1) The administration of my college or university treats me as a mature and responsible adult.

  (2) At my college or university the administration almost always can be counted on to give sufficient consideration to the rights and needs of the students in setting the policy.

Index

A

Academic freedom, 208

Activism: and alienation, 170–172; and authority, 44; changes in, 168; and family background, 27–28, 42–43; and frustration, 203; intervening structure for, 44–45; liberalism versus radicalism in, 168, 171–179, 181–182; models for, 43–44; northern versus southern, 50, 64–65; other studies of, 39–47; as religious alternate, 45; and revolution, 197–198; sources of, 21–47; of students, 156, 160, 187, 196–201; in university, 162, 168, 196–201; and Vietnam, 188; volunteers' prior, 50, 64; of whites, 40, 184. *See also* Civil Rights Movement; Radicalism

ADAMS, J. F., 41n

Administrators of universities, advice to, 207–211

Affluence, 27

Age: and local black support, 78–80; and movement stability, 177; and white opposition, 90

AIKEN, M., 189n, 192n

Alienation, 35–36, 170–172, 201–202; learning of, 204; and social class, 178

ALTBACH, P., 41, 45, 203–204n

American Civil Liberities Union, 13

ANGELL, R. C., 164

Anonymity of replies, 10

Apathy, 76, 97, 115

ARONSON, E., 157n

Arrest of volunteers, 132

ASH, R., 121n, 130n

Atheism, 29

Attitude change. *See* Change in volunteers

Attitude measurement, 213–220

Authority and activism, 44

B

Background of volunteers, 25–28, 62–65

BENDIX, R., 195n

Bitterness, 175, 177

Black Panthers, 168

Black power: and grass roots organization, 194–196; meaning of, 213; and militancy, 127, 134; roots of, 6, 58, 86, 153; shift to, 99, 115, 122, 124, 147–148. *See also* Negroes

BLOCK, J., 41

BLUMBERG, P., 119n

BOHRNSTEDT, G. W., 138n

BORGATTA, E. F., 138n

BOTTOMORE, T. D., 179n

BRINK, W., 194n

Bureaucracy, 112, 190, 208

221